A GUIDE TO
DAILY PRAYER

A GUIDE TO
DAILY PRAYER

William Barclay

HARPER & ROW, PUBLISHERS
New York, Evanston, San Francisco, London

FIRST HARPER & ROW paperback edition published in 1974.

ISBN: 0-06-060401-8

This book is published in Great Britain
under the title of *More Prayers for the Plain Man*.

LIBRARY OF CONGRESS CATALOG CARD NUMBER: 62-11473

CONTENTS

FOREWORD

It is not very long ago since *The Plain Man's Book of Prayers* first appeared in this series of Fontana Books. Since then the number of people who have read it and used it has never ceased to astonish me. And now this second volume appears. It is written in the same way, and it is intended to be used in the same way, as the first volume; but there are certain differences.

The prayers are a very little longer. I felt that those who had used the first volume, and who had formed the habit of praying every day, might want just a little more. And, therefore, in this volume the prayers are a little fuller than in the previous volume.

Prayers are given for forty mornings and for forty evenings. The reason is that I felt that it would be wise to provide some prayers which could be used as alternatives to the prayer for the day. It might be that the prayer for the day does not always express the needs, the feelings and the desires of the person who wishes to use it. And so in this volume the extra prayers will provide alternatives when the prayer of the day is not the prayer that the reader wishes to pray.

The number of prayers for special occasions and for individual people is greatly increased. Nothing will make such a difference to the ordinary, everyday routine of life as to be able to take our own particular, individual job to God. I have tried to provide prayers for those who are engaged in the many activities of the world's work. To make this complete was obviously impossible; and, if the reader should find that his or her work is not represented at all in these prayers, then I should be very happy if he or she would write to tell me so, and other prayers could be included in future editions of this book. Life would be very different, if each one of us could take the whole of life to the whole of God.

I would like to say a word about one way in which many people have found it helpful to use *The Plain Man's Book of*

7

Prayers. Many people found it helpful, when they were separated from their friends and loved ones, for instance, when they were in hospital, or abroad, or on holiday, or working away from home, to arrange that both they and those left at home should have a copy of the book, and to arrange that at the same time in the morning and in the evening in their different places they should together pray the same prayer. Many people have found a feeling of being together, even when they were separated, in knowing that at the same time they were offering to God the same prayer. Even though distance separated them, they met at the mercy seat of God.

I should like to think that those who use this book, unknown as they are to each other, and separated as they may be from each other, might feel themselves bound together in a praying fellowship, when morning and evening they keep their brief appointment with God.

William Barclay

WHEN WE PRAY

Sir Thomas Browne once gave to man a very strange title; he called man "the great amphibian." He meant that man is a creature of two worlds. He is a creature of this visible world of space and time, but he is also a creature of an unseen world, which every now and again breaks in upon his consciousness. Studdert Kennedy put it into verse:

> *I'm a man, and a man's a mixture,*
> *Right down from his very birth,*
> *For part of him comes from heaven,*
> *And part of him comes from earth.*

It is possible to try to explain man entirely in terms of this world. It is possible to make a chemical analysis of a man. The average man contains enough fat to make seven bars of soap; enough iron to make a medium sized nail; enough sugar to fill a sugar-sifter; enough lime to whitewash a henhouse; enough potassium to explode a toy cannon; enough magnesium for a dose of magnesia; enough phosphorus to make tips for two thousand two hundred matches; and a very little sulphur. And, as Harry Emerson Fosdick says, you could buy the whole lot for two dollars, for less than a pound. That is certainly true, but the simple answer is, Take your pound note or your two dollar bills, and go out and buy these chemicals and try to make a man. One of the curious facts which used to fascinate even the ancient Greeks is the fact that a living body and a dead body of the same person weigh exactly the same—but something is gone, and that something is the something which makes the body into a living human being, a person. Man is unquestionably a creature of two worlds.

Every now and then man becomes aware of that other world of which he also forms a part. The theologians talk of what they call the *numinous*. There are situations and places, for instance, to take the simplest example, in the dark, when a man feels that there is something there, that there is something, as it were, looking over his shoulder. At such a time a physical tremor can go through a man's body and the hair can rise on his scalp. That is the consciousness of the numinous, and that is what we might call the raw material of all religion.

This consciousness can break in upon a man anywhere, on a hilltop, on a lonely road, in the face of a · sunset, in the middle of the night, in a cathedral or a church, in the face of some experience. It can come to the most irreligious man and to the most matter-of-fact man and to the man who has no contact with organised religion at all. It is part of the human situation.

This awareness of what another theologian called " the wholly other " in life comes to us especially in the times of crisis which at some time invade every life. It comes in the time of sorrow, when we know we need help from outside to go on. It comes in a time of special effort, when we know that we must pass the breaking-point and somehow not break. It comes in a time of danger in the face of which we feel helpless. That is why the sailors in Shakespeare's play say in their terror : " All's lost! To prayers! To prayers!" During the war a story used to be told of a sergeant who one evening was insisting that he was an uncompromising atheist and that he had no use whatever for any belief in God. The very next day he and some of his men were caught in a dive-bombing raid. There was nothing to do but desperately to scrabble out a fox-hole in the earth and wait. While they waited in their shallow shelter the sergeant was busy praying and praying unashamedly out loud. A soldier with him said : " I thought you were an atheist." " Son," said the sergeant, who was an honest man, " there are no atheists in fox-holes." The simple fact is that when anyone is in trouble he quite instinctively prays. That is why even the agnostic was compelled to pray reluctantly : " O God, if there is a God, save my soul, if I have a soul!" Prayer is unquestionably the natural human reaction to a situation which has got beyond us. That is why even someone who has no connection with any church will send for someone " to say a prayer " when a member of the family is dying, and will wish a funeral service at which the prayers of the Church are said.

It needs no argument to prove that prayer is the universal reaction to any crisis and to any desperate situation. In one sense it is true to say that for many of us that is precisely our error about prayer. We tend to connect prayer with the extraordinary, the abnormal, the hour and the moment when life goes disastrously wrong, and when there is nothing that we or anyone else on earth can do about it. Of course, at such a time prayer is an absolute essential. But prayer should be an activity which is a constant part of life. If we keep prayer for the crisis, then it can happen that, when the crisis comes, we cannot pray. That is why some people have to send for someone to say a prayer for them at such a time. Prayer is simply taking life to God. Prayer is simply remembering that God is not only the rescuer when things get beyond us, but the Friend with whom we live day by day. "A man," said Dr. Johnson, "should keep his friendship in constant repair." And prayer is keeping our friendship with God in constant repair. Many people work on the unconscious assumption that they can do without God when they do not specially need him, and then call him in when everything else has failed. Certainly God will help even then, but in a time of crisis it is so much easier to go to someone who is your well-loved, constantly visited, familiar friend. And that is why prayer should be a daily activity of life. What, then, should this daily prayer be like? Let us ask and try to answer a series of questions about it.

1. *How should we pray?* The way in which we ought to pray is settled once and for all by the name which Jesus gave to God, the name by which he enabled us to address God. When Jesus was praying in Gethsemane he addressed God as: Abba, Father. Twice Paul says that that is the way in which the Christian through Christ is able to address God (Romans 8.15; Galatians 4.6). *Abba* is much more than *father*. *Abba* was the word by which a little Jewish child addressed his father in the privacy and the intimacy of the home circle, as *jaba* is in Arabic to-day. There is no way in which this can be

translated into English without it appearing bizarre and almost grotesque, for the only possible translation of *Abba* is *Daddy*. This is the way in which we can talk to God. We can talk to God with the same intimacy, and confidence, and trust as a little child talks to his father. Because of what Jesus was, because of what he told us, because of what he did, no one is easier to talk to than God.

All kinds of things are settled by this. We do not need to talk to God in any special kind of religious or theological language. Certainly we do not need to talk to him in Elizabethan and archaic English. That is why in this book I have always used *you* in speaking to God, and not *thou*. We do not need to talk to God in any special position. Kneeling, standing, sitting, lying, it is all the same. As a child runs to his father and tells him everything in the days when he is very young and very innocent and very trusting, so we can talk to God.

It is not that God is any the less God. It is simply that God for us has become the friend of all friends. Once, it is said, a Roman Emperor was celebrating a triumph. He was parading his armies, his captives and his trophies through the streets of Rome. The streets were crowded. At one place on the route there was a little platform where the Empress was sitting with her children. As the Emperor's chariot passed this place the Emperor's little son jumped down, dived through the crowd and was about to run out to the road to his father. One of the Roman legionaries who were lining the pavement stopped the boy. He swung him up in his arms. "You can't do that," he said. "Don't you know who that is? That's the Emperor." The boy looked down at him and laughed. "He may be your Emperor," he said, "but he's my father." God is God but God is *Abba* too.

We must once and for all get rid of the idea that prayer is something stilted and unnatural. It is the most natural thing in the world. It is a child talking to his father, as he did when he was very young.

II. *When should we pray?* Paul would have answered: Always and continually. "Pray without ceasing," he said (1 Thessalonians 5.17). The perfect friend is the friend to whom we can go at any time without ever feeling a nuisance. And God is like that. If God is the friend of our lives, then we will be continually speaking to him.

Should there be set times for prayer? That set times bring their own danger is clear. It is possible, as it were, to pray to a schedule, to keep, as it were, a score of the time we spend in prayer, and thus to make prayer a mechanical thing. That may be so, but it is also true that the danger about a thing which can be done any time is that it will be done no time. It is, therefore, well to have in life a fixed time for prayer, although prayer will be very far from being confined to that time. Bertram Pollock was Bishop of Norwich and as busy as a bishop must be; but, no matter how busy he was, he had three set times each day when he prayed, just as Daniel prayed three times a day with his windows open towards Jerusalem (Daniel 6.10). Once just when the Bishop was about to have his brief time of prayer a rather important visitor came asking to see him. Gently and courteously the Bishop said to his servant: "Put him in an anteroom, and ask him if he will please wait. I have an appointment with God." Daily we should have our appointment with God.

Such an appointment cannot be a formal duty; it can never be a formal duty to spend a moment or two in the company of our best friend. Such an appointment must not become a fetish. Florence Allshorn was the well-loved Principal of a women's missionary college, where sometimes there were people who observed a kind of hot-house piety; and she used to criticise gently those who always discovered that their quiet time was due just when volunteers were needed to wash the dishes! Our appointment with God must be neither a religious convention nor a religious fetish but the time without which the activities of no day are complete.

III. *Where should we pray?* Sometimes the Jews used to say that prayer was not really valid and effective unless it was offered in the Synagogue; but the great Jewish teachers also said that he who prays in his own house and home surrounds it with a wall of iron. The simple answer is that we should pray everywhere. It is quite true that there are certain places in which we are bound to feel closer to God than anywhere

else. But, as Stephen said, God does not dwell in temples
made with hands (Acts 7.48), and as Whittier, the Quaker
poet, put it, the whole round earth is the temple of God.

We can pray anywhere, in the quiet of our own room, or,
if we have not got a room of our own, on the street, in the
train, on the bus, in some quiet church into which we can
slip for a moment. Someone has spoken of what he called
"arrow prayers," just words, phrases, half sentences spoken
anywhere to God. If God is everywhere, then we can meet
him anywhere. Brother Lawrence used to say that he felt just
as near to God when he was washing the dirty dishes in the
monastery kitchen and going about the tasks of the scullery
as ever he did when he was kneeling at the Blessed Sacra-
ment. The set appointment must be kept, but anywhere and
everywhere there is a door to the presence of God which no
man can ever shut.

iv. *Why should we pray?* It is here that we come to one
of the misunderstandings of prayer. There are many people
who think of prayer almost entirely in terms of asking God
for things. Prayer can never be a monologue; prayer must be
a dialogue. Prayer is at least as much listening to God as it is
talking to God. Prayer is at least as much accepting the will
of God as asking God for what our will desires. Prayer is a
conversation between us and God, and no conversation can be
worth while if one party in it never gives the other party the
opportunity to speak. A good conversationalist has at least as
big a gift for listening as he has for talking. There are too
many people whose prayer is essentially saying to God : Your
will be changed, rather than : Your will be done. In all our
prayers there should be a time of silence in which we listen,
for prayer is man listening to God even more than it is God
listening to man. We lose far more than half the value of
prayer when we speak so much that we do not even give God
the chance to speak.

v. *What should we pray for?* This is a question which
answers itself. The most revealing test of anything is to take
it into the presence of God. The test of any wish or desire or
ambition or aim is exactly this—Can I pray for it? It may
often be that we see just how wrong a thing is when we realise

how impossible it is to pray for it. And it may often be that our prayer must be, not to receive what we desire, but to be cleansed from desiring it. We can, in a word, pray for anything for which we can really feel that it is right to ask God.

That is not to say that there are things which we cannot bring to God. We can tell God about the temptations about which we cannot even speak to anyone else. We can tell God about the problems which we cannot share with anyone else. There are things which we try to hide from other people; and there are things in our minds and hearts from which we even try sometimes to avert our own eyes. All this we can take to God, because God, who is the searcher of the hearts of men, knows it all already, and God who in Jesus Christ took our human life upon him knows all about it.

We can pray to receive anything for which with a clear conscience and unashamedly we can ask God; and, as for the other things, we can tell God about them, and pray to be freed from the desire for them.

VI. *What can we expect from prayer?* It is here that we come to the very centre and the essence of prayer; and it is here that we come to the reason why so many people fail to make of prayer what prayer can be; it is, in fact, here that we come on the reason why so many people abandon prayer. There are two basic facts which must always be remembered about prayer.

Prayer is not escape; prayer is the way to conquest. Prayer is not flight; prayer is power. Prayer does not deliver a man from some terrible situation; prayer enables a man to face and to master the situation. When Jesus prayed that the bitter cup of the Cross might pass from him, that cup was not taken away from him. He had to drain it to its last agonising dregs. But he was enabled to come through the Cross and to emerge on the other side of it in triumph. So often people pray to be delivered from a problem, to be rescued from a situation, to be saved from a disaster, to be spared a sorrow, to be healed from a sickness, to be freed from a mental or a physical agony. Sometimes, it is true, that deliverance comes; but far more often the answer is that we are given the strength which is not our strength to go through it, and to come out at the other side of it, not simply as a survivor, but with a faith that is strengthened and deepened and a mind and a life and a character which are purified and ennobled. Prayer does not provide a means of running away from the human situation; prayer provides a way of meeting the human situation.

Prayer is not the easy way out. Prayer is not an easy way of getting things done for us. So many people think of prayer as a kind of magic, a kind of talisman, a kind of divine Aladdin's lamp in which in some mysterious way we command the power of God to work for us. Prayer must always remain quite ineffective, unless we do everything we can to make our own prayers come true. It is a basic rule of prayer that God will never do for us what we can do for ourselves. Prayer does not do things for us; it enables us to do things for ourselves.

Any wise parent knows that real parenthood does not mean doing things for the child; it means enabling the child to do things for himself. One of the great stories of history concerns Edward the First and his son the Black Prince. In battle the prince was sorely pressed. There were courtiers who came to the king to tell him that his son was up against it. "Is he wounded or unhorsed?" asked the king. When they said no, the king replied: "Then I will send him no help. Let him win his spurs." To take the matter on a much more everyday level, it is much easier for a parent, when his child asks help with a school exercise, to do the exercise and then to allow the child to copy out the answer. But by that way the child will make no progress at all. By far the wiser way is to teach and to encourage the child to do it for himself. Prayer is not so much God doing things for us as it is we and God doing things together.

We cannot expect escape from prayer, and we cannot expect the easy way out. What we can expect is a strength not our own to do the undoable, to bear the unbearable and to face the unfaceable. What we can expect is that divine help in which everything becomes victory. "In the world ye shall have tribulation," said Jesus, "but be of good cheer; I have overcome the world" (John 16.33).

Now that we have asked and tried to answer our questions about prayer, three great things remain to be said.

I. Prayer must never be selfish. There is a real sense in which no man prays as an individual, but always as a member of a community. It is for that reason that it is not enough to pray at home and by ourselves; we should also in God's house pray in fellowship and in union with God's people. No man can pray to receive something the getting of which will involve someone else's disappointment and loss. To be selfish in prayer is to erect a barrier through which our prayers cannot pass.

II. The man who prays must necessarily lift himself out of time and put himself in touch with eternity. To pray before we go out to work in the morning is to put ourselves in touch with a larger world and a larger life; it is to be lifted above the littleness of life. Robert Louis Stevenson tells of a Scottish byreman who all his life worked amidst the earthy dirt of the cowsheds and the stables. Stevenson asked the man if he never grew weary of this often unpleasant work, the same day in and day out. The man answered: " He that has something ayont need never weary." He who has something beyond need never weary. The man who prays daily puts himself in touch with that which is beyond, and comes back refreshed to life and living.

III. We have thought much of prayer as it affects ourselves; and now at the very end we think of prayer as it affects other people. The greatest thing that we can do for any man is to pray for him. Alexander Whyte told a story of a servant girl who was a member of his congregation. When she came asking to become a member, he asked her what she could do for her church and for the work of Jesus Christ. It was in the old days when the work of a domestic servant lasted all day and half the night. " I haven't much time to do things," the girl said, " but at night, when I go to bed, I take the morning newspaper with me." " Yes," said Whyte, wondering what could possibly be coming next. " And," the girl went on, " I read the birth notices, and I pray for the little babies who have just come into the world. I read the marriage notices, and I pray that God will give these people happiness.

I read the death notices, and I pray that God will comfort those who are sad." No one in this world will ever know what blessing to unknown people came from an attic bedroom from one who prayed. If we love someone, then surely we cannot help praying for them.

It is my prayer that this little book will help others to pray, and it is my prayer that they will go far beyond the words which are written in it, and that day by day they will offer their own prayers to God for themselves and for others, as a man talks with his friend.

PRAYERS WITH BIBLE READINGS
FOR FORTY MORNINGS
AND EVENINGS

In the Morning

Help me, O God, to meet in the right way and in the right spirit everything which comes to me to-day.

Help me to approach my work cheerfully, and my tasks diligently.

Help me to meet people courteously, and, if need be, to suffer fools gladly.

Help me to meet disappointments, frustrations, hindrances, opposition, calmly and without irritation.

Help me to meet delays with patience, and unreasonable demands with self-control.

Help me to accept praise modestly, and criticism without losing my temper.

Keep me serene all through to-day.

All this I ask for Jesus' sake. AMEN.

In the Evening

O God, bless those whose faces come into my mind as I come into your presence.

Bless those whom I love; if it be possible, let nothing happen to them.

Bless my friends, and the people beside whom I work; let nothing come between me and them.

Bless those whom I know to be ill; give them restful and healing sleep to-night.

Bless those whom I know to be sad; and comfort them.

Bless those who are being very foolish; keep them from doing anything that would wreck life for themselves and for others.

Bless the poor, the homeless, the friendless, those in prison, in misfortune and in disgrace.

Bless my absent friends; bless those who are away from home.

You are the Father of all. In your fatherly love bless all who need your blessing.

This I ask for your love's sake. AMEN.

Daily Reading

JOHN I: 1-5, 11-14

In the beginning was the Word, and the Word was with God, and the Word was God. The same was in the beginning with God. All things were made by him and without him was not any thing made that was made. In him was life; and the life was the light of men. And the light shineth in darkness; and the darkness comprehended it not. He came unto his own, and his own received him not. But as many as received him, to them gave he power to become the sons of God, even to them that believe on his name: which were born, not of blood, nor of the will of the flesh, nor of the will of man, but of God. And the Word was made flesh, and dwelt among us, (and we beheld his glory, the glory as of the only begotten of the Father,) full of grace and truth.

In the Morning

O God, help me to-day to think of the feelings of others as much as I think of my own.

If I know that there are things which annoy the people with whom I live and work, help me not to do them.

If I know that there are things which would please them, help me to go out of my way to do them.

Help me to think before I speak, so that I may not thought-lessly or tactlessly hurt or embarrass anyone else.

If I have to differ with anyone, help me to do so with courtesy.

If I have to argue with anyone, help me to do so without losing my temper.

If I have to find fault with anyone, help me to do so with kindness.

If anyone has to find fault with me, help me to accept it with a good grace.

Help me all through to-day to treat others as I would wish them to treat me : through Jesus Christ my Lord. AMEN.

In the Evening

O God, bless the people who are thinking of me and praying for me to-night,

  my parents, my family, my friends, my loved ones.

Bless those who have no one to remember them, and no one to pray for them,

  the aged, the lonely, the friendless, those who have no one to love and no one to love them.

Bless those who specially need my remembrance and my prayers,

  those in illness and in pain, those whose life is in the

balance, those who are dying, those who are in bewilderment, those who are in regret and remorse, those who have been driven to despair.

Bless me before I sleep, and grant me now
    A grateful heart for all your gifts;
    A contrite heart for all my sins;
    A heart at peace, because it rests in you.
Hear this my prayer for your love's sake. AMEN.

Daily Reading

PSALM 46

God is our refuge and strength, a very present help in trouble.

Therefore will not we fear, though the earth be removed, and though the mountains be carried into the midst of the sea;

Though the waters thereof roar and be troubled, though the mountains shake with the swelling thereof. Selah.

There is a river, the streams whereof shall make glad the city of God, the holy place of the tabernacles of the most High. God is in the midst of her; she shall not be moved: God shall help her, and that right early.

The heathen raged, the kingdoms were moved: he uttered his voice, the earth melted.

The Lord of hosts is with us; the God of Jacob is our refuge. Selah.

Come, behold the works of the Lord, what desolations he hath made in the earth.

He maketh wars to cease unto the end of the earth; he breaketh the bow, and cutteth the spear in sunder; he burneth the chariot in the fire.

Be still, and know that I am God: I will be exalted among the heathen, I will be exalted in the earth.

The Lord of hosts is with us; the God of Jacob is our refuge. Selah.

In the Morning

All through to-day, O God, help me to be,
  Quick to praise, and slow to criticise;
  Quick to forgive, and slow to condemn;
  Quick to share, and slow to refuse to give.

Grant me all through to-day,
  Complete control over my temper,
    that I may be slow to anger;
  Complete control over my tongue,
    that I may speak no hasty word.

So grant that all through to-day I may help everyone and hurt
no one, so that I may find true joy in living: through Jesus
Christ my Lord. AMEN.

In the Evening

O God, my Father, as I lay me down to sleep,
  Relax the tension of my body;
  Calm the restlessness of my mind;
  Still the thoughts which worry and perplex.
Help me to rest myself and all my problems in the clasp of
your everlasting arms.
Let your Spirit speak to my mind and my heart while I am

asleep, so that, when I waken in the morning, I may find that
I have received in the night-time,

Light for my way;
Strength for my tasks;
Peace for my worries;
Forgiveness for my sins.

Grant me sleep to-night, and to-morrow power to live.
This I ask through Jesus Christ my Lord. AMEN.

Daily Reading

MATTHEW 10: 24-31

The disciple is not above his master, nor the servant above his
lord. It is enough for the disciple that he be as his master,
and the servant as his lord. If they have called the master
of the house Be-elzebub, how much more shall they call
them of his household? Fear them not therefore: for there is
nothing covered, that shall not be revealed; and hid, that
shall not be known. What I tell you in darkness, that speak
ye in light: and what ye hear in the ear, that preach ye upon
the housetops. And fear not them which kill the body, but
are not able to kill the soul: but rather fear him which is
able to destroy both soul and body in hell. Are not two
sparrows sold for a farthing? and one of them shall not
fall on the ground without your Father. But the very hairs
of your head are all numbered. Fear ye not therefore, ye are
of more value than many sparrows.

In the Morning

Equip me to-day, O God, with

The humility, which will keep me from pride and from conceit;

The graciousness and the gentleness, which will make me both easy to live with and a joy to meet;

The diligence, the perseverance, and the reliability, which will make me a good workman;

The kindness which will give me a quick eye to see what I can do for others, and a ready hand to do it;

The constant awareness of your presence, which will make me do everything as unto you.

So grant that to-day men may see in me a glimpse of the life of my Blessed Lord.

This I ask for your love's sake. AMEN.

In the Evening

Thank you, O God, for all the help you have given me to-day.

Thank you for

Keeping me safe all through to-day;

Helping me to do my work all through to-day;

Giving me strength to conquer my temptations all through to-day.

Thank you for

My home and all that it has been to me;

My loved ones and all the circle of those most dear;
My friends and comrades with whom I have worked and
   talked.

Thank you for
   Any kindness I have received;
   Any help that was given to me;
   Any sympathy that was shown to me.

Help me to lay myself down to sleep to-night with a glad and
grateful heart.

This I ask through Jesus Christ my Lord. AMEN.

Daily Reading

PSALM 63 : 1-7

O God, thou art my God; early will I seek thee: my soul
   thirsteth for thee, my flesh longeth for thee in a dry and
   thirsty land, where no water is;
To see thy power and thy glory, so as I have seen thee in the
   sanctuary.
Because thy lovingkindness is better than life, my lips shall
   praise thee.
Thus will I bless thee while I live: I will lift up my hands
   in thy name.
My soul shall be satisfied as with marrow and fatness; and
   my mouth shall praise thee with joyful lips:
When I remember thee upon my bed, and meditate on thee in
   the night watches.
Because thou hast been my help, therefore in the shadow of
   thy wings will I rejoice.

In the Morning

O God, help me all through to-day
  To do nothing to worry those who love me;
  To do nothing to let down those who trust me;
  To do nothing to fail those who employ me;
  To do nothing to hurt those who are close to me.

Help me all through this day
  To do nothing which would be a cause of temptation to
  someone else or which would make it easier for someone
  else to go wrong;
  Not to discourage anyone who is doing his best;
  Not to dampen anyone's enthusiasms, or to increase anyone's doubts.

Help me all through this day
  To be a comfort to the sad;
  To be a friend to the lonely;
  To be an encouragement to the dispirited;
  To be a help to those who are up against it.

So grant that others may see in me something of the reflection
of the Master whose I am and whom I seek to serve.

This I ask for your love's sake. AMEN.

In the Evening

Forgive me, O God, if to-day
  By being irritable and unreasonable, I made trouble in the
  family circle;

By being careless and slack and inefficient at my work, I
made the tasks of others more difficult;
By being self-willed and stubborn and too set on my own
way, I was a problem to my friends and my companions.

Forgive me if to-day
I was too impatient with someone who was doing his best;
I have been too quick to take offence, and to see slights
where no slight was intended;
I did things badly, and caused others trouble, because I was
not attending to my instructions and to my work as I
ought to have been.

Help me to-morrow to be more strict with myself; more understanding to others; more faithful to my work than ever before : through Jesus Christ my Lord. AMEN.

Daily Reading

MATTHEW 13: 31-34

Another parable put he forth unto them, saying, The kingdom
of heaven is like to a grain of mustard seed, which a man
took, and sowed in his field; which indeed is the least of all
seeds : but when it is grown, it is the greatest among herbs,
and becometh a tree, so that the birds of the air come and
lodge in the branches thereof. Another parable spake he unto
them : The kingdom of heaven is like unto leaven, which a
woman took, and hid in three measures of meal, till the whole
was leavened. All these things spake Jesus unto the multitude in parables; and without a parable spake he not unto
them.

In the Morning

O God, I know that I am going to be very busy to-day. Help me not to be so busy that I miss the most important things.

Help me not to be too busy to look up and to see a glimpse of beauty in your world.

Help me not to be too busy listening to other voices to hear your voice when you speak to me.

Help me not to be too busy to listen to anyone who is in trouble, and to help anyone who is in difficulty.

Help me not to be too busy to stand still for a moment to think and to remember.

Help me not to be too busy to remember the claims of my home, my children, and my family.

Help me all through to-day to remember that I must work my hardest, and also to remember that sometimes I must be still.

This I ask for Jesus' sake. AMEN.

In the Evening

O God, sometimes I begin to worry, especially when I sit at the end of the day and think.

I begin to worry about my work.
Help me to know that with your help I can cope.

I begin to worry about money, and about making ends meet.

Help me to remember that, though money is important, there are things that money cannot buy—and these are the most precious things of all.

I begin to worry about my health.
Help me to remember that worrying makes me worse, and that trusting always makes me better.

I begin to worry about the things which tempt me.
Help me to remember that you are with me to help me to conquer them.

I begin to worry about those I love.
Help me to do everything I can for them, and then to leave them in your care.

Give me to-night your peace in my troubled heart: through Jesus Christ my Lord. AMEN.

Daily Reading

PSALM 51: 7-12

Purge me with hyssop, and I shall be clean: wash me, and I shall be whiter than snow.
Make me to hear joy and gladness; that the bones which thou hast broken may rejoice.
Hide thy face from my sins, and blot out all mine iniquities.
Create in me a clean heart, O God: and renew a right spirit within me.
Cast me not away from thy presence; and take not thy holy Spirit from me.
Restore unto me the joy of thy salvation; and uphold me with thy free Spirit.

In the Morning

Lord Jesus, help me to walk with you all through to-day.

Give me to-day
  Something of the wisdom that was in your words;
  Something of the love that was in your heart;
  Something of the help that was on your hands.

Give me to-day
  Something of your patience with people;
  Something of your ability to bear slights and insults and
    injuries without bitterness and without resentment;
  Something of your ability always to forgive.

Help me to live in such a way to-day that others may know
that I began the day with you, and that I am walking with
you, so that, however dimly, others may see you in me.

This I ask for your love's sake. AMEN.

In the Evening

O God, I think to-night of those in special trouble and distress of body, mind, or heart.

  Bless the homes in which someone has died, and in which
    those who are left are bewildered and sad.

  Bless the homes where to-night there are those who must
    sit by the bed of a loved one and wait for the end to
    come.

  Bless those who are ill, and whose pain seems worst of all
    in the slow night hours.

Bless homes into which bad news has come, homes in which some member of the family has brought shame upon himself and sorrow to those who love him.

Bless those who are sitting alone with some bitter disappointment, with some dream that has ended, and which will now never come true.

Bless those for whom life has fallen in.

Bless those who are wrestling with some temptation, and those who have lost the battle.

Bless those who are separated from those they love, and who are lonely and anxious.

Where there is trouble of any kind, be there to comfort and support.

This I ask for your love's sake. AMEN.

Daily Reading

MATTHEW II: 25-30

At that time Jesus answered and said, I thank thee, O Father, Lord of heaven and earth, because thou hast hid these things from the wise and prudent, and hast revealed them unto babes. Even so, Father: for so it seemed good in thy sight. All things are delivered unto me of my Father: and no man knoweth the Son, but the Father; neither knoweth any man the Father, save the Son and he to whomsoever the Son will reveal him. Come unto me, all ye that labour and are heavy laden, and I will give you rest. Take my yoke upon you, and learn of me; for I am meek and lowly in heart; and ye shall find rest unto your souls. For my yoke is easy, and my burden is light.

In the Morning

O God, Lord of all good life, help me to use to-day well.

Help me to use to-day
  To know you a little better;
  To do my work a little more diligently;
  To serve my fellowmen a little more lovingly;
  To make myself by your help a little more like Jesus.

Help me to make to-day a day of progress in my life, and to become a little more like what you want me to be.

This I ask for Jesus' sake. AMEN.

In the Evening

Forgive me, O Father, for anything I refused to do to-day which I might have done.

Forgive me for any help I might have given to-day, and did not give.

Forgive me for being so wrapped up in my own troubles and my own problems that I had no time for those of anyone else.

Forgive me for being so immersed in my own work that I had no time to give anyone else a helping hand.

Forgive me for selfishly hoarding my own leisure and comfort, and for refusing to give them up to help others, or to help your Church and your people and your work.

Help me to learn the lesson—I know that it is true—that selfishness and happiness can never go together; and help me to find happiness in trying to forget myself, and in trying to bring help and happiness to others : through Jesus Christ my Lord. AMEN.

Daily Reading

PSALM 34 : 1-8

I will bless the Lord at all times : his praise shall continually be in my mouth.

My soul shall make her boast in the Lord; the humble shall hear thereof, and be glad.

O magnify the Lord with me, and let us exalt his name together.

I sought the Lord, and he heard me, and delivered me from all my fears.

They looked unto him, and were lightened : and their faces were not ashamed.

This poor man cried, and the Lord heard him, and saved him out of all his troubles.

The angel of the Lord encampeth round about them that fear him and delivereth them.

O taste and see that the Lord is good : blessed is the man that trusteth in him.

In the Morning

Give me this day, O God,
The energy I need to face my work;
The diligence I need to do it well;
The self-discipline, which will make me work just as hard,
even if there be none to see, and none to praise, and
none to blame;
The self-respect which will not stoop to produce anything
which is less than my best;
The courtesy and the considerateness, which will make me
easy to live with and easy to work with.

Help me so to live to-day that I may make this world a
happier place wherever I may be: through Jesus Christ my
Lord. AMEN.

In the Evening

Give me this night, O Father, the peace of mind which is
truly rest.

Take from me
All envy of anyone else;
All resentment for anything which has been withheld from
me;
All bitterness against anyone who has hurt me or wronged
me;

All anger against the apparent injustice of life;
All foolish worry about the future, and all futile regret
about the past.

Help me to be
At peace with myself;
At peace with my fellowmen;
At peace with you.

So indeed may I lay myself down to rest in peace : through
Jesus Christ my Lord. AMEN.

Daily Reading

MATTHEW 6: 27-34

Which of you by taking thought can add one cubit unto his
stature? And why take ye thought for raiment? Consider
the lilies of the field, how they grow; they toil not, neither do
they spin : and yet I say unto you, That even Solomon in all
his glory was not arrayed like one of these. Wherefore, if God
so clothe the grass of the field, which to-day is, and to-
morrow is cast into the oven, shall he not much more clothe
you, O ye of little faith? Therefore take no thought, saying,
What shall we eat? or, What shall we drink? or, Where-
withal shall we be clothed? (For after all these things do the
Gentiles seek :) for your heavenly Father knoweth that ye
have need of all these things. But seek ye first the kingdom
of God, and his righteousness; and all these things shall be
added unto you. Take therefore no thought for the morrow :
for the morrow shall take thought for the things of itself.
Sufficient unto the day is the evil thereof.

In the Morning

O God, give me strength and wisdom to live this day as I
ought.

Give me
> Strength to conquer every temptation which will come to
> me;
> Strength to do every task which is assigned to me;
> Strength to shoulder every responsibility which is laid upon
> me.

Give me
> Wisdom to know when to speak, and when to keep silent;
> Wisdom to know when to act, and when to refrain from
> action;
> Wisdom to know when to speak my mind, and when to
> hold my peace.

So bring me to the end of this day in goodness, in happiness
and in content: through Jesus Christ my Lord. AMEN.

In the Evening

O God, I know that there is nothing so precious as friendship
and that there is nothing so enriching as love.

Thank you for all the friends whom I have met to-day.

Thank you for all the people with whom I travelled, with whom I walked, with whom I worked, with whom I talked, with whom I ate.

Thank you for the people with whom I listened to music, or watched plays or pictures, or watched games or played games.

Thank you for those who are even closer to me than my friends, those whom I love, and those who love me; those whose hands serve my needs and care for my comfort; those whose love surrounds me all my days.

Help me always to be loyal to my friends and true to those who love me : through Jesus Christ my Lord. AMEN.

Daily Reading

PSALM 90 : 12-17

So teach us to number our days, that we may apply our hearts unto wisdom.

Return, O Lord, how long? and let it repent thee concerning thy servants.

O satisfy us early with thy mercy; that we may rejoice and be glad all our days.

Make us glad according to the days wherein thou has afflicted us, and the years wherein we have seen evil.

Let thy work appear unto thy servants, and thy glory unto their children.

And let the beauty of the Lord our God be upon us; and establish thou the work of our hands upon us; yea, the work of our hands establish thou it.

In the Morning

O God, I want to try to begin to-day by thinking not of myself but of others.

Bless those for whom to-day is going to be a difficult day :
  Those who must make decisions;
  Those who must wrestle with temptations;
  Those who have some special problem to solve.

Bless those for whom to-day is going to be a sad day :
  Those who are meeting the day with tears in their eyes
    and with sorrow and loneliness in their hearts;
  Those who to-day must lay some dear one to rest in death;
  Those who awake to the morning with no work to do.

Bless those for whom to-day is going to be a happy day :
  Those who are happy and who are eagerly looking forward
    to to-day;
  Those who are to be married to-day;
  Those who will walk in the sunshine of life to-day.

Give me all through to-day sympathy and love for all, that I may always try to weep with those who weep and to rejoice with those who rejoice : through Jesus Christ my Lord. AMEN.

In the Evening

O God, I thank you for to-day.
I thank you that you gave me

  Health and strength and ability to do my work;

Friends with whom to walk and talk;
Those who love me, who care for me, and who pray for me.

I thank you
    For the times when you made me able to overcome my
      temptations;
    For the times when you made me able to choose the right
      and to refuse the wrong;
    For the times when you spoke to me, and gripped me, and
      kept me from doing something which would have
      brought me shame or regret.

I thank you for Jesus,
    For his example;
    For his presence with me;
    For the friendship I have with you because of him.

Help me to show my gratitude by loving you more and by
serving and obeying you better: through Jesus Christ my
Lord. AMEN.

Daily Reading

JOHN 14: 1-6

Let not your heart be troubled: ye believe in God, believe
also in me. In my Father's house are many mansions: if it
were not so, I would have told you. I go to prepare a place
for you. And if I go and prepare a place for you, I will
come again, and receive you unto myself; that where I
am, there ye may be also. And whither I go ye know,
and the way ye know. Thomas saith unto him, Lord,
we know not whither thou goest; and how can we know the
way? Jesus saith unto him, I am the way, the truth, and the
life; no man cometh unto the Father, but by me.

In the Morning

O God, thank you for giving me another day, and another gift of time.

Help me all through to-day not to put off until to-morrow that which I ought to do to-day.

Help me not to put things off
  Because I can't be bothered doing them;
  Because I don't want to do them;
  Because I don't like doing them;
  Because I am afraid to do them.

Help me to do each task, to face each duty, to shoulder each responsibility as it comes to me, so that, if life should end to-night for me, there will be no loose ends, no things half-finished, no tasks undone: through Jesus Christ my Lord. AMEN.

In the Evening

When I sit down and think at night, O Father, before I go to sleep, I always feel that there never has been a day when I have done all that I meant to do, and when I have been all that I meant to be. Somehow the day is never long enough, and my strength of will is never strong enough.

Even in spite of my many failures keep me from discouragement; keep me from lowering my ideals; keep me from abandoning hope and from giving up.

Help me to try still harder; to trust still more and more in you, and less and less in myself.

This I ask for your love's sake. AMEN.

Daily Reading

PSALM 95: 1-6

O come, let us sing unto the Lord : let us make a joyful noise to the rock of our salvation.
Let us come before his presence with thanksgiving, and make a joyful noise unto him with psalms.
For the Lord is a great God, and a great King above all gods.
In his hand are the deep places of the earth : the strength of the hills is his also.
The sea is, and he made it : and his hands formed the dry land.
O come, let us worship and bow down : let us kneel before the Lord our maker.

In the Morning

O God, my Father, I am very fortunate in my home, my parents, my family, my friends, my work, my church, my country. To-day, before I go out to work, I want to remember before you those for whom life is not nearly so happy as it is for me,

Refugees who have no home, no place to call their own;

Coloured people in lands in which coloured people have no rights;

Those who love freedom in lands where freedom is lost;

Christians in lands where Christians are persecuted;

Those who are unhappy in their work, badly paid, compelled to work in bad conditions;

Those who are treated at home without sympathy, and even with cruelty;

Those who live or work in a situation in which it is very difficult to be a Christian at all;

The friendless, the lonely, and the sad;

Those in hospitals and in places for those whose minds have lost the light of reason;

Those in prison and in disgrace.

O God, grant that my own happiness may never make me blind to the need and forgetful of the unhappiness of others: This I ask for your love's sake. AMEN.

In the Evening

Forgive me, O God,

If to-day I have been too impatient, especially with people;

If to-day I have made anyone feel a nuisance;
If to-day in my heart of hearts I have thought people fools
—and have shown them that I did;
If to-day there were times when I was too aggressively sure
that I was right;
If to-day I have ridden rough-shod over the feelings of
someone else;
If to-day I have been
Unapproachable to talk to;
Difficult to work with;
Unsympathetic to appeal to;
Critical in my outlook;
Harsh in my judgment.

I cannot undo what I have done, but help me to-morrow to be
more loving and more kind—more like Jesus.

This I ask for your love's sake. AMEN.

Daily Reading

JOHN 15: 1-5

I am the true vine, and my Father is the husbandman. Every
branch in me that beareth not fruit he taketh away; and every
branch that beareth fruit, he purgeth it, that it may bring
forth more fruit. Now ye are clean through the word which
I have spoken unto you. Abide in me and I in you. As the
branch cannot bear fruit of itself, except it abide in the vine;
no more can ye, except ye abide in me. I am the vine, ye are
the branches: he that abideth in me, and I in him, the same
bringeth forth much fruit: for without me ye can do nothing.

45

In the Morning

O God, my Father, as I go out to life and work to-day,

I thank you for the world's beauty:
For the light of the sun;
For the wind on my face;
For the colour of the flowers;
And for all glimpses of lovely things.

I thank you for life's gracious things:
For friendship's help;
For kinship's strength;
For love's wonder.

I remember this world's evil and its sin.
Help me to overcome every temptation, and make my life like a light which guides to goodness. And, if anyone has fallen, help me to sympathise and to help rather than to judge and condemn.

I remember this world's sorrow.
Help me to-day to bring comfort to some broken heart, and cheer to some lonely life.

So grant that, when evening comes, I may feel that I have not wasted this day.

Hear this my prayer through Jesus Christ my Lord. AMEN.

In the Evening

O God, my Father, to-night I bring to you myself, my life and all that is in it.

I bring to you
My sins for your forgiveness;
My hopes, my aims, my ambitions for your blessing;
My temptations for your strength;
My tasks, my duties, my responsibilities for your help;
My friends, my dear ones, my loved ones for your care and your protection;
And I bring everything with a thankful and a grateful heart for all that you have done for me.

So grant to me to sleep to-night with the everlasting arms underneath and about me: through Jesus Christ my Lord. AMEN.

Daily Reading

P S A L M 100

Make a joyful noise unto the Lord, all ye lands.
Serve the Lord with gladness: come before his presence with singing.
Know ye that the Lord he is God: it is he that hath made us, and not we ourselves; we are his people, and the sheep of his pasture.
Enter into his gates with thanksgiving, and into his courts with praise: be thankful unto him, and bless his name.
For the Lord is good: his mercy is everlasting; and his truth endureth to all generations.

In the Morning

O God, my Father, keep me from all failure all through to-day.

Keep me from
  Failure in gratitude to those to whom I owe so much;
  Failure in diligence to those to whom I owe my duty and my work;
  Failure in self-control, when temptation comes and when passions are strong.

Keep me from
  Failure to give my help to those who need my help;
  Failure to give an example and a lead to those who need support in goodness;
  Failure in kindness to those who are in trouble of any kind.

Help me this day perfectly to fulfil my responsibilities to myself, to my loved ones, to my employers, to my fellowmen and to you.

This I ask for Jesus' sake. AMEN.

In the Evening

O God, you are the Father of all, and I ask your blessing on all those who are in trouble to-night.

I ask you to bless and help
  Little children who are afraid of the dark;
  Sufferers who cannot sleep for their pain;
  Those who in sorrow are lonelier than ever they thought it possible to be.

I ask you to bless and help
  Those in prison and in disgrace;

Those who have suddenly realised the mess they have made of life for themselves and for others;

Those who have been hurt, wounded, failed, by those whom they trusted, those in whom they believed, those whom they loved;

Those who have newly come to see the sorrow and the heartbreak of which their thoughtlessness has been the cause.

O God, my Father, bless me now before I sleep.

Thank you for to-day and for all the happy things that were in it.

Forgive me for anything in it which was wrong, and which grieved others or hurt you.

Give me now a good night's rest and quiet sleep.

This I ask for Jesus' sake. AMEN.

Daily Reading

LUKE 9: 57-62

And it came to pass, that, as they went in the way, a certain man said unto him, Lord, I will follow thee whithersoever thou goest. And Jesus said unto him, Foxes have holes, and birds of the air have nests; but the Son of man hath not where to lay his head. And he said unto another, Follow me. But he said, Lord, suffer me first to go and bury my father. Jesus said unto him, Let the dead bury their dead: but go thou and preach the kingdom of God. And another also said, Lord, I will follow thee; but let me first go bid them farewell, which are at home at my house. And Jesus said unto him, No man, having put his hand to the plough, and looking back, is fit for the kingdom of God.

In the Morning

Eternal and everblessed God, whom to know is life eternal,

Help me daily to know you better, that daily I may more fully enter into real life, and may more fully know the meaning of life.

Eternal and everblessed God, whom to serve is perfect freedom,

Grant that I may daily serve you more faithfully, so that in doing your will I may find my peace.

Eternal and everblessed God, whom to love is fulness of joy,

Help me day by day to love you more, so that I may come a little nearer to loving you as you first loved me.

Hear this my prayer, through Jesus Christ my Lord. AMEN.

In the Evening

O God, forgive me for allowing any wrong thoughts to enter into my mind to-day.

Forgive me for allowing my eyes to linger on things at which I should not even have looked.

Forgive me for speaking words which I should never have allowed to soil my lips.

Forgive me for needlessly giving temptation a chance to attack me.

Forgive me for all the things for which I am sorry now, and grant to me, before I sleep, the sense of being forgiven and the kiss of pardon and of peace.

This I ask for your love's sake. AMEN.

Daily Reading

PSALM 124

If it had not been the Lord who was on our side, now may Israel say;

If it had not been the Lord who was on our side, when men rose up against us:

Then they had swallowed us up quick, when their wrath was kindled against us:

Then the waters had overwhelmed us, the stream had gone over our soul:

Then the proud waters had gone over our soul.

Blessed be the Lord, who hath not given us as a prey to their teeth.

Our soul is escaped as a bird out of the snare of the fowlers; the snare is broken, and we are escaped.

Our help is in the name of the Lord, who made heaven and earth.

In the Morning

O God, Father and Protector of all, bless all those for whom this will be a worrying and a difficult day:

People in hospital, waiting to undergo an operation to-day;
People who must take some very important decision to-day;
Scholars at school, students at university, who must sit some examination to-day;
Those who are leaving home for the first time to-day, to go to some place that is new and strange, and people who are beginning a new job to-day;
Those who have to face some interview to-day, the result of which will make a very big difference to them;
Those for whom to-day
Work will be specially hard;
Temptation will be specially strong;
People will be specially difficult.

Bless all such people, and bless me. Grant that they and I may be so strengthened and guided that we may come to the end of the day with no mistakes and with no regrets: through Jesus Christ my Lord. AMEN.

In the Evening

O God, I thank you for the things which I have discovered to-day:
For any new thing which I know now which I did not know this morning;
For anything that has been added to my store of knowledge and of experience;

For books that I have read and places that I have seen : •
I thank you, O God.

I thank you for all the people I have discovered to-day :
For the friends I have known for long;
For new acquaintances whom I have made;
For people I met who have the same interests as I have, and
to whom it was a joy to talk :
I thank you, O God.

I thank you specially for people whom I did not like and
whom now for the first time I am beginning to understand.

Amidst all the changes of life I thank you for Jesus who is
always the same, yesterday, to-day and forever.

Hear this my evening thanksgiving, and help me to try to
deserve it all a little better : through Jesus Christ my Lord.
AMEN.

Daily Reading

LUKE 10: 38-42

Now it came to pass, as they went, that he entered into a
certain village : and a certain woman named Martha received
him into her house. And she had a sister called Mary, which
also sat at Jesus' feet, and heard his word. But Martha was
cumbered about much serving, and came to him, and said,
Lord, dost thou not care that my sister hath left me to serve
alone? bid her therefore that she help me. And Jesus
answered and said unto her, Martha, Martha, thou art careful
and troubled about many things : but one thing is needful :
and Mary hath chosen that good part, which shall not be taken
away from her.

In the Morning

O God, bless all those who have very responsible jobs to do
to-day:

Teachers who mould the minds and lives of boys and girls;

Doctors and surgeons whose skill makes people well again
and eases their pain;

Lawyers who interpret the law, policemen who enforce the
law, judges who administer justice;

Those in whose employment and control there are many
workers, and whose decisions affect many lives;

Those on the roads, on the railways, at sea, and in the air,
in whose hands are the lives and the safety of those who
travel and journey;

Scientists who control decisions and discover powers which
can bring life and death;

Statesmen whose decisions affect the welfare of the nations
and of the world;

Preachers who tell the story of Jesus in this land and in
lands across the sea;

Parents to whom there has been given the privilege and the
responsibility of a child.

Help them and support them in their work, and help me
to-day to do well every task, however humble, which is given
me to do: through Jesus Christ my Lord. AMEN.

In the Evening

O God, forgive me for all to-day's mistakes.

When I look back, I think of
The things I would do much better, if I had the chance to
do them again;

The people to whom I would be so much kinder and so
much more courteous, if I could meet them again;
The things that I wish I had not done, and the words that
I wish I had not spoken;
The things I failed to do, and the chance to do which may
never come back again;
The fine impulses which I would turn into action, if I had
to-day again.

O God, give me sleep to-night; and in the days to come give
me strength and grace to do what I know I ought to do, and
to live in the way I know I ought to live: through Jesus
Christ my Lord. AMEN.

Daily Reading

PSALM 136: 1-5, 23-26

O give thanks unto the Lord; for he is good: for his mercy
endureth for ever.
O give thanks unto the God of gods: for his mercy endureth
for ever.
O give thanks to the Lord of lords: for his mercy endureth
for ever.
To him who alone doeth great wonders: for his mercy
endureth for ever.
To him that by wisdom made the heavens: for his mercy
endureth for ever.
Who remembered us in our low estate: for his mercy endureth for ever.
And hath redeemed us from our enemies: for his mercy
endureth for ever.
Who giveth food to all flesh: for his mercy endureth for ever.
O give thanks unto the God of heaven: for his mercy
endureth for ever.

In the Morning

O God, my Father, give me patience all through to-day.

Give me patience with my work,
  so that I may work at a job until I finish it or get it right,
  no matter how difficult or how boring it may be.

Give me patience with people,
  so that I will not become irritated or annoyed,
  and so that I may never lose my temper with them.

Give me patience with life,
  so that I may not give up hope
  when hopes are long in coming true;
  so that I may accept disappointment without bitterness
  and delay without complaint.

Hear this my morning prayer for your love's sake. AMEN.

In the Evening

O God, as I lay myself down to rest to-night, I pray for all those who do not like the night;

  Bless little children who are afraid of the dark.

Bless those in illness and in pain, for whom the night hours are very slow and very long.

Bless those who are lonely, and who in the stillness of the night feel their loneliness all the more.

Bless those who are sad, and who in the night time miss someone who is gone from them more than at any other time.

Bless those who are away from home in hospitals and in infirmaries, in journeyings and in distant places.

Bless those who are worried, and whose thoughts will not let them sleep.

O God, give me to-night a heart content and a mind at rest, so that I may sleep in peace and rise in strength: through Jesus Christ my Lord. AMEN.

Daily Reading

JOHN 10: 7-11

Then said Jesus unto them again, Verily, verily, I say unto you, I am the door of the sheep. All that ever came before me are thieves and robbers: but the sheep did not hear them. I am the door: by me if any man enter in, he shall be saved, and shall go in and out, and find pasture. The thief cometh not, but for to steal, and to kill, and to destroy: I am come that they might have life, and that they might have it more abundantly. I am the good shepherd: the good shepherd giveth his life for the sheep.

In the Morning

O God, grant that to-day
  I may not disappoint any friend;
  I may not grieve any loved one;
  I may not fail anyone to whom I have a duty;
  I may not shame myself.

Grant that to-day
  I may do my work with honesty and fidelity;
  I may take my pleasure in happiness and purity.

Grant that to-day
  I may lead no one astray;
  I may not make goodness and faith harder for anyone.

Help me to-day to be a help and example to all, and to bring strength and encouragement, wherever I may be: through Jesus Christ my Lord. AMEN.

In the Evening

O God, at the end of the day it is not so much the things that I have done which worry me as the things which I have not done.

Forgive me for the tasks into which I did not put my best, for work that was shoddy, and for workmanship of which any true craftsman would be ashamed.

Forgive me for the things I did not do, and for the help I did not give.

Forgive me for the word of praise and the word of thanks I did not speak.

Forgive me for my failure in courtesy and in graciousness to those with whom I live and work.

Help me each day to do better, so that each night I may have fewer regrets: through Jesus Christ my Lord. AMEN.

Daily Reading

ISAIAH 6: 1-8

In the year that king Uzziah died I saw also the Lord sitting upon a throne, high and lifted up, and his train filled the temple. Above it stood the seraphim: each one had six wings; with twain he covered his face, and with twain he covered his feet, and with twain he did fly. And one cried unto another, and said, Holy, holy, holy, is the Lord of hosts: the whole earth is full of his glory. And the posts of the door moved at the voice of him that cried, and the house was filled with smoke. Then said I, Woe is me! for I am undone; because I am a man of unclean lips, and I dwell in the midst of a people of unclean lips: for mine eyes have seen the King, the Lord of hosts. Then flew one of the seraphim unto me, having a live coal in his hand, which he had taken with the tongs from off the altar: and he laid it upon my mouth, and said, Lo, this hath touched thy lips; and thine iniquity is taken away, and thy sin purged. Also I heard the voice of the Lord, saying, Whom shall I send, and who will go for us? Then said I, Here am I; send me.

In the Morning

O God, help me to-day and every day to use life as you would have me to use it.

Help me to use whatever gifts and whatever strength I have to help others, and to make a useful contribution to the life and the work of the world, wherever I am.

Help me to use whatever money I have, not selfishly, but generously.

Help me to use my time wisely in honest work; help me to use my spare time, not altogether selfishly, and not altogether for my own pleasure, but to do something in it for others.

Help me to use my mind to get new knowledge and to improve myself; help me never to stop learning, and not to be entirely taken up with light and frivolous things.

Help me to use to-day in such a way that in it I may improve myself, help others and please you : through Jesus Christ my Lord. AMEN.

In the Evening

O God, when I sit and think at the end of the day, I realise how unsatisfactory I am.

So often I do not give my employers my best work.

So often I only make use of my home, and I am more disobliging and more discourteous to those who love me most than to anyone else.

So often I expect far more from my friends than I am prepared to give to them.

So often I find pleasure in things in which I shouldn't.

So often I allow thoughts and pictures to come into my mind, and feelings to come into my heart, which should never be allowed to find an entry there.

So often I refuse to give my Church the help and the service I could well give, even if it does mean giving up something of my time or money.

So often I shirk work, evade decisions, refuse duties, and run away from responsibilities.

Forgive me, O God. Help me to try harder and to do better. Give me your strength to do the things which I cannot do myself. This I ask for Jesus' sake. AMEN.

Daily Reading

2 CORINTHIANS 5 : 17-21

Therefore if any man be in Christ, he is a new creature: old things are passed away; behold, all things are become new. And all things are of God, who hath reconciled us to himself by Jesus Christ, and hath given to us the ministry of reconciliation; to wit, that God was in Christ, reconciling the world unto himself, not imputing their trespasses unto them; and hath committed unto us the word of reconciliation. Now then we are ambassadors for Christ, as though God did beseech you by us: we pray you in Christ's stead, be ye reconciled to God. For he hath made him to be sin for us, who knew no sin; that we might be made the righteousness of God in him.

In the Morning

O God, this morning I have come into the quietness and still-ness of your presence to begin the day, so that out of this moment I may take with me a quiet serenity which will last me through the rough and tumble of this day's life.

I have come to find wisdom,
  so that to-day I may not make any foolish mistakes.

I have come to find peace,
  so that nothing may worry or upset me all through to-day.

I have come to find love,
  so that all through to-day nothing may make me bitter or unforgiving or unkind.

I have come to begin the day with you, to continue it with you, and to end it with you, so that it will be a day which will have in it nothing to regret.

Hear this my morning prayer for Jesus' sake. AMEN.

In the Evening

O God, I started out to-day with all kinds of high hopes and resolutions, but it has just been another of these days.

I have been just as easily irritated and annoyed as ever I was.

I have been just as easily worried and flustered and upset as ever I was.

I have been just as impatient with people, just as quick in temper and tongue as ever I was.

I have been no kinder, no more considerate, no more like Jesus.

O God, it would be easy to make excuses, to put the blame on others, to say that it was not all my fault. But I don't want to say that, because it would not really be true. All I want to say is : Forgive me, help me not to be discouraged, and not to give up the battle for goodness, and help me to do better to-morrow.

All this I ask for your love's sake. AMEN.

Daily Reading

ISAIAH 53 : 1-6

Who hath believed our report? and to whom is the arm of the Lord revealed? For he shall grow up before him as a tender plant, and as a root out of a dry ground : he hath no form nor comeliness; and when we shall see him, there is no beauty that we should desire him. He is despised and rejected of men, a man of sorrows, and acquainted with grief : and we hid as it were our faces from him; he was despised, and we esteemed him not. Surely he hath borne our griefs, and carried our sorrows : yet we did esteem him stricken, smitten of God, and afflicted. But he was wounded for our transgressions, he was bruised for our iniquities : the chastisement of our peace was upon him; and with his stripes we are healed. All we like sheep have gone astray; we have turned every one to his own way; and the Lord hath laid on him the iniquity of us all.

In the Morning

O God, you know me, and you know that I don't want to go out at all to-day.

> I am tired before I start. There are people I don't want to meet; there are jobs I don't want to do. There are tasks which I will have to do, and I am not nearly as well prepared for them as I ought to be.

> I would much rather stay at home, or run away from it all. But I can't do that, and I know I can't do that. I know quite well life has got to go on, no matter how I feel about it.

Lord Jesus, come with me, and help me to feel you beside me all day, so that I will not only get grimly through to-day, but that I may know the joy of living with you.

This I ask for your love's sake. AMEN.

In the Evening

O God, bless all my friends and my loved ones to-night.

Bless those whose lives are interwoven with mine, and without whom life could never be the same. Bless those to whom I owe my comfort, and without whom life would be very lonely.

Bless the one to whom I have given my heart to keep, and who has given me his/her heart to keep, and keep us for ever loyal, for ever loving, and for ever true to one another.

Bless my absent friends and loved ones, from whom for a time I am separated. Guard them, guide them, protect them, and grant that we may soon meet again.

I know that all for whom I am praying are also praying for me. Help me just now to feel very near to them, and not only to them, but even to those whom I have loved and lost awhile, and who have gone to be with you.

Hear this my prayer for your love's sake. AMEN.

Daily Reading

I CORINTHIANS 3: 18-23

Let no man deceive himself. If any man among you seemeth to be wise in this world, let him become a fool, that he may be wise. For the wisdom of this world is foolishness with God. For it is written, He taketh the wise in their own craftiness. And again, The Lord knoweth the thoughts of the wise, that they are vain. Therefore let no man glory in men. For all things are yours; whether Paul, or Apollos, or Cephas, or the world, or life, or death, or things present, or things to come; all are yours; and ye are Christ's; and Christ is God's.

In the Morning

O God, my Father, make me more appreciative of others.

Help me never to fail to say thanks for everything that is done for me, and never to take anything for granted, just because it comes to me unfailingly every day.

Help me always to be ready to speak a word of praise, whenever a word of praise is possible—and sometimes even when it is not possible.

Help me to be quick to notice things. Help me to be quick to see when someone is depressed and discouraged and unhappy. Help me to be quick to see it when someone is lonely and shy and is left out of things.

O Lord Jesus, all through to-day help me to see people with your eyes.

This I ask for your love's sake. AMEN.

In the Evening

Forgive me, O God, for all the trouble I have caused to-day.

Forgive me
if I made a nuisance of myself by being stupidly obstinate, or needlessly obstructive, or foolishly fussy.

Forgive me
if I have caused other people trouble by keeping them waiting for me, or by being late with my work, or by failing to keep a promise.

66

Forgive me
   if I have annoyed others by trying to be funny at the wrong
   time, by making jokes about the wrong things, or by being
   cross, irritable, bad-tempered, discourteous.

Forgive me
   if I could see no point of view but my own, or if I was
   hard to work with, or difficult to live with.
To-night, O God, forgive me. To-morrow is another day;
help me to make a better job of it than I did of to-day.

This I ask for your love's sake. AMEN.

Daily Reading

ISAIAH 55: 6-11

Seek ye the Lord while he may be found, call ye upon him
while he is near: let the wicked forsake his way, and the
unrighteous man his thoughts: and let him return unto the
Lord, and he will have mercy upon him: and to our God,
for he will abundantly pardon. For my thoughts are not your
thoughts, neither are your ways my ways, saith the Lord. For
as the heavens are higher than the earth, so are my ways
higher than your ways, and my thoughts than your thoughts.
For as the rain cometh down, and the snow from heaven,
and returneth not thither, but watereth the earth, and maketh
it bring forth and bud, that it may give seed to the sower,
and bread to the eater: so shall my word be that goeth forth
out of my mouth: it shall not return unto me void, but it
shall accomplish that which I please, and it shall prosper in
the thing whereto I sent it.

67

In the Morning

O God, so help me to-day that nothing may make me lose my temper.

So help me that nothing may make me lose my serenity, that I may be proof alike against the big blows and the petty pinpricks of life.

So help me that nothing may make me lose my patience either with things or with people.

So help me that I may not get flustered or excited, but that I may take things easily and just as they come.

So help me to work that I may do things when they ought to be done, and as they ought to be done, so that there will be no last-minute rush to-day.

So help me that nothing may make me take offence or differ in bitterness with anyone to-day.

To-day, O God, garrison my heart with your peace and equip my life with your strength.

This I ask for your love's sake. AMEN.

In the Evening

Forgive me, O God,
    if I have behaved to-day as if I was the only person who
    was busy, and as if I was the only person who had a lot to
    do.

Forgive me
>if I have behaved as if I was the only person for whom things were difficult and hard, and as if life was unkinder to me than to anyone else.

Forgive me
>if I have behaved as if I was the only person who was misjudged or misunderstood, and as if I was the only person who ever got a raw deal.

Forgive me for magnifying my troubles and for forgetting my blessings.

Help me from now on to get things in their right proportions by thinking far more of others and far less of myself.

This I ask for your love's sake. AMEN.

Daily Reading

I CORINTHIANS 15: 53-58

For this corruptible must put on incorruption, and this mortal must put on immortality. So when this corruptible shall have put on incorruption, and this mortal shall have put on immortality, then shall be brought to pass the saying that is written, Death is swallowed up in victory. O death, where is thy sting? O grave, where is thy victory? The sting of death is sin; and the strength of sin is the law. But thanks be to God, which giveth us the victory through our Lord Jesus Christ. Therefore, my beloved brethren, be ye steadfast, unmoveable, always abounding in the work of the Lord, forasmuch as ye know that your labour is not in vain in the Lord.

In the Morning

O God, my Father, give me to-day
Courage, to do the things I am afraid to do;
Conscientiousness, to do the things I do not want to do;
Grace to get alongside the people I do not like and who
do not like me.

Grant that even in the dull routine of the day's work I may
find a thrill, because I remember that I am doing it with you,
so that even the uninteresting things may become interesting,
and so that even things which seem not to matter may become
important.

Help me to be happy all through to-day, and to make others
happy too.

This I ask for Jesus' sake. AMEN.

In the Evening

O God, I thank you for to-day.

I thank you
that I was able to do the work which earns the pay to
support myself and those whom I love and who are depen-
dent on me.

I thank you
for the people I met, and whose company I enjoyed.

I thank you
for any temptation you made me able to overcome;
for any new thing which I have learned;
for any useful thing I was able to do;
for anyone I know better, and to whom I have come closer
to-day.

Help me now to go to sleep with a quiet mind, and to wake
to-morrow glad to meet another day: through Jesus Christ
my Lord. AMEN.

Daily Reading

JEREMIAH 31: 31-34

Behold the days come, saith the Lord, that I will make a new
covenant with the house of Israel, and with the house of
Judah: not according to the covenant that I made with their
fathers in the day that I took them by the hand to bring
them out of the land of Egypt; which my covenant they
brake, although I was a husband unto them, saith the Lord:
but this shall be the covenant that I will make with the house
of Israel: After those days, saith the Lord, I will put my law
in their inward parts, and write it in their hearts; and will be
their God, and they shall be my people. And they shall teach
no more every man his neighbour, and every man his brother,
saying, Know the Lord: for they shall all know me, from
the least of them unto the greatest of them, saith the Lord:
for I will forgive their iniquity, and I will remember their
sin no more.

In the Morning

I thank you, O God, for health and strength to go out and to do my work; and I remember before you those who cannot go out to work to-day.

I remember
> Those who are ill and in pain at home and in the hospitals and the infirmaries and nursing-homes;
> Those who are helpless and paralysed;
> Those whose nerves and minds have collapsed under the strain of living;
> Those who are slowly recovering from a long illness.

I remember
> Those who are old, and whose day's work is done, and who are feeling useless;
> Those who are in disgrace;
> Those who are unemployed, and who have no work to do, and who are worried about what is to happen to their homes and to their loved ones.

Bless all the people who are like that. And, even if my work is dull, or worrying, or hard, or badly paid, or unappreciated, help me to remember how fortunate I am to have the health and strength to do it, and help me not to forget to be grateful to you.

This I ask for Jesus' sake. AMEN.

In the Evening

O God, help me to-night to relax in body and in mind.

Take from me the tension which makes rest impossible.

Take from me the worries which fill my mind with thoughts which destroy sleep.

Take from me the fears which lurk at the back of my mind, which come to haunt me when work is laid aside, and when there is too much time to think.

Help me to-night really and truly to cast my care upon you, really and truly to feel the everlasting arms underneath and about me.

Help me to sleep to-night, not just the sleep of tiredness, but the sleep of peace; through Jesus Christ my Lord. AMEN.

Daily Reading

2 CORINTHIANS 12: 7-10

And lest I should be exalted above measure through the abundance of the revelations, there was given to me a thorn in the flesh, the messenger of Satan to buffet me, lest I should be exalted above measure. For this thing I besought the Lord thrice, that it might depart from me. And he said unto me, My grace is sufficient for thee: for my strength is made perfect in weakness. Most gladly therefore will I rather glory in my infirmities, that the power of Christ may rest upon me. Therefore I take pleasure in infirmities, in reproaches, in necessities, in persecutions, in distresses for Christ's sake: for when I am weak, then am I strong.

In the Morning

O God, give me the things which will make me able to live well to-day.

Give me
   A sense of proportion,
      that I may see what is important and what is not important, and that I may not get all hot and bothered about things which do not matter;

   A sense of humour,
      that I may learn to laugh,
      and especially to laugh at myself, and not to take myself too seriously;

   A sense of responsibility,
      that I may look on each task as something which I am doing for the general good and for you.

Give me
   A new sensitiveness of spirit,
      that I may see when I am hurting people,
      and that I may not blindly and thoughtlessly trample on the feelings of others.

Give me, too, a continual awareness of the presence of Jesus, that I may do nothing which it would grieve him to see, and nothing which it would hurt him to hear.

This I ask for your love's sake. AMEN.

In the Evening

O God, I thank you for to-day.

   I thank you for any lovely thing that I have seen or experienced.

I thank you for anything which happened to me which made me feel that life is really and truly worth living.

I thank you for all the laughter which was in to-day.

I thank you, too, for any moment in which I saw the seriousness and the meaning of life.

I thank you very specially for those I love, and for those who love me, and for all the difference it has made to me to know them, and for all the happiness it brings to me to be with them.

O God, my Father, forgive me for anything in to-day which has vexed others, which has shamed myself, which has disappointed my friends, or which has grieved you.

Give me the sense of being forgiven, that I may lay me down to sleep in peace : through Jesus Christ my Lord. AMEN.

Daily Reading

JOEL 2 : 28-32

And it shall come to pass afterward, that I will pour out my spirit upon all flesh : and your sons and your daughters shall prophesy, your old men shall dream dreams, your young men see visions : and also upon the servants and upon the handmaids in those days will I pour out my spirit. And I will shew wonders in the heavens and in the earth, blood, and fire, and pillars of smoke. The sun shall be turned into darkness, and the moon into blood, before the great and the terrible day of the Lord come. And it shall come to pass, that whosoever shall call on the name of the Lord shall be delivered : for in mount Zion and in Jerusalem shall be deliverance, as the Lord hath said, and in the remnant whom the Lord shall call.

In the Morning

O God, all through to-day make me quicker to praise than to criticise.

Help me never to forget to thank people for anything that they do for me.

Make me always ready to speak a word of praise and of appreciation.

Grant that I may take no service for granted, and that I may allow no help to pass unnoticed.

Make me quick to notice when people are upset or depressed, and give me the ability to speak the word which will help and cheer them.

All through to-day help me to think far less of myself and far more of others, and so to find my own happiness in making others happy.

This I ask for Jesus' sake. AMEN.

In the Evening

Before I sleep to-night, I want to say a prayer for all the people—known to me and unknown to me—for whom this has been a special day of gladness or of grief, of trouble or of joy.

Bless all the homes in which to-day life has ended or life has begun.

Bless all the homes in which a child has been born, and take special care of the mother and the father and the little baby.

Bless those who have been married to-day, and grant that this may be the beginning for them of many years of loyalty and love.

Bless all homes where there has been joy or heartbreak, where there has been happy news of success or sorrowful news of failure, homes to which someone has brought honour and homes to which someone has brought disgrace.

Be very near to any home in which anyone is tempted to do some disgraceful and dishonourable and evil thing, and lay your hand upon his/her shoulder and restrain them from it.

Be in every home to comfort, to encourage, to guide, to restrain; and grant to them all to feel your presence and to know your love: through Jesus Christ my Lord. AMEN.

Daily Reading

GALATIANS 6: 1-5

Brethren, if a man be overtaken in a fault, ye which are spiritual, restore such a one in the spirit of meekness; considering thyself, lest thou also be tempted. Bear ye one another's burdens, and so fulfil the law of Christ. For if a man thinks himself to be something, when he is nothing, he deceiveth himself. But let every man prove his own work, and then shall he have rejoicing in himself alone, and not in another. For every man shall bear his own burden.

77

In the Morning

O God, I know that there are certain dangers which are always threatening me.

Keep me from taking people and all that they do for me for granted, and help me to show them how much I value them, and how much I appreciate all that they do for me.

Keep me from allowing myself to become satisfied with less and less, from lowering my standards, from forgetting my ideals as the days go on.

Keep me from taking sin less and less seriously, from allowing myself things which once I would have refused, from accepting as inevitable things which once would have shocked me.

Help me to walk looking unto Jesus, that I may see all things in the light of his life and of his Cross, so that I may strive to be always on the upward way.

This I ask for your love's sake. AMEN.

In the Evening

O God, I thank you for to-day and for your help all through to-day.

There were things which I thought I would never be able to do,
    but with your help I managed to do them.

There were things of which I was frightened as I looked forward to them,
    but with your help I found them not so terrible after all.

I thank you for the pleasure I found in the company of people whom up to now I thought uninteresting, or whom up to now I did not like.

I thank you that life is just as full of unexpected joys as it is of unexpected sorrows.

I thank you for the friends who grow dearer to me every day, and without whom life would never be the same.

I thank you for the people who have given me the generous love which I have done so little to deserve.

Help me to fall asleep to-night counting my blessings.

Hear this my prayer for Jesus' sake. AMEN.

Daily Reading

MICAH 6: 6-8

Wherewith shall I come before the Lord, and bow myself before the high God? shall I come before him with burnt offerings, with calves of a year old? Will the Lord be pleased with thousands of rams, or with ten thousand rivers of oil? shall I give my firstborn for my transgression, the fruit of my body for the sin of my soul? He hath shewed thee, O man, what is good; and what doth the Lord require of thee, but to do justly, and to love mercy, and to walk humbly with thy God?

In the Morning

O God, my Father, I thank you that this morning I am able to rise and to go to my work.

I thank you that I can move and walk, and see and hear, and think with my mind and work with my hands.

As I think of the health which I enjoy, I remember those who are blind and deaf, lame and helpless and bedridden, those who have lost their reason and whose minds are darkened and whose senses are gone.

I remember those who long to work but who are unemployed, whose talents and gifts and skills are wasting in an idleness which they hate.

Help me, O God, to live to-day in such a way that I may show my gratitude for all the gifts and blessings you have given me : through Jesus Christ my Lord. AMEN.

In the Evening

This morning, O God, I thanked you that I was able to rise from sleep and to go out to my work. It is good to go out, but it is still better to come home.

I thank you for keeping me safe to-day on the busy streets, and on my journeys to and from my work.

I thank you for any temptation which you made me able to conquer to-day.

I thank you that I was able to do the work which I was given to do.

I thank you for everyone who helped me and who was kind to me to-day.

I am sorry if I did any of my work badly, or if I hurt or disappointed anyone.

Now guard and keep me while I sleep, and waken me strengthened and refreshed to-morrow morning: through Jesus Christ my Lord. AMEN.

Daily Reading

HEBREWS 4: 12-16

For the word of God is quick, and powerful, and sharper than any two-edged sword, piercing even to the dividing asunder of soul and spirit, and of the joints and marrow, and is a discerner of the thoughts and intents of the heart. Neither is there any creature that is not manifest in his sight: but all things are naked and opened unto the eyes of him with whom we have to do. Seeing then that we have a great high priest, that is passed into the heavens, Jesus the Son of God, let us hold fast our profession. For we have not a high priest which cannot be touched with the feeling of our infirmities; but was in all points tempted like as we are, yet without sin. Let us therefore come boldly unto the throne of grace, that we may obtain mercy, and find grace to help in time of need.

In the Morning

O God, it is you who have given me another day of life. Unless you help me, I know that this day will go all wrong.

Control my tongue.
Keep me from saying things which make trouble, and from involving myself in arguments which only make bad situations worse and which get nowhere.

Control my thoughts.
Shut the door of my mind against all envious and jealous thoughts; shut it against all bitter and resentful thoughts; shut it against all ugly and unclean thoughts.

Help me to live to-day in purity, in humility and in love.

All through to-day grant that no wrong thought may enter my mind and no wrong word come from my mouth : through Jesus Christ my Lord. AMEN.

In the Evening

O God, my Father, to-night in the quiet time I have many people in my mind and in my heart.

Those I love :
Help me never to hurt or to disappoint them, and never to drift apart from them. Bless them and keep them safe.

My friends :
Help me never to be too selfish and too demanding with my friends; never to try to make use cf them; always to try to do something to enrich their lives, as I wish that they may enrich mine.

The people with whom I work:
Make me easy to work with. Help me never to make the work of others harder by dodging or shirking the work I ought to be doing. Help me never to be needlessly slow to learn, or impatiently unwilling to show others how to do things, or to help them to do them.

All people in pain, in sadness, in loneliness, in trouble, in disgrace:
Help those who cannot help themselves, and bless those for whom their fellowmen can do little to comfort or to support.

Bless me, and make me for ever sure of your love and your care.

This I ask for your love's sake. AMEN.

Daily Reading

EXODUS 20: 1-7

And God spake all these words, saying, I am the Lord thy God, which have brought thee out of the land of Egypt, out of the house of bondage. Thou shalt have no other gods before me. Thou shalt not make unto thee any graven image, or any likeness of anything that is in heaven above, or that is in the earth beneath, or that is in the water under the earth: thou shalt not bow down thyself to them, nor serve them: for I the Lord thy God am a jealous God, visiting the iniquity of the fathers upon the children unto the third and fourth generation of them that hate me; and shewing mercy unto thousands of them that love me, and keep my commandments. Thou shalt not take the name of the Lord thy God in vain; for the Lord will not hold him guiltless that taketh his name in vain.

In the Morning

O God, I will meet all kinds of people to-day; help me to help them all.

If I meet any who are sad,
    help me to comfort them, even if I can do no more than say a word of sympathy and shake their hand.

If I meet any who are depressed,
    help me to cheer them up, and to send them on their way happier because they met me.

If I meet any who are tempted,
    help me to help them to resist temptation by showing them an example, or by speaking a gentle word of warning to them.

If I meet any who are worried,
    help me to ease their anxiety as far as I can.

If I meet any who are overworked,
    help me to lend them a hand, if I possibly can, even if it means extra work for me, and even if I have to go a long way out of my way to do so.

If I meet any who are disgruntled and discontented,
    help me to help them to feel that things are not as bad as they think they are.

If I meet any who are happy,
    help me to share in their joy, and never to grudge it to them.

Make me able to enter into the mind and heart of all whom I meet to-day, and to bring joy and happiness wherever I go : through Jesus Christ my Lord. AMEN.

In the Evening

O God, you know how I feel, and you know that to-night I am so tired that I can hardly stay awake to pray.

But, before I go to sleep, I must say thank you for to-day and I must ask your forgiveness for everything in it that was not right.

Help me now to fall asleep thinking about you, and to waken to-morrow to live for you.

This I ask for your love's sake. AMEN.

Daily Reading

EXODUS 20 : 8-17

Remember the sabbath day, to keep it holy. Six days shalt thou labour, and do all thy work; but the seventh day is the sabbath of the Lord thy God : in it thou shalt not do any work, thou, nor thy son, nor thy daughter, thy manservant, nor thy maidservant, nor thy cattle, nor the stranger that is within thy gates; for in six days the Lord made heaven and earth, the sea, and all that in them is, and rested on the seventh day : wherefore the Lord blessed the sabbath day, and hallowed it. Honour thy father and thy mother : that thy days may be long upon the land which the Lord thy God giveth thee. Thou shalt not kill. Thou shalt not commit adultery. Thou shalt not steal. Thou shalt not bear false witness against thy neighbour. Thou shalt not covet thy neighbour's house, thou shalt not covet thy neighbour's wife, nor his manservant, nor his maidservant, nor his ox, nor his ass, nor any thing that is thy neighbour's.

In the Morning

Help me, O God, to-day,
    To shirk no duty that I should face,
    or word that I should speak.

To avoid no person whom I ought to meet,
or any decision which I ought to take.

To postpone no task that I ought to do,
nor to delay the answer to any request to which I should
    respond.

Help me,
    To do each thing as it comes to me,
    And to do it faithfully, wisely and well.

Keep me alike,
    From delaying the things I ought to do,
    And from rushing into the things, about which I ought to
    think before I act.

All through to-day grant me the wisdom which will keep me
from all mistakes and save me from all regrets: through
Jesus Christ my Lord. AMEN.

In the Evening

Thank you, O God, for making me able to do my work
to-day, and for bringing me back home at evening time.

Thank you for the times to-day when you guided me to do what I ought to do, and when you strengthened me to resist the temptation to do what I ought not to do.

Thank you for anyone you made me able to help to-day, and for anyone to whom I have come closer.

Thank you for those who have helped me to-day, for those who have cheered me when I was depressed, for anyone who went out of his way to help me, for anyone who made me feel that after meeting him life was better than I thought.

Help me to sleep well to-night and to work well to-morrow: through Jesus Christ my Lord. AMEN.

Daily Reading

LUKE 10: 25-28

And, behold, a certain lawyer stood up, and tempted him, saying, Master, what shall I do to inherit eternal life? He said unto him, What is written in the law? how readest thou? And he answering said, Thou shalt love the Lord thy God with all thy heart, and with all thy soul, and with all thy strength, and with all thy mind; and thy neighbour as thyself. And he said unto him, Thou hast answered right: this do, and thou shalt live.

In the Morning

Give me, O God, all through to-day a strong sense of duty,
   so that I will not be able to shirk any task,
   to evade any decision,
   or to avoid any responsibility.

Help me to do my duty to myself,
   so that I will never lose my self-respect.

Help me to do my duty to others,
   so that I may be among my fellowmen as one who serves.

Help me to do my duty to you,
   by giving myself to you body, soul and spirit,
   so that you can use me as you wish.

At the same time give me joy in all things, so that duty may
not be a grim and joyless thing, but so that I may do everything as unto you.

This I ask for your love's sake. AMEN.

In the Evening

O God, you are the God of peace, and I am a worrier. Take
away my worry and give me some of your peace.

Help me not to waste my time worrying about things about
   which there is nothing to be done, but help me to accept
   them, and to make the best of them, and to overcome them.

Help me not to worry about things which I myself can mend,
   but to do something about them, even if it means a great
   effort, and even if it means that which is still more difficult

—the confessing of my error and the humbling of my pride.

Help me not to worry about the past. Although I am a sinner, help me to know and to remember that I am a forgiven sinner.

Help me not to worry about the future, but to know that I will never be tried above what I am able to bear.

Help me to-night to sleep in peace, and to waken to-morrow sure that I can face life, and all that life can demand from me, and all that life can do to me.

Hear this my prayer for Jesus' sake. AMEN.

Daily Reading

I CORINTHIANS 13: 1-7

Though I speak with the tongues of men and of angels, and have not charity, I am become as sounding brass, or a tinkling cymbal. And though I have the gift of prophecy, and understand all mysteries, and all knowledge; and though I have all faith, so that I could remove mountains, and have not charity, I am nothing. And though I bestow all my goods to feed the poor, and though I give my body to be burned, and have not charity, it profiteth me nothing. Charity suffereth long, and is kind; charity envieth not; charity vaunteth not itself, is not puffed up, doth not behave itself unseemly, seeketh not her own, is not easily provoked, thinketh no evil; rejoiceth not in iniquity, but rejoiceth in the truth; beareth all things, believeth all things, hopeth all things, endureth all things.

In the Morning

O God, as this day begins for me, I want to remember before you those for whom it will be hard and sad and difficult.

Bless those
  Who have no work to do, and for whom the hours will be
    empty;
  Who to-day will have to watch a loved one pass from this
    life, or lay a dear one to rest;
  Who will go out to sadness and come home to loneliness;
  Who will be stricken with sudden illness;
  Who have to undergo an operation to-day
    or who must spend it waiting for one;
  Who will receive bad news;
  To whom this day will bring disappointment and heart-
    break.

Grant that all in sorrow, in difficulty, and in hardship may find in you a refuge and strength, and a very present help in their trouble.

This I ask through Jesus Christ my Lord. AMEN.

In the Evening

Take from me to-night, O God,
  The worries which would keep me from sleeping;
  The tension which would keep me from relaxing;
  The envies and the jealousies and the wrong memories,
    which would make my heart bitter.

Forgive me for the things which I regret and for which I am sorry now; and help me here and now to make up my mind to take the first step to try to put things right to-morrow with anyone whom I have hurt or wronged, or anyone with whom I finished to-day at variance.

Help me to-night to sleep in peace, sure of your love and care surrounding me; and grant that to-morrow I may waken with my mind clear, with my body refreshed, and with my heart at peace with men and with you: through Jesus Christ my Lord. AMEN.

Daily Reading

I CORINTHIANS 13: 8-13

Charity never faileth: but whether there be prophecies, they shall fail; whether there be tongues, they shall cease; whether there be knowledge, it shall vanish away. For we know in part, and we prophesy in part. But when that which is perfect is come, then that which is in part shall be done away. When I was a child, I spake as a child, I understood as a child, I thought as a child: but when I became a man, I put away childish things. For now we see through a glass, darkly; but then face to face: now I know in part; but then shall I know even as also I am known. And now abideth faith, hope, charity, these three; but the greatest of these is charity.

In the Morning

O God, help me to make to-day a perfect day, a day at the end of which I will have nothing to regret.

Help me
    To do my work as well as it can possibly be done;
    To treat everyone with perfect courtesy and kindness;
    To conquer every temptation and to say no to everything that is wrong.

Help me
    Not to annoy anyone else and not to allow myself to become annoyed;
    Not to lose my temper and not to do things which will make others lose theirs;
    Not to do anything that is foolish or thoughtless, cruel or unkind.

Help me
    To be cheerful and kind;
    To be brave and strong;
    To be pure and true.
This I ask for your love's sake. AMEN.

In the Evening

O God, this morning I set out with such good resolutions and with such high intentions to make this a perfect day—but it didn't work out that way.

I am sorry for all the time that I have wasted;
I am sorry for all the people at whom I snapped;
I am sorry that I did silly things, when I wasn't thinking
what I was doing.

There are so many things which I said and did to-day for
which I am sorry now. I am sorry that I was needlessly
annoying, bad-tempered and unkind.

Help me before I go to sleep to feel that you understand how
difficult it is, and to feel that you have forgiven me. And help
me to do better to-morrow, and never to give up trying:
through Jesus Christ my Lord. AMEN.

Daily Reading

MATTHEW 5: 43-48

Ye have heard that it hath been said, Thou shalt love thy
neighbour, and hate thine enemy. But I say unto you, Love
your enemies, bless them that curse you, do good to them
that hate you, and pray for them which despitefully use you,
and persecute you; that ye may be the children of your Father
which is in heaven: for he maketh his sun to rise on the evil
and on the good, and sendeth rain on the just and on the
unjust. For if ye love them which love you, what reward have
ye? do not even the publicans the same? And if ye salute
your brethren only, what do ye more than others? do not even
the publicans so? Be ye therefore perfect, even as your
Father which is in heaven is perfect.

In the Morning

O God, help me this morning to count my blessings before I start on the day.

I thank you that I have a job to go to and work to do.

I thank you that I have the health and the strength and the skill to do it.

I thank you for my home, and for those who are very near and dear to me.

I thank you for the friends whom I will meet to-day, as I travel, at my work, at my meals, and when my work is done.

I thank you for everything in which I will find pleasure to-day, for work, for games, for books, for pictures, for films, for plays, for music, for dancing, for talks with my friends, and for times with those who are more than friends, and whom I love.

I thank you for Jesus, and for the promise that he is always with me.

Help me in that promise to find my inspiration to goodness, and my protection from sin.

Hear this my prayer for your love's sake. AMEN.

In the Evening

O God, before I sleep to-night, I want to bring to you in my prayer those whom I know who specially need your help.

Bless those in sickness, in illness, and in pain. Give them the cheerfulness, the serenity, the faith which will help them to get well.

Bless those who are sad. Comfort them; take away the ache of their loneliness, and help them to find comfort in going on.

Bless those who are worried. Help them to find the peace of mind which comes from the certainty that they will never be tested beyond what they can bear.

Bless those who are tempted. Give them grace to resist; and give your warning to those who are foolishly playing with fire.

Bless those who are far from home and far from friends, and protect them in body, mind and spirit.

Bless all those who are praying for me to-night as I am praying for them.

Hear this my prayer for your love's sake. AMEN.

Daily Reading

JOHN 13: 31-35

Therefore, when he was gone out, Jesus said, Now is the Son of man glorified, and God is glorified in him. If God be glorified in him, God shall also glorify him in himself, and shall straightway glorify him. Little children, yet a little while I am with you. Ye shall seek me : and as I said unto the Jews, Whither I go, ye cannot come; so now I say to you. A new commandment I give unto you, That ye love one another; as I have loved you, that ye also love one another. By this shall all men know that ye are my disciples, if ye have love one to another.

In the Morning

O God, keep me from the things which are bound to cause trouble.

Keep me from
    The self-will which unreasonably insists on its own way;
    The self-conceit which cannot stand the slightest criticism;
    The touchiness which sees offence where no offence was
        ever intended.

Keep me from
    The tale-bearing tongue;
    From all delight in malicious gossip;
    From repeating that which was said in confidence.

Keep me from
    The eyes which can see nothing but faults;
    The mind which can think only the worst;
    The tongue whose delight it is to criticise.

Help me
    To think with kindness;
    To speak with courtesy;
    To act in love.

Help me to live as one who has been with Jesus.

This I ask for your love's sake. AMEN.

In the Evening

O God, thank you for to-day.

Thank you
For happy things which came to me quite unexpectedly;
For things which turned out to be not nearly so bad as I expected;
For difficult things which became quite manageable when I faced up to them.

Forgive me for the things I did not do,
For the letter which is still not answered;
For the promise which is still not kept;
For the decision which is still delayed;
For the habit which is still not given up.

Make me honest enough to see myself as I am, and humble enough to seek from you the help I need, so that what I cannot do, your grace may do for me: through Jesus Christ my Lord. AMEN.

Daily Reading

PROVERBS 3: 13-18

Happy is the man that findeth wisdom, and the man that getteth understanding. For the merchandise of it is better than the merchandise of silver, and the gain thereof than fine gold. She is more precious than rubies; and all the things thou canst desire are not to be compared unto her. Length of days is in her right hand; and in her left hand riches and honour. Her ways are ways of pleasantness, and all her paths are peace. She is a tree of life to them that lay hold upon her; and happy is every one that retaineth her.

In the Morning

O God, grant that all through to-day I may never find any request for help a nuisance.

Help me never to find a child a nuisance,
   when he wants me to help him with his lessons,
   or play with him in his games.

Help me never to find a sick person a nuisance,
   if he would like me to spend some time with him,
   or do some service for him.

Help me never to find someone who is old a nuisance,
   even if he is critical of youth,
   settled immovably in his ways,
   demanding of attention.

Help me never to find a nuisance anyone who asks me,
   To show him how to do things;
   To help him in his work;
   To listen to his troubles.

Grant, O God, that I may neither be too immersed in work or too fond of my own pleasure, that I may never be too busy and never too tired, to help those who need help, even if they are the kind of people who get on my nerves and whom I instinctively dislike.

Help me to help, not only when it is pleasant to help, but when help is difficult and when I don't want to give it: through Jesus Christ my Lord. AMEN.

In the Evening

O God, the thing that hurts me most to remember at night is how I hurt others through the day.

Forgive me
For cruelly and mercilessly criticising others;
For laughing at people;
For thinking people fools, and for letting them see that I
thought they were.

Forgive me
For any request that I refused;
For any sympathy that I did not give;
For any disloyalty which brought pain to the heart of a
friend.

O God, I know that so often I have not treated others as I
would wish them to treat me; I have treated them as I would
hate to be treated.
Forgive me and help me to be kinder to-morrow: through
Jesus Christ my Lord. AMEN.

Daily Reading

PHILIPPIANS 2: 5-11

Let this mind be in you, which was also in Christ Jesus; who,
being in the form of God, thought it not robbery to be equal
with God: but made himself of no reputation, and took upon
him the form of a servant, and was made in the likeness of
men; and being found in fashion as a man, he humbled
himself, and became obedient unto death, even the death of
the cross. Wherefore God also hath highly exalted him, and
given him a name which is above every name: that at the
name of Jesus every knee should bow, of things in heaven,
and things in earth, and things under the earth; and that
every tongue should confess that Jesus Christ is Lord, to the
glory of God the Father.

99

IN TIME OF A DISASTER

O God, I remember before you those on whom at this time disaster has come.

Bless those whose dear ones have been killed, and those whose dear ones have lost their lives in seeking to save the lives of others.

Bless those who have lost their homes, and those who have seen all that they toiled for a lifetime to build up lost in an hour.

Help us always to remember those whose job it is to risk their lives to rescue others or to keep them safe—those in the fire-service, in the lifeboat service, in the police service, in the mountain-rescue service, in the medical service.

We will forget this disaster, but we ask you in your love always to remember those who will never forget because life for them can never be the same again.

This we ask for your love's sake. AMEN.

AT THE TIME OF A
HOLIDAY TRAGEDY

O God, Father of all comfort and God of all grace,

Bless those for whom the joy of holiday time has turned to tragedy;

Those who have lost dear ones in accidents on the roads, on the beaches and at sea, in the hills, on the railways, in the air, by the sudden and unexpected coming of death into their family circle.

Help us to remember that there is always someone who is sad, that never morning wore to evening but some heart did break, and comfort those for whom happy days in the sunshine turned suddenly to the midnight of a broken heart.

This I ask for your love's sake. AMEN.

FOR A HAPPY ANNIVERSARY

O God, to-day I am happy as I look back and remember.

I thank you for that day . . . years ago which was the beginning of joy for me.

I thank you for the happy years you have given to me in my home, at my work, within my Church.

I thank you for all the friends and the comrades and the loved ones with whom throughout the years my life has been intertwined.

This day, as you have commanded me, I remember all the way by which you have brought me to this present hour, and I thank you for it.

Hear this my thanksgiving through Jesus Christ my Lord. AMEN.

FOR A SAD ANNIVERSARY

O God, to-day brings me memories that are sad.

Sometimes in the busy world and at my work I can forget. But you have given us hearts which are so vulnerable, and the sight of a place, a photograph, a tune, the sound of a word, and above all a day like this sets my heart throbbing with pain again, and I feel again the blank in life which nothing can fill.

Help me not to sorrow overmuch as those who have no hope. Help me still to face life with steady eyes, remembering that the one I loved is not gone for ever, but that another has been added to the unseen cloud of witnesses who compass me about.

And bring quickly the time when the memories which make me cry will be the memories which make me smile: through Jesus Christ my Lord. AMEN.

FOR A WEDDING ANNIVERSARY

O God, I thank you that you have given us another year of life together.

I thank you
> For the love which grows more precious and for the bonds which grow more close each day.

I thank you
> For the happiness we have known together;
> For the sorrows we have faced together;
> For all the experiences of sunshine and of shadow through which we have come to to-day.

I ask your forgiveness
> For any disloyalty on my part;
> For any times when I was difficult to live with;
> For any selfishness and inconsiderateness;
> For any lack of sympathy and of understanding;
> For anything which spoiled even for a moment the perfect relationship which marriage should be.

Spare us to each other to go on walking the way of life together, and grant that for us it may be true that the best is yet to be: through Jesus Christ my Lord. AMEN.

A BIRTHDAY PRAYER

O God, I thank you for giving me another year of life.

I thank you for all the people who have remembered me to-day, and who have sent me cards, and letters, and good wishes, and presents.

I thank you for everything which I have been enabled by you to do and to be in the past year.

I thank you for all the experiences of the past year;
    For times of success which will always be happy memories;
    For times of failure which reminded me of my own weakness and of my need of you;
    For times of joy when the sun was shining;
    For times of sorrow which drove me to you.

Forgive me
    For the hours I have wasted;
    For the chances I failed to take;
    For the opportunities I missed in the past year.

Forgive me that I have not made of life all that I might have made of it and could have made of it; and help me in the days which lie ahead to make this the best year yet, and in it to bring credit to myself, happiness to my loved ones, and joy to you.

This I ask for Jesus' sake. AMEN.

Thank you, O God, for the success which you have given me to-day.

Help me not to rest on my oars because I achieved something, but to work still harder, to aim still higher, to do still better.

Keep me from becoming conceited. Help me always to think, not of what I have done, but of what I still must do; not of the few things in which I have succeeded, but of the many things in which I have failed.

Help me to be happy in the joy of achievement, but save me from a boastful and a foolish pride.

This I ask for Jesus' sake. AMEN.

O God, you know how badly I have failed in the task which I attempted, and which was given me to do, and in which I so much wanted to do well.

Don't let me become too depressed and discouraged; help me to have the determination to try again and to work still harder.

Don't let me try to put the blame on everyone and on everything except myself.

Don't let me be resentful and bitter about this failure; but help me to accept both success and failure with a good grace.

Don't let me be envious and jealous of those who have succeeded where I have failed.

Don't ever let me talk about giving up and giving in; but help me to refuse to be beaten.

Help me to learn the lesson which you want me to learn even from this failure; help me to begin again, and not to make the same mistakes again.

Maybe it is hardest of all to meet the eyes of those who are disappointed in me. Help me even yet to show them that I deserve their trust and to let them see what I can do.

This I ask for your love's sake. AMEN.

O God, somehow nowadays I am always tired. I go to sleep tired and I get up still tired.

Things take longer than they used to take, and I get behind with my work, and with the things I ought to do.

I come home tired, and that makes me cross and bad-tempered and irritable and impatient with my own family and my own people.

Everything has become an effort and a labour.

O God, help me to keep going, and help me to find something of the rest which you alone can give. Refresh me with your presence, and give me back the joy of living and the thrill of working: through Jesus Christ my Lord. AMEN.

O God, there are things about which I can't talk to anyone except to you. There are things in me about which no one knows except myself and you.

The things which I should not even want fascinate me. The thoughts which I should never allow into my mind, I cannot keep out.

So far I have resisted the wrong things, but I know my own weakness, and I am afraid of myself.

O God, come to me with your cleansing power, and make me able to overcome evil and to do the right.

I ask even more—fill me with such a love of you that I will not even want to sin any more.

This I ask for Jesus' sake. AMEN.

FOR ONE WHO HAS FALLEN
TO TEMPTATION

O God, I know that there is nothing which I can hide from you. I can hide my failure and my shame from others, but I cannot hide them from you. You know what I have done, and you know how sorry I am for it.

I am sorry more than anything else for the way in which I have hurt and disappointed and failed those who hoped in me, and believed in me, and love me.

I have come to you to ask for your forgiveness, to ask for strength and grace and courage to face up to things, to try even yet to redeem myself.

Forgive me. Keep me from doing the same wrong thing again. Help me to live from now on in that purity and that honesty and that goodness which you alone can give, and which you alone can preserve.

Hear this my prayer for your love's sake. AMEN.

O God, I come to you for comfort.

You know how lonely I am without . . . There are so many things which keep reminding me of . . . , and of all that I have lost.

O God, keep me from living too much in the past. Keep me from living too much with memories and too little with hopes.

Keep me from being too sorry for myself. Help me to remember that I am going through what many another has gone through. Help me not to sorrow as those who have no hope.

Help me to find comfort in my work, and, because I have gone through sorrow myself, help me to help others who are in trouble. Help me to keep trying to face life with gallantry, until I meet again the loved one whom I have lost awhile.

This I ask for your love's sake. AMEN.

FOR ONE WHOSE NERVES
HAVE BROKEN DOWN

O God, I have come to the stage when I cannot face life any longer.

I get so tense that I cannot relax. Always at the back of my mind there is the fear that I will get worse than I am now.

I know that nothing can help me, unless I help myself. I cannot help myself, and so, because things have got beyond me, I come to you.

Help me to feel that you know, that you understand, and that you care.

I used to love my work, but now I am frightened of it. I used to love life, but now I am afraid of it.

Give me the peace which comes from stopping struggling and from leaving things to you. Help me really to cast myself and my burden on you. Give me the courage to face my life, myself, my work, and the world again. Help me to win this battle which I know that by myself I can only lose.

Hear this my prayer, for your love's sake. AMEN.

O God, in my heart of hearts, when I stop and think, I know that I am selfish.

I always want things done for me. I always want my own way. I demand from others far more than I am prepared to give. If I am honest, I have got to admit that I try to make use of people. I never think of the trouble that I give to others. I know that I am thoughtless, and I know that I am often careless of the feelings of others, that I often hurt them because I am thinking of myself and of no one else. I know that I am so often ungrateful, that I forget how much I owe to others, and that I very seldom make any attempt to repay it.

O God, make me aware, not just at odd moments, but all the time, how ugly this selfishness is. Fix before my eyes the example and the Cross of my Lord, who, though he was rich, yet for my sake became poor. Help me to dethrone self, and to enthrone him within my heart, so that I may learn from him to love others and not myself.

This I ask for your love's sake. AMEN.

O God, I know that my besetting sin is pride.

So often I find myself looking down on others, and even despising them. I find myself thinking of my own cleverness, and of my own triumphs and achievements. I find myself thinking that I am sensible, and that other people are fools.

O God, take away my pride and my self-conceit.

Help me not to compare myself with other people, but to compare myself with Jesus, so that, when I set myself in the light of his goodness and of his beauty, I may never again be satisfied with myself. Help me to set myself in the light of his holiness, so I may see how unworthy, how inadequate, how ignorant I am.

And, when shame replaces pride, give me your grace, so that through it I may find in you the things I know I need and have not got.

Hear this my prayer, for your love's sake. AMEN.

FOR ONE WITH A QUICK TEMPER

O God, I know that my temper is far too quick.

I know only too well how liable I am to flare up, and to say things for which afterwards I am heartily sorry.

I know only too well that sometimes in anger I do things which in my calmer moments I would never have done.

I know that my temper upsets things at home; that it makes me difficult to work with; that it makes me lose my friends; that far too often it makes me a cause and source of trouble.

O God, help me. Help me to think before I speak. When I feel that I am going to blaze out, help me to keep quiet just for a moment or two, until I get a grip of myself again. Help me to remember that you are listening to everything I say, and seeing everything I do.

O God, control me and my temper too.

This I ask for your love's sake. AMEN.

FOR SOMEONE WHO
PUTS THINGS OFF

O God, I know how apt I am to put things off.

Sometimes it is because I am too lazy to do them. Sometimes it is just because I am afraid to do them. Sometimes it is because I just can't make up my mind, and I shilly-shally, and can't make a decision. Sometimes it is because I say to myself that to-morrow will be time enough.

I know that I have got into this bad habit, and I know that it causes trouble for myself and for other people, and I am only too well aware that because of it things that ought to have been done have never been done—and some of them can never be done at all now.

O God, help me to do better.

Help me to remember that for all I know to-morrow may never come.

Give me resolution to make up my mind, and strength and courage to act on my decision.

Help me never to leave until to-morrow what I ought to do to-day; and help me within each day to do the tasks and to make the decisions which the day demands.

Hear this my prayer for your love's sake. AMEN.

FOR ONE WHO IS IN
TOO BIG A HURRY

O God, I know that I am in far too big a hurry.

I dash at things with far too little preparation, and without thinking of the consequences of them. Far too often I speak and act without thinking. Far too often I start something without counting the cost.

I am far too impatient both with things and with people. I have never learned to wait. I try to do things as quickly as I can and not as well as I can. My life is full of sudden enthusiasms which blaze up and just as quickly die down.

The result of all this is that my life is full of things I began and never finished, and took up and never continued, and which have to be done all over again because they were done in far too big a hurry. My frantic efforts to save time just waste time in the end.

Help me to take a grip of myself. Help me to take time to think. Give me patience to wait and perseverance to continue. Help me to think of how slowly and patiently you work, and to remember that it is better to do things well than to do them quickly.

Hear this my prayer for your love's sake. AMEN.

O God, keep me from grumbling.

I am quite well aware—from experience—that there is no one harder to put up with than someone who is always complaining. Don't let me become like that. Don't let me have discontentment written all over my face, and the whine of the east wind for ever in my voice.

If I can't get my own way,
don't let me sulk about it.

If I can't get what I want,
help me to make the best of what I can get, and of what I have.

Don't let me become one of these people who take offence far too easily, and who go off in the huff, even when nothing unpleasant was ever intended.

Help me all day every day
to look on the bright side of things,
and to see the best in people.

And help me to live in the certainty that you are working all things together for good, if I have only the trust to accept them, and the patience to wait for your purposes to work out.

This I ask for your love's sake. AMEN.

THAT I MAY NOT WASTE
THE PRECIOUS THINGS
OF LIFE

O God,
    Help me not to waste my time. Don't let me always be in a hurry and a fuss, but help me to go on quietly and without haste, filling every minute with the work which is given me to do.

Help me not to waste my strength. Help me to see quite clearly the things which matter and the things which don't matter. Give me a sense of proportion that I may not get all hot and bothered about things which are of no importance, and so make myself too tired and exhausted to do the things which really matter.

Help me not to waste my money. Don't let me be mean and miserly, but help me to spend wisely and to give generously, and to try to use everything I have remembering that it belongs, not to me, but to you.

Above all, help me not to waste my life. Help me to use the talents you have given me, to seize the opportunities you are sending to me, so that some day you may be able to say to me: Well done!

You are the Lord and Master of all good life; hear this my prayer and help me to live well: through Jesus Christ my Lord. AMEN.

O God, you have given us your own day to worship and to rest. Bless all those who to-morrow will preach and proclaim your word.

Give them a message from you to their people. Grant that on their lips the old themes may become new, and the old story as vivid as if it had never been told before.

Give them such a love of truth that they will think of nothing but to speak it; but give them also such a love and care for their people that they will speak the truth in sympathy and in love.

Give them, as they speak,
    A word of comfort
      for the sad in heart;

    A word of certainty and of light
      for the seeking and the searching and the doubting mind;

    A word of strength
      for those who are wrestling with temptation;

    A word of grace
      for those who are very conscious of their sin.

Bless all who to-morrow will worship in your house.

Grant that their time of worship may not be a nuisance which must be endured, or a respectable convention which must be observed. Grant that they may come in joy, in faith, and in expectation; and make them very sure that none will be sent empty away.

Bless all Church members who will not worship in your house to-morrow.

If they are held at home by sickness or by the care of the sick, by the care of children and of household things, by weakness or by age, because they must work even on Sunday, or because they were too sad to come, make them to know that you and we remember them. If they stayed away because they did not wish to come, make them to remember their vows and to worship as they ought.

Bless those to whom the Church is nothing, and who will never even think of coming.

If they have forgotten you, we know that you have not forgotten them; and help us to bring your lost children back into the family of the Church.

Hear this my prayer through Jesus Christ my Lord. AMEN.

PRAYERS BEFORE GOING
TO CHURCH

O God, bring me to your Church in the right spirit to-day.

Grant that in my heart there may be no bitterness to anyone, and help me to remember that I cannot be at one with you, if I am not at one with my fellowmen.

Take from me the critical and fault-finding spirit, so that I may really and truly go to Church only to worship.

Take from me the selfish and the self-centred spirit, so that I may think, not only of what I am going to get out of this service, but also of what I am going to give and to bring to it.

Bless my minister. Give him a message for his people to-day, and uphold and support him in the high task you have given him to do.

Grant that in Church to-day I may seek for nothing but to hear your truth and to see Jesus.

This I ask for your love's sake. AMEN.

O God, help me this morning to worship you in spirit and in truth.

Make me willing to listen to the truth, even if the truth hurts and condemns me.

Keep my thoughts from wandering, and help me to concentrate on listening to you.

Help me not only to listen to the prayers, and not only to repeat them, but really to share in them.

Put out of my heart every bitter and unforgiving thought which would be a barrier between me and you. Help me to remember that I cannot have your friendship, if I am out of friendship with my fellowmen.

Help me to go to Church to-day with no other purpose than to listen to your word to me. Take from me the critical spirit and give me the mind and heart which are ready and open to receive.

Bless the preacher; and give him a message this morning for his waiting people, and give him strength and courage, grace and winsomeness to deliver it. Grant that this morning the whole congregation may be saying: Sir, we would see Jesus.

This I ask for your love's sake. AMEN.

O God, don't let me forget everything that I heard and felt in Church to-day.

Don't let me think that any word of warning and rebuke was meant for other people but not for me.

Don't let me forget that moment when I really did feel that you were near and close to me.

Don't let me forget the sorrow and the regret and the repentance which in that moment I really did feel for the wrong things in life; and don't let me forget the way in which I did feel that I must, with your help, be better.

Don't let the fact that to-day I met Jesus and listened to your word all go for nothing.

This I ask for your love's sake. AMEN.

Prepare me in mind and heart, O God, to listen to and to receive what your word has to say to me.

Bind me in loving fellowship with this group of people with whom I study, so that we may all be able to talk with freedom, knowing that no one will misunderstand, and no one will take offence.

Guard me from the prejudices which would blind me to the truth. Keep me from reading into your word what I want to hear, and rather help me humbly to listen to what you want to say to me.

Help me to bring to the study of your word all the help that the saints and the scholars of the past and the present can give to me to help me to understand it better; and grant that I may fearlessly follow the truth wherever it may lead me.

And then, when I have learned from your word what you want me to do, give me grace and strength to go out and to do it : through Jesus Christ my Lord. AMEN.

PRAYERS FOR DIFFERENT
OCCUPATIONS

A CHURCH OFFICE-BEARER'S
PRAYER

O God, to whom the Church belongs, thank you for giving me a special task and a special place within it.

Help me never to think of my office in the Church as a position of honour; help me always to think of it as an opportunity of service. Help me never to think of it as a privilege without thinking of it as a responsibility. Help me never to think of it as an opportunity to rule others; help me always to think of it as an obligation to serve others. So grant that my position may never make me proud, but that it may always keep me humble.

Help me never to make trouble, but always to make peace. So help me always to speak the truth, but always to speak it in love.

Help me never to stand on the letter of the law; never to be concerned with my own rights, my own place, my own importance. Help me to remember that he who would be chief must be the servant of all.

Make me faithful in my duty to the members of this congregation, and help me always to uphold the hands of my minister in sympathy and in prayer.

And out in the world at my day's work and in my pleasure make me a good advertisement for the Church which it is my honour to serve : through Jesus Christ my Lord. AMEN.

A CHOIR MEMBER'S
AND AN ORGANIST'S
PRAYER

Thank you, O God, for giving me the privilege of leading the praise of your people in your house to-day.

Help me always to remember that this is not an opportunity to show my talents but to serve you and your people in your house. So banish from my heart every thought of self and pride, and help me to sing and to make music only because I truly love you with my whole heart.

Help me to remember that there are those whose hearts can be reached and touched by music even more than by speech, and so help me to remember that I too have my ministry and I too to-day can bring someone to you.

This I ask for Jesus' sake. AMEN.

A SUNDAY SCHOOL TEACHER'S
PRAYER

Lord Jesus, I remember that you said: Let the little children come to me, and never try to stop them. I thank you that you have honoured me by giving me the task of bringing boys and girls to you.

Help me to do this great work as it ought to be done.

Grant that I may never meet these boys and girls unprepared. Help me to remember that, if I am teaching, I must be always learning. Help me to remember that, if I am a teacher, I must never stop being a scholar.

Grant that I may wisely and lovingly combine the discipline which will make the boys and girls respect me, and the kindness which will make them love me. Help me never to lose patience and never to lose my temper, however inattentive and troublesome they may be. Help me never to stop loving them. And help me throughout the weeks to build up a relationship with them in which they will come and ask me about anything which is worrying them, sure that I will always be ready to listen to them and always ready to understand and to sympathise.

Grant that I may always respect them and be strictly honest with them, and that I may never to save bother tell them something which they will afterwards have to unlearn.

Help me
  To teach them to think;
  To teach them to live;
  To teach them to love.

And at all times help me to teach more by what I am than by what I say.

This I ask for your love's sake. AMEN.

A BIBLE CLASS LEADER'S
PRAYER

O God, you have given me a very difficult job to do within your Church.

Help me never to face these young people unprepared.

Help me to be absolutely honest with them. Help me never to dodge their questions, and never to evade their problems.

Help me to try to understand them before I criticise them. Keep me from the foolishness of looking for old heads on young shoulders, and help me to remember that the ways of one generation are not the ways of another, and that things are different since I was their age.

Help me never to laugh at them, and never to lose patience with them. Help me to be wise enough to know when they need control and discipline, and when it is better to let them have their own way.

Help me to help them to think, to worship and to pray.

Help me to remember that, whether I like it or not, and whether I know it or not, they will judge the Church by me, and that this is the grave responsibility that is laid upon me.

Even if I see no result, help me not to be discouraged. Help me to remember that it takes a long time for a seed to become a tree, and help me to sow the seed and to leave its growth to you.

Grant that what I am may never undo all that I say. You have given me this part of your work to do—help me to do it well.

This I ask for your love's sake. AMEN.

Lord Jesus, you have very specially called me to be a fellow-worker with you.

Make me diligent in my preparation to preach, determined never to offer to you or to my people that which cost me nothing.

Make me faithful in my visitation, a shepherd who bears each one of his flock upon his heart.

Make me constant in prayer, so that I may never go out to meet men until I have met you.

Help me to meet opposition, obstruction, misunderstanding, misrepresentation with your gentleness, your love, and your forgiveness.

Help me never to lose faith and hope even when nothing seems to be happening, but help me to be content to sow the good seed and to leave the increase to you.

Help me never to lose my temper, never to speak in irritation, never to be on terms of enmity with any man.

Give me firmness and resolution to stand for what I believe to be right, yet give me sympathy and tolerance to understand the point of view of others.

Help me never to make anyone feel a nuisance when he comes to see me, and help me to suffer even fools gladly.

Make me like you, among my fellowmen as one who serves.

This I ask for your love's sake. AMEN.

O God, bless all those who have gone out to bring the message of the gospel to other lands.

I remember before you
Those who have to endure hardship and discomfort;
Those who have to face peril and danger;
Those who have had to leave their families and their children behind while they went out to other lands;
Those who have to struggle with a new language and with new ways of thought;
Those whose health has broken down under the strain, and who have had to come home, not knowing whether they will ever be fit for their task again;
Those who have to face constant discouragement in a situation in which no progress ever seems to be made.

Especially bless those who work in countries where new nations are being born, and where there is strife and trouble and bitterness in the birth-pangs of the new age.

Bless those who preach in the villages and the towns and the cities; those who teach in the schools and the colleges; those who work in the hospitals and among the sick; those who have laid their gifts of craftsmanship or administration on the altar of missionary service.

Help us at home never to forget them and always to pray for them. And help us to give generously of our money to their work so that it may go where we ourselves cannot go.

And bring quickly the day when the knowledge of you will cover the earth as the waters cover the sea: through Jesus Christ my Lord. AMEN.

A PRAYER
FOR THOSE WHO ARE
NEWLY MARRIED

O God, we two want to begin our life together with you, and we want always to continue it with you.

Help us never to hurt and never to grieve one another.

Help us to share all our work, all our hopes, all our dreams, all our successes and all our failures, all our sorrows and all our joys. Help us to have no secrets from one another, so that we may be truly one.

Keep us always true to one another, and grant that all the years ahead may draw us ever closer to one another. Grant that nothing may ever come between us, and nothing may ever make us drift apart.

And, as we live with one another, help us to live with you, so that our love may grow perfect in your love, for you are the God whose name is love.

This we ask for your love's sake. AMEN.

A MOTHER'S PRAYER

O God, help me always to remember that you have given to me the most important task in the world, the task of making a home.

Help me to remember this when I am tired of making beds, and washing clothes, and cooking meals, and cleaning floors, and mending clothes, and standing in shops. Help me to remember it when I am physically tired in body, and when I am weary in mind with the same things which have to be done again and again, day in and day out.

Help me never to be irritable, never to be impatient, never to be cross. Keep me always sweet. Help me to remember how much my husband and my children need me, and help me not to get annoyed when they take me for granted, and when they never seem to think of the extra work they sometimes cause me.

Help me to make this home such that the family will always be eager to come back to it, and such that, when the children grow up and go out to their own homes, they will have nothing but happy memories of the home from which they have come.

This I ask for your love's sake. AMEN.

O God, help me to be true to the great privilege and the great responsibility which you have given to me.

Help me to be an example and a friend to my children, and a real partner to my wife.

Don't let me get so busy with work and with outside things that I am almost a stranger in my own home, and that I take no interest in household things.

Don't let me take all that is done for me for granted, and help me to keep love alive within the home.

Keep me from habits which make the work of the house harder, and from ways which irritate and annoy, or which get on the nerves of those who live with me.

Give me health and strength and work to do, to earn a living for those who depend on me and whom I love so much; but help me to remember that love is always more important than money.

O God, you have given me the name of father; you have given me your own name; help me to be true to it.

This I ask for your love's sake. AMEN.

Thank you, O God, for the home and for the parents you have given me.

Thank you for

All the loving care which I received when I was a child and when I could not care for myself;

All that was provided for me—food and clothes and shelter —in the years before I could earn my own living and support myself;

All the opportunities of education and of learning which my parents gave to me;

All the security I have enjoyed, the door of home always open, the sympathy and the love when I was hurt or discouraged or depressed.

Thank you for all the loving care with which I have been surrounded ever since I was born.

Forgive me, if I have done anything to hurt or to grieve my parents, and, if, as I have grown older, I have drifted away from them until we are almost strangers.

or,

Thank you, if the passing of the years has made me understand my parents better, and has made me love them more, and has drawn me closer and closer to them.

Forgive me, if I have taken everything for granted, if sometimes I just made use of my home, if I took everything and gave nothing.

Forgive me, if sometimes I have been difficult to live with, irritable, rebellious, disobedient, uncommunicative, impatient of advice, angry at restraint.

Help me at least to try to do something to show my gratitude, and to try to repay the debt I owe, even if it never can be fully repaid.

Help me so to value my home, so to love my parents, so to show them that I love them, that some day, when they are gone and I look back, I may have nothing to regret.

Hear this my prayer for Jesus' sake. AMEN.

Lord Jesus, when you lived and worked and talked amongst men in Palestine, they called you Teacher.

Help me to remember the greatness of the work which has been given to me to do.

Help me always to remember that I work with the most precious material in the world, the mind of a child. Help me always to remember that I am making marks upon that mind which time will never rub out.

Give me patience with those who are slow to learn, and even with those who refuse to learn.

When I have to exercise discipline, help me to do so in sternness and yet in love. Keep me from the sarcastic and the biting tongue, and help me always to encourage and never to discourage those who are doing their best, even if that best is not very good.

Help me to help these children, not only to store things in their memories, but to be able to use their minds, and to think for themselves.

And amidst all the worries and the irritations and the frustrations of my job, help me to remember that the future of the nation and of the world is in my hands.

This I ask for your love's sake. AMEN.

Lord Jesus, when you were on earth, you healed all those who had need of healing.

Help me always to remember that you have honoured me by giving me the task of continuing your healing work.

Give me skill in my mind, gentleness on my hands, and sympathy in my heart.

Help me always to remember that often when people come to me, they are frightened and nervous, and help me always to try to bring to them, not only healing for their bodies, but also calm to their minds.

Make me patient yet firm with the foolish malingerer who wastes my time.

When I must tell people that there is nothing that human skill or hands can do for them, give me a wise gentleness to break the news to them.

Help me never to lose the thrill of bringing new life into the world, and never to become callous to the pathos of the parting of death.

Give me something of your skill to heal men's diseases, to ease men's pains, and to bring peace to men's troubled minds.

This I ask for your love's sake. AMEN.

A PRAYER
FOR THOSE WHO SERVE
THE COMMUNITY

*in Town and District Councils, and in Parliament,
in Trades Unions, and in all Public Service*

O God, grant that in all the public work which has been given to me to do my only motive may be to serve my fellowmen, and my only master may be my conscience.

Help me to set loyalty to the right things above all loyalty to party or to class.

Grant that the importance of my work may never make me full of my own self-importance, but rather that it may make me humbly eager to serve and to help the people whom I represent.

Give me wisdom in my mind, clearness in my thinking, truth in my speaking, and always love in my heart, so that I may try always to unite people and never to divide them.

Help me always to set the interests of the community above those of the party; the interest of the nation above the interest of the community; and faithfulness to you above everything else.

So grant that at the end of the day I may win the approval of my own conscience, the respect of men, and your Well done! This I ask for the sake of Jesus who was among his fellowmen as one who served. AMEN.

A PRAYER FOR THOSE
IN AUTHORITY

for Masters, Employers, Managers, Foremen, Directors

O God, you have given me the great responsibility of being in authority over my fellowmen.

Help me always to act fairly and justly; but to justice help me always to add mercy and sympathy. Help me to know when to enforce discipline and when to relax it. Help me never to be guilty of prejudice against any man or favouritism for any man.

Help me to remember that people are always more important than things, and that men are always more important than machines.

Keep me from exercising my authority in harshness or in tyranny, and keep me also from being afraid to exercise it at all, and help me by my presence and my example to make myself and those who work under me one united band of brothers.

Help me to remember that, though I am called master, I too have a Master, even Jesus Christ.

Hear this my prayer for your love's sake. AMEN.

O God, you are the source and the giver of all wisdom and of all truth. I lay no claim to the name of scholar, but life has set me in this University/College/School, where I must learn and where I must teach.

Give me diligence, perseverance, accuracy in my study, and help me to seek for truth as blind men long for light.

Give me clarity, sympathy, enthusiasm in my teaching, and grant that I may ever seek to open the minds of those whom I teach to beauty and to truth. And grant that I may never wish those whom I teach to think as I think, but that I may ever seek to teach them to think for themselves.

Grant that my life within this place of learning may not separate and isolate me from the life and work of the world of business and of trade and of industry and of commerce.

Grant that at the end of the day I may have taken a little further the torch of knowledge and of truth which was handed on to me.

This I ask for your love's sake and for your truth's sake. AMEN.

A FARMER'S OR
A GARDENER'S PRAYER

O God, I thank you for the gifts which the garden, the fields and the orchards bring to us.

I thank you for the green of the grass and the colours of the flowers, and for all the loveliness of nature which is more beautiful than the robes of kings. I thank you for all the growing things which bring food and health to men.

I thank you for the sleep of the winter, the rebirth of the spring, the golden glory of the summer, for the harvest of the autumn.

Grant that the mysterious way in which growth goes on, silently and unseen, night and day, may always make me think of you, the giver of it all.

I thank you that you gave to me the love of the soil and of all growing things, and the gift of green fingers which know nature's ways and secrets.

Help me in nature's life to see you who are the giver of all life, and to catch a glimpse of the endless life which death can never destroy: through Jesus Christ my Lord. AMEN.

O God, I thank you for your gift to men of music.
I thank you

For the music which tells of the sorrows of the human heart, and which can also soothe them;

For the music which expresses human joy;

For the music which thrills and challenges the spirit of man;

For the music which says things which words are powerless to say.

I thank you that you gave me the ability to enjoy music and to understand it. I thank you for the ability to create it. I thank you alike for the music which makes the feet of men dance and for the music which makes the hearts of men pray.

Help me to worship and to serve you in your gift of music, and grant that I may always be ready to use this gift of mine for your service and for the joy of men: through Jesus Christ my Lord. AMEN.

A PRAYER FOR
SHOP ASSISTANTS
and for all who serve the Public

Lord Jesus, you have given me the task of serving the public —and it isn't always easy.

Help me to be patient with the time-wasting.

Help me to be courteous to the discourteous.

Help me to be forbearing to the unreasonable.

Help me to be always cheerful, always obliging, always willing to go the extra mile in service.

Make me such that people will go away happier and smiling because I served them to-day.

Hear this my prayer for your love's sake. AMEN.

AN OFFICE-WORKER'S PRAYER

O God, my work is with the typewriter and the comptometer and the ledger and the accounts and the invoices and things like that.

It isn't work that is much in the limelight or that people see very much of. I am just like a very small cog in a very big machine. But help me to remember that no machine can run well unless even the smallest part of it is doing its job.

So help me to be careful and punctual in my work. Help me to be interested in my work and to take a pride in it. Keep me from making careless mistakes which hold things up and which mean that things have to be done over again and which waste everyone's time. Help me to be willing and easy to work with.

And help me always to be courteous and cheerful so that this office will be a happier place, because I work in it: through Jesus Christ my Lord. AMEN.

A NURSE'S PRAYER

Lord Jesus, help me to love my job, and help me to feel that
I am really doing your work, and really helping you, when I
look after people who are sick.

Help me at all times to have
    Patience with the unreasonable, the querulous and the irri-
        tating;
    Sympathy with the frightened and the nervous;
    And never let me neglect those who are quiet and uncom-
        plaining.

When people telephone or come to ask how their friends or
loved ones are getting on, help me to remember how worried
and anxious they are, and to do my best to help them.
Give me a steady nerve when difficult things have to be done.
Make me very attentive to orders and instructions and very
obedient in carrying them out; and in an emergency make me
able to think for myself and to come quickly to a decision.

    Give me skill; but give me gentleness.
    Give me efficiency; but make me kind.
    Make me firm; but make me understanding too.

Help me to study with diligence and to work with willingness; and help me to love my work and to love the people
whom it is my work to help.

This I ask for your love's sake. AMEN.

A PRAYER
FOR THOSE WHO ADMINISTER
THE LAW

O God, I know that it is from you that men have learned what goodness and justice are.

Give me a mind that is fair and impartial, and give me the power to judge and to decide with wisdom and with equity. Grant that nothing may ever make me pervert the course of justice, neither the promise of reward nor the threat of vengeance. Grant that I may never be influenced either by the fear or the favour of men.

Make me to know that there are times when mercy is greater than justice, and when love is better than law.

Help me to help others rather to settle their disputes and differences in peace and friendship than to pursue them in bitterness and contention; and make me, not only an expert in the law, but also a wise counsellor to those who come to me for help and for advice: through Jesus Christ my Lord. AMEN.

O God, you have given me the task of maintaining law and order in this community. It is a much more dangerous and frustrating task than once it was.

Give me the courage and the resolution at all times to do my duty, and give me such a love and respect for justice that neither promise nor threat will ever make me depart from it. Help me in a real sense to be the Guardian and the Friend of the whole community, a friend to the children, an example to youth, a counsellor and adviser to all good citizens.

Give me the skill and the wisdom and the strength I need to capture the evil-doer and to keep him from his misdeeds. And give me at all times wisdom to know when to enforce and when to relax the letter of the law.

Help me to be a personal example of the honesty, the goodness, the justice which it is my duty to maintain; and help me to win the authority which comes from respect: through Jesus Christ my Lord. AMEN.

A PRAYER FOR THOSE
IN THE FIRE SERVICE AND
THE LIFE-BOAT SERVICE

*and for all those
whose task it is to rescue others*

O God, you have given to me the task of rescuing those who are in trouble and in danger. Help me to find pride and pleasure in the thought that there is no greater task than the task of saving others.

Sometimes I have to risk my own life in seeking to save the life and the property of others. When I think of the perils which I must face, and when I remember those who gave their lives in facing them, help me to remember that Jesus said: Greater love hath no man than this, that a man lay down his life for his friends.

Others may have better-paid jobs, and jobs which are safer and in which the hours and the work are easier, but no one has a bigger and a more important job than I have.

Lord Jesus, you are the Saviour of the world; help, strengthen and protect me that in my own way and in my own sphere I too may be ready to risk all to save others.

This I ask for your love's sake. AMEN.

O God, you have given me a share in the administration of this country. I don't hit the headlines in the newspapers; people don't know my name as they know the names of the famous politicians, and members of Parliament, and members of the government. But help me always to have the great satisfaction of knowing that they would be helpless without the ordinary routine work which I have to do, and that without it the life of the country would come to a stop. So give me joy and pride in my work, even if it is unseen.

Help me to be efficient, but not soulless.

Help me always to remember that, although I usually never see them, I am dealing with real flesh and blood people with hearts that can be hurt and minds which can be bewildered, and not with names on a schedule or numbers on a card index.

Give me courtesy, even when I have to enforce regulations which dishonest people are trying to dodge.

In all my work help me to remember that I am a human being dealing with human beings.

This I ask for your love's sake. AMEN.

A PRAYER FOR
A WELFARE WORKER OR
A SOCIAL WORKER

O God, I sometimes think that I have the hardest job of all, because what I am really trying to do is to make bad people good and to make foolish people wise—and it is a hard job.

Help me
  Never to lose patience;
  Never to abandon hope;
  Never to regard anyone with loathing or contempt;
  Never to stop caring.

Help me always to love the sinner, however much I may hate the sin. And help me always to try to understand what makes people act as they do; and help me sometimes to stop and think what I would be like, if I had had as little chance as some of them have had.

  Make me always
    Sympathetic to failure;
    Patient with folly;
    Firm with shiftlessness;
    Stern to cruelty;
    Resolute against those who make vice and evil easier for others.

Help me to be wise enough to know
  When to be kind and when to be stern;
  When to encourage and when to rebuke;
  When to give and when to refuse.
Above all, never let love grow cold within my heart.

Lord Jesus, you came to seek and to save that which was lost, and it is your work that I am still trying to do.

Hear this my prayer for your love's sake. AMEN.

O God, you have set me under discipline. Make me not only at all times obedient to my leaders, but give me the self-discipline which will make me always obedient to the voice of conscience, and to the command of the highest that I know.

Help me always and everywhere to behave in such a way that I will be an honour and a credit to the traditions of my regiment and to the uniform and the badge which I wear.

Bless and protect those whom I love and those who love me, and, when the call of duty separates me from them, keep me true to them and them true to me.

If so it be that some day I must fight, help me to fight only to make peace, only to protect the helpless and the weak, only to support that which is just and right.

Help me at all times to fear you and to honour the Queen.

This I ask for Jesus' sake. AMEN.

O God, I ask you to take me into your care and protection along with all those who go down to the sea in ships.

Make me alert and wise in my duties. Make me faithful in the time of routine, and prompt to decide and courageous to act in any time of crisis.

Protect me in the dangers and the perils of the sea; and even in the storm grant that there may be peace and calm within my heart.

When I am far from home and far from loved ones and far from the country which I know, help me to be quite sure that, wherever I am, I can never drift beyond your love and care.

Take care of my loved ones in the days and weeks and months when I am separated from them, sometimes with half the world between them and me. Keep me true to them and keep them true to me, and every time that we have to part, bring us together in safety and in loyalty again.

This I ask for your love's sake. AMEN.

O God, I thank you that I live in an age in which things that even my father never dreamed of have become commonplace.

I thank you that you have given me the power to travel higher than the clouds and faster than the wind across the sky.

Give me a fit body, a clear eye, a steady nerve and a mind able to make instant decisions.

Protect me in my journeyings, and bring me always safely to my flight's end; and help me, as I journey far above the clouds in the vast spaces of the sky, to feel your presence near: through Jesus Christ my Lord. AMEN.

O God, give me in all my work the spirit of reverence.

As I search for the secrets of the universe,
And as I seek to discover nature's laws,
Help me to see behind it all your creative power and pur-
pose.
Help me to love nothing so much as the truth,
And fearlessly to follow wherever truth may lead me.

Give me at all times
The spirit of service,
That I may think and calculate, experiment and search,
Never for power to destroy,
But always for power
To lighten men's burdens;
To feed men's hunger;
To ease men's pain;
To make the world a better place to live in,
Nearer to men's hearts' desire,
And closer to what you meant it to be.

And above all
Give me the humility
Which will make me,
Not proud of what I have discovered,
But conscious of all that I do not know,
And which will always make me think of truth,
Not as something I have found,
But as something which you have given me,
And which must be used
As you would have it to be used.

This I ask for your love's sake. AMEN.

I thank you, O God, for giving me a body which is specially fit and strong, and for making me able to use it well.

In my training
  Help me never to shirk the discipline which I know that I need and that I ought to accept.

In my leisure and in my pleasure
  Help me never to allow myself any indulgence which would make me less fit than I ought to be.

When I compete with others
  Help me, win or lose, to play fair. When I win, keep me from boasting; when I lose, keep me from making excuses. Keep me from being conceited when I succeed, and from being sulky when I fail. And help me always with good will to congratulate a better man who beat me.

Help me so to live that I will always have a healthy body and a healthy mind.

This I ask for your love's sake. AMEN.

O God, every time I drive my car, help me to remember that I am responsible, not only for my own life, but also for the lives of others.

Give me patience, when progress is annoyingly and frustratingly slow, so that I may not endanger my own life and the lives of others by taking a chance to save a minute or two.

Give me courtesy, so that I may think of the other driver as well as of myself.

Keep me always alert, and give me wisdom to know when it is time to stop and rest.

Help me never to indulge in any habit or in any pleasure which would make me a danger to others on the road.

Help me to do everything that one man can do to make life safer on the roads on which I drive: through Jesus Christ my Lord. AMEN.

A TRADESMAN'S
OR A CRAFTSMAN'S
PRAYER

O God, it is you who gave me skill in my hands. You gave me the ability to make wood and metals and the materials out of which things are made obedient to my hands and to my will.

Give me pride in my work. Give me such self-respect that I will always be ashamed to turn out any inferior bit of workmanship or a shoddily done job.

Make me at all times absolutely honest in my work, more concerned to do a job as well as it can be done than with reckoning how much I will get out of it, or how long it will take me to do it.

Help me to work, not to satisfy the clock, but to satisfy my own conscience. Lord Jesus, you were a craftsman in Nazareth, working with the tools of your trade; make me as good a workman as you were.

This I ask for your love's sake. AMEN.

A PRAYER FOR A WRITER,

*an Author, or a Journalist, for all whose craft it is
to use words which many will hear or read*

O God, you gave me the gift and the responsibility of using
words. Help me in all my writing and my speaking to be the
servant of goodness, of beauty and of truth. Help me never
to write or to say anything which would injure another's
innocence or take another's faith away.

Help me never to write or say anything which would make
that which is wrong more attractive, or which would soil the
mind of anyone who reads or hears it.

Help me never to pander to that which is low, never to seek
popularity at the expense of truth, never to be more concerned with sensations than with facts, and always to respect
the feelings and the rights of other people.

Grant that all that I write or say be such that it can stand the
scrutiny of my own conscience, and such that I could with a
clear conscience offer it to you.

This I ask for your love's sake. AMEN.

A PRAYER
FOR ONE WHO IS HELPLESS
OR BED-RIDDEN

O God, life has taken a good deal from me, but I want to begin by thanking you for all that life has left me.

I can see and read; I can hear and listen; I can talk and speak with my friends. Though my body must stay in the one place, I can still send my mind and my imagination in adventurous travel. Once I was too busy doing things to think. Now I can think until I reach you and the things which really matter.

I have still books which I can read, music I can listen to, wireless and television which I can hear and watch, even games which I can play in bed.

For all that, O God, I need your help more than I need anything else. Keep me cheerful even when it is very difficult. Keep me content when my whole being naturally wants to be resentful. Let me not become querulous, complaining, demanding. Keep me from self-pity. Help me to be truly grateful for all that is done for me; and, even when it is the last thing that I feel like doing, help me to smile.

Bless the doctors and the nurses and the people who care for me and who look after me; and give them skill to find a cure some day even for people like me.

When I feel that I am useless and a burden to others, help me to remember that I can still pray, and so help me constantly to uphold the hands of those I love, and constantly to bear them and myself to your throne of grace.

All this I ask for your love's sake. AMEN.

A PRAYER
FOR ONE WHO IS DEAF

O God, life has taken away from me the power to hear, and there is much that I have lost.

I miss the voices of my friends, the music that I loved, the many lovely and homely sounds which others hear.

Sometimes my deafness makes me avoid company, and sometimes it makes things very awkward for me. Sometimes I think that deaf people get less sympathy than anyone else, and that people regard us deaf people as something of a nuisance. It is very easy for a deaf person like me to become lonely and suspicious and to avoid meeting people.

O God, help me to bear it all with a good grace. After all I have got something to be thankful for. I can sleep anywhere, because noise doesn't disturb me, and I can concentrate on my work because sounds don't distract me. When I think about it, I have got some blessings to count!

Help me to do my best to conquer this handicap. Help me at least to be sensible enough to do what I can about it. I thank you very specially for hearing-aids, and for the skill of those who have done so much to help us deaf people to hear.

Help me to do my work and to enjoy my life, even although I cannot hear without my hearing-aid.

This I ask for Jesus' sake. AMEN.

A PRAYER
FOR ONE WHO IS BLIND

O God, I have to live in the dark now, and there is much that I can't help missing.

I can't help missing the faces of my loved ones and my friends, and the colour of the flowers. I can't help feeling it difficult not to see the road that I must walk and the scenes I loved.

O God, help me to face all this with courage and with cheerfulness.

I thank you for all that is done for us blind people. I thank you for books in braille, for guide-dogs wonderfully trained to be wise, for special training to make us able to do a useful job, for the sympathy and the kindness and the consideration which nearly everyone shows to us.

I thank you that my memory has still its gallery of pictures and that the eyes of my mind can still see. Even if I can no longer see the things that are visible, I can still see the things that are invisible.

Keep me from pitying myself, and help me not to let this thing beat me. Help me bravely to train myself to be as independent as it is possible for me to be. I know that no trial ever came to any man without bringing with it the power to bear it. Help me to bear and to conquer this.

This I ask for the sake of him who is the light of the world, for Jesus' sake. AMEN.

O God, you have made all living things, and you love them all.

Bless all living creatures, especially those in the service and in the homes of men.

Grant that no man may ever be thoughtlessly, callously, or deliberately cruel to the dumb animals who have no voice to speak and no power to defend themselves from the actions of men.

Grant that those who keep animals as pets within their homes may care for them as they ought to be cared for, may never neglect them, or cause them needless suffering and pain.

Bless all animals in captivity, and grant that their masters and their trainers may always be kind.

The animals have given to men their strength and their work, and often even their devotion and their love; grant that men may give to them the care which they deserve as creatures whom your hands have made and for whom your heart cares.

This I ask for your love's sake. AMEN.

75 76 77 78 79 10 9 8 7 6 5 4 3 2

AGITATION
FOR FREEDOM:
The Abolitionist Movement

EDITED BY

Donald G. Mathews
University of North Carolina

John Wiley & Sons, Inc.
New York • London • Sydney • Toronto

Library of Congress Catalogue Card Number: 77—177256

ISBN 0-471-57623-9 (cloth) ;   ISBN 0-471-57624-7 (paper)

Printed in the United States of America.

10 9 8 7 6 5 4 3 2 1

SERIES PREFACE

This series is an introduction to the most important problems in the writing and study of American history. Some of these problems have been the subject of debate and argument for a long time, although others only recently have been recognized as controversial. However, in every case, the student will find a vital topic, an understanding of which will deepen his knowledge of social change in America.

The scholars who introduce and edit the books in this series are teaching historians who have written history in the same general area as their individual books. Many of them are leading scholars in their fields, and all have done important work in the collective search for better historical understanding.

Because of the talent and the specialized knowledge of the individual editors, a rigid editorial format has not been imposed on them. For example, some of the editors believe that primary source material is necessary to their subjects. Some believe that their material should be arranged to show conflicting interpretations. Others have decided to use the selected materials as evidence for their own interpretations. The individual editors have been given the freedom to handle their books in the way that their own experience and knowledge indicate is best. The overall result is a series built up from the individual decisions of working scholars in the various fields, rather than one that conforms to a uniform editorial decision.

A common goal (rather than a shared technique) is the bridge of this series. There is always the desire to bring the reader as close to these problems as possible. One result of this objective is an emphasis on the nature and consequences of problems and events, with a de-emphasis of the more purely historiographical issues. The goal is to involve the student in the reality of crisis, the inevitability of ambiguity, and the excitement of finding a way through the historical maze.

Above all, this series is designed to show students how experienced historians read and reason. Although health is not contagious, intellectual engagement may be. If we show students something significant in a phrase or a passage that they otherwise may have missed, we will have accomplished part of our objective. When students see something that passed us by, then the process will have been made whole. This active and mutual involvement of editor and reader with a significant human problem will rescue the study of history from the smell and feel of dust.

Loren Baritz

ACKNOWLEDGMENTS

I acknowledge with thanks the permission of Yale University's Office of Teacher Training to reproduce here an edited version of my paper, "The Radicalism of American Abolitionists," which was published in the report of the Thirteenth Yale Conference on the Teaching of Social Studies in 1968.

I am particularly grateful to my wife, Jane DeHart Mathews, who encouraged me to compile this book. I also thank Mrs. Nicholas G. Cameron of Princeton University's Firestone Library for her gracious help and interest in my work and Dianne Taylor for her cheerful endurance of my importunate demands upon her secretarial skills. I am especially indebted to Elizabeth Farrior Buford who assisted me in this project with infectious good humor and incomparable care.

One note about the editing: I have reproduced the abolitionists' words as they spoke, wrote, capitalized and italicized them. This accounts for the lower case of many words that are capitalized today and the abundant italicization which was so characteristic of nineteenth century partisan journalism.

DONALD G. MATHEWS

CONTENTS

AGITATION FOR FREEDOM:
The Abolitionist Movement

I. INTRODUCTION: THE RADICALISM OF THE ABOLITIONISTS

Radicalism and abolitionism were synonymous to many nineteenth century Americans. Of the so-called "ultraisms" that enlivened the antebellum United States, the abolitionist crusade against slavery, because of its familiarity and political implications, represented all the erratic notions, extreme positions, and eccentric values associated in the popular mind with "wild attempts to make the world over." Uncritical journalists often lumped "Fanny Wrightism," perfectionism, Fourierism, and abolitionism together into one threatening un-American conspiracy against the Union. This facile identification of abolitionism and all other radicalism obscured issues in the nineteenth century just as do similar assumptions about contemporary dissent. To be sure, the anthill activity of the 1830s created a general entrepreneurial thrust in dissent as well as canals, banks, and railroads, and not a few abolitionists were engaged in protesting forms of oppression that were only indirectly related to their assault on slavery. But they were not all united in a general radical criticism of everything in American society. In fact, the identification of abolitionism with radicalism may seem naive and simplistic to a generation wrestling with the problems of a mass, technological society, and confronting ever-more probing and strident groups of dissenters. Compared with latter-day radicals, abolitionists seem fairly tame. Although there were exceptions, for the most part, they prized private property when it was not in the form of human beings; they believed in the sanctity of inherited values, had no overriding, profound quarrel with capitalism, and shared their fellow countrymen's vision of the untrammelled individual's creating his own institutions in anticipation of the Millennium.

Why, then, were abolitionists identified with all sorts of radicalism, indeed, identified as radicalism itself? Simply because they challenged the almost universal racist assumptions of American society, put abstract moral values above political and constitutional considerations, and were influential enough to endanger the Union. Moreover, abolitionists were among the most successful radicals in our history. Success is, of course, a relative condition, and abolitionists have not always been considered paragons of victorious achievement. They wanted peaceful abolition of slavery and the popular renunciation of racism: but, as is so painfully evident today, neither goal was accomplished. Because abolitionists did not get what they wanted in the way in which they would have preferred to get it, and because they were usually flagrantly disrespectful of people in authority, they have not, until the past few years, been very popular with historians. They have been dismissed as "fanatics," or as neurotic people who attempted to compensate for their inability to manage their own lives by attempting to manage the lives of others—in this case slaveholders. They have also been accused of being less idealistic than they claimed and, on the other hand, of being too idealistic. The first charge is meant to cast doubt on their devotion to racial equality; the second is meant to raise serious questions about their effectiveness as agitators—indeed, to question agitation as a socially desirable action. The viewpoint represented in this book of readings takes issue with these derogatory views of agitation and the abolitionists. When viewed in the context of what they set out to accomplish, the character of their opposition, and the means that they had at their disposal, abolitionists, it may be argued, used American institutions in an expert way to achieve remarkable success. To explain this thesis, it is necessary to discuss the nature of abolitionist radicalism, its tactics, and the meaning of its success.

ABOLITIONISTS AGAINST A RACIST SOCIETY

Differences in tactics, style, and perspective drew abolitionists toward four centers of gravity. There were in the first place those remarkably articulate and single-minded people associated with William Lloyd Garrison and Wendell Phillips, whose arguments against slavery were developed into criticism of all invidious social distinctions and an appeal for freedom in all social relationships. In some instances, Garrisonians were drawn into pacifism, and from there into something very much like Christian anarchism. Impressed by the vision of a perfect society whose solidarity resulted from the moral purity of individuals rather than from the force of "corrupted" institutions, Garrisonians professed to rely on "moral suasion" alone to change public opinion and to achieve their ends. Disgusted with the temporizing of political parties and churches, these energetic and willful people could be counted on for the most hostile statements, the least compromising positions in the abolition movement. They acted as a prod for their ideological comrades and, although not all intellectuals, provided many of the ideas and set the terms of discussion that unified the movement. The second and third centers of abolitionist gravitation did not draw people so disillusioned with institutions as were the Garrisonians. Some abolitionists actually leapt into politics (while holding their noses) in order to found the Liberty Party in 1840, and they never quite relinquished their appreciation for the power that "moral suasion" might possibly have if based on solid electoral victories. James G. Birney, whom the Liberty Party nominated for president in 1840 and 1844, was one of the pioneers; Joshua Giddings, an antislavery Congressman from Ohio, and Frederick Douglass, the black abolitionist leader, were two other important figures. Convinced that political pressure was necessary to put moral principles into action, they were never successful in establishing an effective abolition party even though they provided continuity between the passion of Garrison and the pragmatic calculations of Free Soilers and Radical Republicans. As a source of pressure on these later parties, they were often more effective than as a mobilizing force in their own right.

Probably more successful on their own terms than the political abolitionists were those associated with various evangelical Protestant denominations. Although usually identified as adherents of the Congregationalist American Missionary Association, they were actually more active in moving the larger Protestant churches toward more satisfactory antislavery—but not abolitionist—positions. Scattered throughout the North, they often endured the scorn of the New England-oriented Garrisonians for remaining

loyal to churches that would not condemn slaveholders; but by
the end of the antebellum period, they had schooled hundreds of
thousands of Americans in the ideas and rhetoric if not the
commitment of the abolition crusade. A fourth abolitionist
"party" included people in the other three groups, yet maintained
their own separate identity. These were the black abolitionists who
taught Garrison much of what he knew about the American
Colonization Society, who acted as agents and lecturers for the
antislavery movement, and who constantly had to teach their
white friends that paternalism was no more attractive among
white abolitionists than among white slaveholders. Bound by their
racial and cultural identity, black abolitionists often spoke in tones
that revealed their bitterness and alienation. What did the Fourth
of July mean to them? August First—the date of British Emancipation in the West Indies—had much more meaning for them, as
they were careful to point out.[1] The division of the abolition
movement into white and black, like the other divisions, did not
prevent the cooperation or a shifting of personnel or even an
appreciation of the different roles that each group played. Diverse
and mutually antagonistic as these abolitionists often were, they
belonged together in a dynamic division of labor—Garrisonians
and blacks as the hardcore, militant irreconcilables, the institutional abolitionists as the "reasonable" moderates.[2]

At the beginning of the antislavery movement, very few people
thought any abolitionist reasonable; they were all too radical, or
in the phraseology of the day, "ultraistic." The reasons are not
difficult to find and included abolitionists' views on race and
slavery, their suspicion of American institutions, and their conception of the role and tactics of reform. From the abolitionists'
assault on slavery flowed all their other views and attitudes.
Historians have smugly accused abolitionists of confused and
inconsistent thinking because they professed to be pacifists but

[1] Benjamin Quarles, *Black Abolitionists*, New York, 1969, *passim* and pp. 123ff.
[2] For a discussion of the abolitionist crusade, see Gilbert H. Barnes, *The
Antislavery Impulse 1830-1844*, New York, 1933; James M. McPherson, *The Struggle for
Equality*, Princeton, 1964; Dwight Dumond, *Antislavery: the Crusade for Freedom in
America*, Ann Arbor, 1961; Louis Filler, *The Crusade Against Slavery 1830-1860*, New
York, 1960; Donald G. Mathews, *Slavery and Methodism: A Chapter in American Morality
1780-1845*, Princeton, 1965.

yielded to glorifying war, often disdained "union with slaveholders" but joined in a crusade to restore them to the nation, and expressed an exalted loyalty to the principles of the Declaration of Independence but burned the constitution. In a somewhat different manner, other historians have characterized antislavery thought as anti-institutional, individualistic, abstract, and infused with guilt.[3] Both views are in large part true; and both also have the same merit as one would expect from a discussion of Marxism that ignored its opposition to capitalism or, at least, took it for granted. Certainly, it has been argued that abolitionist opposition to slavery "goes without saying." But the truth of the matter is that it does not "go without saying." One should be chary of building a paradigm of abolitionist thought or of analyzing the consistency of abolitionist thinking without taking seriously first and foremost that what held the abolition movement together was its opposition to slavery and race prejudice. Abolitionists were obsessed with slavery and with the place of the Negro in American life, and they tried to inflict their views on others by whatever means dictated by the logic of the situation and the power at their disposal. Furthermore, it must be remembered that abolitionists were engaged in a social movement that labored under the dynamics of collective behavior rather that the logic of the academy. There were many voices, there was much anger, not a little frustration, and a great deal of hastily expended energy in the abolition movement as well as the opposition to slavery. To bring unity out of diversity and to explain the reason for the contradictions, one must take seriously the enormity of the task that the abolitionists set for themselves.

They confronted a racist America. The North no less than the South had heavily penalized the Negro for being so thoughtless as to be captured by African slavetraders. The more philanthropic Northerners suggested the colonization of free Negroes to Africa in order to escape race prejudice, which everyone agreed existed; but colonizationists were not enthusiastic about standing up against race prejudice. Not a few were so ensnared in their self-induced fantasies about racial amalgamation as to share the antipathies of the people from whom they were presumably trying to save

---

[3] See especially, Stanley Elkins, *Slavery: A Problem in American Institutional and Intellectual Life*, Chicago, 1959, pp. 147ff.

Negroes. If philanthropists were compromised by race prejudice, one can easily imagine how other people felt; and a brief glance at Northern laws and customs would almost confirm the worst his imagination could present. The status of the black man in the United States was simply that he was not a citizen, not even a second-class citizen. True, Negroes had a few rights of citizenship in some Northern states, but the Dred Scott decision in 1857 symbolized the plight of the American Negro throughout the antebellum period—he was not considered a citizen of the United States: he could not be naturalized; he could not automatically receive whatever benefits were accorded other Americans, for instance, the ones conferred on men who had served in the army or navy—he was always a special case. When the logic of a situation seemed to say that the Negro was a citizen, someone had to explain away the implications. When, for example, someone asked if Negro veterans of the War of 1812 could qualify for land bounties as had their white comrades, Attorney-General William Wirt replied in the affirmative. But he added that he did not think that Negroes should have been in the military in the first place. Such contradictions were gradually being resolved, but to the Negro's disadvantage: to deprive him of western lands and, finally, to deprive him of the protection that the uncertainty about his legal position afforded. The Dred Scott decision explicitly stated what most Americans had known for a long time—that the Negro had no rights that the white man was bound to respect. And he had, of course, many liabilities. Many states had anti-immigration laws to keep Negroes out, most refused to allow a black man to testify against a white, most refused to allow him to vote or to go to school with whites. Churches were segregated as were cemeteries, streetcars, and railway coaches. Hotels and inns were closed to him, and intermarriage was considered a monstrous parody of an honorable institution. The wonder of this society was that more Negroes did not applaud or express the sentiments of one black man who cursed: "I can hate this Government without being disloyal because it has stricken down my manhood. . . . I can join a foreign enemy and fight against it, without being a traitor, because it treats me as an ALIEN and a STRANGER. . . ."[4]

---

[4] Leon F. Litwack, *North of Slavery: The Negro in the Free States, 1790-1860,* Chicago, 1961, p. 266 and pp. 64ff.

It had also enslaved him. Slavery was a national institution, abolitionists claimed; and by this, they meant not that Northerners literally held slaves or engaged in the domestic slave trade, although some did. They meant that slavery claimed the North's allegiance as well as that of the South. It had slipped into the American consciousness as a possibly tragic institution about which nothing could be done. But it was more. It was an insistent reminder of the failure of American principles, although not in a constant, conscious, or very clear way. Submerged in the subconscious, feelings of guilt were expressed in the defensiveness that Americans exhibited about their peculiar institution, and more especially were expressed in defining the lessons that they had learned about its irrepressible, inexorable existence. In the first place, they had learned that direct antislavery activity was fruitless, and worse—it made slavery's defenders even more implacable. In the great revivals following the Revolution, and in the contagious effects of speaking so valiantly of liberty during the war, American antislavery advocates had worked prodigiously to spread their new egalitarian, Republican, evangelical gospel of freedom. But they had failed. In the North where emancipation was achieved, the people who ran things had not been engaged in slaveholding—but in the South they were, and they did not take kindly to any amount of antislavery activity. When the foremost antislavery people—most of them evangelicals—tried to demand the emancipation of slaves held by Christians, the answer was a forthright "No!" And the retreat was on. Antislavery men soon found that they could not even require kind treatment of slaves as a matter of discipline, nor the integrity of marriage, nor the solidarity of the family. No meddling of any kind was to be allowed.[5] Reformers learned not only that confrontation with slaveholders was "counterproductive," but that conscious effort to ameliorate the slave's condition was almost impossible. Having learned these lessons, reformers found that the question of slavery in any form would always be a little unsettling—it reminded people of misbegotten optimism and idealism, it was said to remind them of socially adolescent folly; it reminded them also of their shame.

[5] See, for example, Mathews, *Slavery and Methodism*, p. 52.

Another lesson was more important because it was more universal. Americans had learned from the first debates on the Constitution that compromise over slavery was the sensitive scar tissue that covered the wounds of sectional differences while binding the nation together. Slavery was a way of life and power and prestige for the South; for the North it was the constant reminder of the tenuousness of the Union. To preserve the nation in its revolutionary unity, it was necessary to deny the implications of its revolutionary ideology. The force of this axiom of early American political life was emphatically revealed in the bitter Missouri debates in 1819 and 1820. Thereafter, throughout the antebellum period, the discussion of slavery was in bad taste. The South was sensitive on that subject, it was said, and newspapers, legislative bodies, and church consvention all joined in the incantation that explained the price of national unity. The lesson was not the perception of a false consciousness; nor was it learned without a sense of tragedy—but it was learned well. If a man loved the United States of America he would not work against slavery because to do so would endanger the constitutional and political settlement. Northerners did not like to think of slavery as *their* institution—it belonged to the South—but because of the lessons that they had learned about slavery and its opposition, they belonged to slavery even if slavery did not belong to them.

Abolitionist radicalism is immediately apparent when compared with the society it confronted. Abolitionists challenged the conventional wisdom that directed social intercourse, and they placed no value at all on the compromises relating to slavery. On the one hand, they contradicted public opinion—which Alexis de Tocqueville described as so irresistibly tyrannical in a democracy—and on the other, they denied that the American Republic was so virtuous as their fellow citizens claimed. Abolitionist radicalism did not inhere in its attack on slavery per se in the North—although it did in the South—but in its attack on the American commonwealth and commonsense. It was inconceivable to nineteenth century Americans that their pragmatism should be so challenged by abstractions, and to no good purpose, or that anyone should stand up for such pariahs as Negroes. Recent scholarship has revealed the extent of the abolitionists' emphasis on racial equality and their attempts to stamp out racism in the United States. No one has suggested that white abolitionists did not share some of the racial attitudes of their society, they could not avoid doing so. But they thought that Nothern slaveholding principles, or race prejudice, were just as bad as Southern slavery, perhaps worse, because of the hypocrisy involved. Often engaged in quibbling about social intercourse with Negroes or in repeating common fallacies about racial traits, they nevertheless fought laws forbidding intermarriage, built schools to educate Negroes, attacked segregation in public transportation and churches, and even listened to black Americans who accused them of sharing the prejudices of their society. (This last fact may have been the most important of all.[6]) And they constantly appealed to white Americans to try to experience the meaning of prejudice and slavery by imagining themselves as Negroes and slaves. "There never was a more narrow-minded, ignoble, and despicable sentiment," wrote one abolitionist, "than the prevailing prejudice against color. There is no magnanimity, no elevation, no noble-heartedness about it. It is a little, mean, contemptible feeling, fit for no place in the universe save peradventure, the heart of a despot, an aristocrat, or a fop."[7]

Abolitionists' radicalism is found not only in their attack on slavery and prejudice but also in their attitude toward American institutions. This is not to say that they were anti-institutional nor to express regret that they did not try harder to work through available American institutions. As Stanley Elkins has pointed out, there were no national institutions that could make Southern slaveholders do things they did not want to do, that is, free their slaves, or ameliorate their condition at the very least. There were no institutions to which Americans were so loyal that new rules and regulations could make them behave differently from their accustomed racist patterns. Professor Elkins regrets this lack of institutional power, arguing that one of the great faults of the abolitionist crusade was that it could not work through proper, institutional channels. Such a possibility in Elkins' mind would have guaranteed a balanced and relatively easy transition from a slaveholding to a free-labor society.[8] Easy transitions in social history, however, are very rare indeed; and Elkins' view does not adequately represent the social dynamics of the nineteenth cen-

---

[6] McPherson, *Struggle for Equality, passim.*

[7] [Harvey Newcomb] *The "Negro Pew": Being an Inquiry concerning the propriety of Distinctions in the House of God, on Account of Color,* Boston, 1837, p. 101.

[8] Elkins, *Slavery,* pp. 27-37, 193 ff.

tury. Now, it is true that Americans viewed their institutions as servants and, therefore, refused to obey rules of which they did not approve. But it is not true that Americans were opposed to institutions. They employed them as means of social intercourse and integration, as organizations to get things done, and as ways to pass on the values and ideas of one generation to the next. In fact, most Americans valued their peculiar institutions quite highly, since in the early nineteenth century things were happening so rapidly in this country as to require a steady, recognizable, habitual way of getting society organized and keeping it in tact.

The abolitionist's radicalism was not that he shared an antipathy toward institutions with his fellow Americans; his situation was the exact opposite. He endangered the integrity of the institutions that they valued so highly: their churches, political parties, and the Union. And it was this institutional loyalty that abolitionists counted on to change public opinion. Neither at the beginning nor at the end of the abolitionists' crusade did a majority of abolitionists repudiate institutional direction as unnecessary to the functioning of a good society. Historians like Elkins, who have thought so, have apparently kept their attention fixed firmly on Garrison and his friends during the period of their weakest influence. To be sure, one must admit that radicals are quite likely to succumb to that human frailty of making a virtue of unconcealed weakness. Elkins is quite correct in pointing out that not a few abolitionists shared Garrison's discomfort within the limiting framework of institutions that seemed incapable of making the right decisions; but it has yet to be determined that they were in the majority, or that they came to their conclusions happily and as a result of philosophical reflection instead of historical adversity. Whatever the reason, these most anarchistic of abolitionists acted as a reference group to demonstrate to institutional spokesmen that more "moderate" abolitionists' loyalty to institutions had its limits and that, therefore, some accommodation should be arrived at that was more favorable to antislavery opinion. The radicalism of abolitionists was not opposition to institutions as such, but in their insistence that these institutions be judged as to whether or not they supported slavery. The widespread reaction of ecclesiastics, politicians, and thousands of plain people concerned for the prosperity of those institutions that provided order and direction is not evidence of widespread anti-institutionalism in American life so much as it was a sense of anxiety lest those institutions be weakened. Abolitionists found in their peculiar ideology and camaraderie the security and direction that other people were content to find in their institutions. In one sense, the movement—dynamic, unstructured, and difficult to control—acted as a functional equivalent of an institution and allowed abolitionists to manipulate institutions from positions of weakness far more effectively than their small number would presumably have justified. If abolitionists had simply and quietly repudiated institutional ties, and that alone, they would have constituted no threat to a majority of Americans. It was their willingness to be a part of institutions that they judged so harshly that made them appear to be so dangerous.

The third aspect of the abolitionists' radicalism was their conception of the proper role of reformers, represented in their impassioned rhetoric and characteristic slogan: "immediate emancipation without expatriation." These words, like the contemporary rhetoric of Black Power, were characteristic of radical reform movements in several ways. In their provocative words of denunciation and stirring appeals to abstract morality was an annoying attack on the best in the American value system—they sometimes compared churches unfavorably with brothels. They seemed to enjoy overstating their case in broad, picturesque terms, and then pausing to explain away the apparent irrationality of their statements by appealing to what they considered to be a higher rationality. Their rhetoric was meant to expose not conceal, to arouse to action not placate, to confront their opponents and to polarize potentially antagonistic positions rather than to conciliate differences. Often condemned for the impolitic, presumably impractical character of immediate emancipation, abolitionists would reply that any workable process would, of course, require careful planning, perhaps, even an extraordinary amount of government control. But immediatism, they insisted over and over again, was not so much a plan of action as it was a conception of reform. That is, significant social change would result not with the passage of time but with the passage of laws, and the latter would occur when public opinion was sufficiently aroused. And public opinion would be aroused not by careful, reflective argument, but by impassioned agitation. William Lloyd Garrison explained it this way:

"In demanding equal and exact justice we may get partial

redress; in asking for the whole that is due us, we may get a part; in advocating the immediate, we may succeed in procuring the speedy abolition of slavery. But if we demand anything short of justice, we shall recover no damages; if we ask for a part we shall get nothing."[9]

Radical in significant ways as they were, abolitionists were not so alien to American society as to be powerless. Their radicalism was sufficiently familiar to numerous Americans to lay a claim on their conscience, or if not that, at least, their self-image. Abolitionists spoke of slavery as a sin; they spoke as if men could do right if they so desired, and they described the Negro as a child of God—in other words, they could use the common language of evangelicalism against slavery and race prejudice. It would not convince everyone, but it could and did present an authentic mode of discussion. Not a few Americans who could not think of slaveholding as a sin could, because they were accustomed to discussing problems of this kind through the ubiquity of the revivalist churches, think of slavery in moral terms and eventually could be made susceptible to the dramatic impact of *Uncle Tom's Cabin.* Probably even more important was the appeal to American political principles. Abolitionists have been scolded for having made their arguments abstract; but men who would not lift a finger to help a black man might possibly be moved to disapprove of slavery by the realization that some Americans betrayed their revolutionary inheritance of liberty by wielding absolute power over other human beings. Moreover, the abstractions of the American revolution had an evocative impact on many people, and when these values seemed to be threatened by conservative and Southern attacks on the rights of free speech, press, and assembly, there was power in their resentment that radicals could use. Abstractions made it possible for some Americans to transcend the almost overwhelming racism of their society and to fight the symbol of that racism—slavery. Perhaps it was hypocritical of many Northerners—abolitionists said it was—but the radicals sensed that hypocrisy had a certain functional value, and they accepted nonabolitionist antislavery opinion as a feeble step in the right direction. Abolitionists could not have achieved this much

---

[9]Quoted in Donald G. Mathews, "The Abolitionists on Slavery: The Critique Behind the Social Movement," *Journal of Southern History,* (May 1967), 167.

success had it not been for the limitation of slavery to the South. As sectional antagonism increased, Northerners could use antislavery ideas to justify themselves. Radicals had, after 1830, intended to use the North as a base for pressure against the South, hoping that once Northern public opinion was aroused against slavery an isolated South would begin to see the logic and morality of abolition. Federal laws, too, could complement public opinion by abolishing the interstate slave trade, as well as slavery in the District of Columbia. The implications of these tactics abolitionists did not fully admit until the Southern rebellion, since they counted on the South's loyalty to the Union, necessitated, they believed, by that section's reliance on Northern power and trade.

THE TACTICS OF DISRUPTION AND CONFLICT

The conventional historical interpretation of abolitionist tactics emphasizes their reliance on "moral suasion" and their naive sense of betrayal when it did not work. Although Garrison and his ideological friends talked at great length about "moral suasion," they did not practice it—they did not rely on the force of moral arguments alone to win converts. They often claimed to do so, and some even repudiated the use of any institutional or political means in spreading antislavery attitudes. But the style of their rhetoric, the continuous barrage of their propaganda, the ability with which they could take advantage of a crisis situation reveals something other than naive do-gooders awaiting a miraculous conversion of their enemies to great principles and civic righteousness.

Abolitionists had few choices of alternatives once they had made up their minds to do something about slavery. Previous experience had proved that slaveholders would not countenance any piecemeal meddling with slave society. Abolitionists found that indirect moral suasion such as that practiced by the American Colonization Society merely reinforced slavery; the discussion of plans, like the one carried out by Benjamin Lundy in the Genius of Universal Emancipation, merely diverted attention from action to useless speculation; and churches had been compromised by their decisions to ignore slavery as a moral problem. Abolitionists were consequently in a weak position, and their weakness dictated the tactics that were available to them. A small minority in a popular democracy, they had to try to change public opinion, a problem that they solved by adopting the tactics of disruption and conflict. Developed in a dialogue of conflict and confrontation between opposing views in various institutions, abolitionist tactics originated from their earliest frustration and disillusionment with the churches. The ever-increasing success of the evangelical denominations had infused abolitionists with premature raptures of optimism because they chose to believe that people joined churches for moral rather than social reasons; moral suasion, it was concluded, should be a moral force. Whereas radicals in other countries turned to the working class—defined and alienated from authority by political and economic exploitation—to act as the driving force in achieving a just social order, radical abolitionists could not do so. The working classes in this country were primarily white and primarily concerned with their own condition instead of with the condition of blacks whom they looked on as potential if not actual competitors for jobs and social standing. Insecure as they were, American workers had no inclination to aid blacks. On the contrary, they opposed this aid as contrary to their own interests. Therefore, American radicals involved in the race problem turned to the only group of people whom they sensed had the kind of social solidarity and moral commitment to engage in activity on behalf of people less fortunate than themselves; this group was identified at first as those people who were morally sensitive, who wanted to make the world a better place in which to live, that is, regenerate Christians. The adjective "regenerate" was supposed to connote a repudiation of conventional values and a devotion to creating a better society. To reach these people and to make them into a social force to attack slavery and racism, abolitionists used the churches as a base for moral appeal and education through periodicals, pamphlets, lectures, and revivals. Whether or not abolitionists really believed in their heart of hearts that Americans were so loyal to their churches that they would meekly repent of the sins of slaveholding and race prejudice, they talked as if they did—if only for a short while. Almost immediately they learned that they could not get churches to condemn slaveholding as a sin; but at the same time they learned the value of using the churches, and American institutions, in general, as arenas of conflict in which issues important to abolitionists could be developed in conjuction with issues that were important to a greater number of people.

The process of disruption and conflict began in the early 1830s and lasted through the Civil War, although the novelty had worn off by 1840. In the churches and voluntary societies it took the form of abolitionists' asking for root and branch reform immediately in a most "unreasonable," unsophisticated, and insistent way. Impossibilist as they seemed to be, abolitionists never wavered from their attacks on slavery and in their demands for action. Invariably, institutional authorities would try to silence them, an action that would, in turn, raise issues of freedom of opinion and speech; in the resulting realignment of loyalties, friends, if not partisans, would be won to the abolitionists' cause. Continued agitation would bring further cleavage, especially if Southerners were part of the institution. The two largest denominations split specifically over slavery, while the third, the Presbyterian church, divided over issues raised by abolitionist-related activities. The Baptist and Methodist cases are instructive models of abolitionist tactics since, in both, Southerners seceded from national denominational assemblies in reaction to what they perceived were abolitionist tendencies among institutional leadership. To be more specific, in both Baptist and Methodist denominations, abolitionist demands for the excommunication of slaveholders forced Northern church leaders to explain their dissatisfaction with slavery as an institution. They calmly assured Southerners, however, that slaveholding was not to be considered sinful; but, they insisted, it was an arrangement for which Christians should feel considerable regret. Southerners responded by demanding that national ecclesiastical officials be allowed to own slaves. When nonabolitionist authorities refused to honor this demand, Southerners left their respective churches. In neither case were abolitionists any more than a small minority of churchmen involved, but in both they used impossibilist demands and denunciatory language as a wedge to pry from conservative Northerners statements that indicated that slavery could not be considered a happy solution to problems of racial adjustment. These statements, wrung at great effort by abolitionists from Northern institutional spokesmen, helped to develop a confrontation between North and South on issues that were not strictly abolitionist, since in none of the cases did the North take what

could be considered an abolitionist stance; the result was nevertheless a division of the churches. The significance of this process
was that it was a preview of a larger, more far-reaching conflict.
The issue of splitting the denominations would be discussed
throughout the respective communions in thousands of local
churches, focusing on the distinctive differences between North
and South. In the search for a rationale to define and to claim
loyalties, antislavery sentiment could be relied on to fill an
ideological gap. Such a result was not acceptable to abolitionists
as proof of pure motives, but it was indicative of some weakening
of the claim that slavery had on the North.

Direct confrontation between abolitionists and political institutions provided an even more widespread and significant conflict
than the conflict within the churches. The result of the polar-
ization process is well known, of course. But it should also be
remembered how abolitionists played their peculiar role. The
tactics of conflict and confrontation went through various phases
in the political world as the country changed in reaction to a
series of events over which radicals had no control but in which
they played an important part. The first was initiated by abolitionists themselves and involved the question of civil liberties.
In the early days of the antislavery crusade, abolitionists were
often mobbed—one was even killed. Although they were blamed for
causing the riots directed against them, abolitionists persisted, won
a few converts, and succeeded in dramatizing their cause. They
decided to make the right of abolitionists to speak freely a test of
American freedom and the extent of the "slave power." Would
Americans honor the first amendment to the Constitution? Theirs
was a good plan, reflecting the uses that a weak minority may
make of the abstractions of national values when contrasted with
the prejudices and muscular stupidity of an arrogant, excitable
majority. Public opinion, although it was not favorable to them
was, at least, forced to grant them the right to speak.

The abstractions of American freedom of expression were not so
forceful as radicals would have liked, but they were the only
weapons that were available at the time. This was particularly
true of the congressional petition campaign. In the middle 1830s
the abolitionists renewed with skill and vigor the old campaigns to
present the House of Representatives with petitions for the

abolition of slavery in the District of Columbia and for the eradication of the interstate slave trade. When Southern and conservative members of the House passed a rule to lay those petitions on the table without being heard, abolitionists claimed that the right of petition was being denied them by the South and its allies. By making this claim, abolitionists accused the South of repudiating American freedoms, and in the resulting dramatic confrontation they had excellent help from Representative John Quincy Adams, who seemed to enjoy "bugging the establishment" almost as much as did the abolitionists. By confrontation with slavery in as many forms of public discourse as possible, abolitionists were able to dramatize the contradiction of a slaveholding system in a presumably free society, and to help develop the myth of a threatening and arrogant South.

When the abolitionists split in 1840 over whether to work through politics or whether to identify abolitionism with other reforms, their tactics of confrontation and conflict were not seriously affected. In fact, they were enhanced. As purist abolitionists seceded from political parties and Christian churches,they confronted Americans with a species of radicalism to which they were not accustomed—one that seemed to repudiate American society at about the same time that foreign travelers found Americans to be most anxious about their identity. The result of this condition was to force some hard thinking about the truth of abolitionist observations about the South, especially as sectional antagonism began to affect general public debate. Continued abolitionist activity uncompromised by association with official institutions meant that abolitionist ideals and judgments were maintained in tact by a group that doggedly proclaimed that anything less than complete abolition of slavery was wrong. Americans were not allowed to be self-satisfied with the nonextension of slavery or with the renewal of the colonization movement— at least, as far as antislavery radicals were concerned. Every profession of opposition to slavery in the abstract was countered with inquiries as to whether one were opposed to slavery in the South. The existence of a radical element pulled some Americans into more liberal positions. Professing that they were not so extremist as abolitionists, they nevertheless felt that they should be against slavery, in a pragmatic way of course. The abolitionists were a negative reference group for many people, but sometimes they were very much like a minister or priest in relation to his congregation. A minister preaches the truths of his gospel to a people who like to think of themselves as being better than they really are. Parishioners might think the pastor a little strange in his sincerity and "unrealistic" attitude toward life, but in a moment of crisis they may very well have to turn to his ideas and values in order to understand their situation, to find justification, and to move in a significant direction.

Something very much like this happened with the abolitionists and the North. In the developing sectional crisis of the 1850s abolitionists could observe the results of their continuing conflict with a majority of Americans. Political abolitionists had succeeded in making slavery an issue in various ways. Their antagonism toward slaveholders and their explanation of Southern aggressiveness as a threat to the nation were seized on by politicians for their own purposes in debates over the annexation of Texas, the disposition of lands taken in the Mexican war, the fugitive slave law, and the question of whether or not Congress should or could allow slavery in the territories. The developing of slavery as an issue was not the abolitionists' doing alone, of course. Other factors contributed: slavery was seized on by opposing politicians as the symbol of difference between North and South in the sectional struggles because it did make the interests and society of the South different from those of the North, and as demography and power changed within the Union there is no doubt that the South felt threatened. Slavery could very easily become a primary issue in politics during the 1850s, but especially after abolitionists had made their views and fears quite clear through the years of conflict with all the institutions in American society. Theirs was the most radical ideology which could lend potency to another conflict. In times of great crisis and anxiety, when national values seemed threatened, the Union seemed to be splitting apart, and when political parties gave no ideological certainty, citizens could find a way to enhance their sense of purpose and the moral foundation of their own position by borrowing abolitionist phrases and ideas. The best example of this process is, of course, the Civil War.

It is a truism that the civil war began as a war for Southern independence in the South, became a war for the Union in the North, and ended as a victorious crusade against slavery. Emancipation was a commitment made during the war as Northerners sought to justify themselves on ideological grounds and to transform their fight from a conservative denial of the right of revolution into a liberalizing crusade of freedom against slavery. In the process, abolitionists grew in prestige as never before, speaking to crowded houses, running books through several editions, and suggesting policies to politicians in expectation of some success. But the tactics of confrontation and conflict did not end. Abolitionists continued as before to demand equality for the Negro and freedom for the slave. It has been said that they were confused when the war broke out, not knowing what to think about the Union, Lincoln, or the war. Confusion, of course, was endemic to the situation; radicals obviously share human frailty, but they had one goal in view as they always had had: to fight slavery as best they could. Taking advantage of a situation in which growing emancipationist sentiment indicated a greater susceptibility to abolitionist ideas that before, radicals pushed for policies that led to the Thirteenth Amendment and to the abolition of slavery. From the charges of naivete pressed against them, one would have expected that abolitionists would have been satisfied, but they were not. They were instrumental in developing the Freedmen's Bureau, doing careful research into the needs of the newly freed slaves, and in achieving liberal features in the bill that made the bureau a government body. They also helped governmental authorities to see the legitimacy of arming Negro troops and of educating emancipated slaves. What else they did in getting legislation favorable to the Negro would be difficult to specify. It would be too much to claim that abolitionists were primarily responsible for the Fourteenth Amendment and the Fifteenth Amendment because antislavery politicians and the problems of the war directed the logic of much activity leading to their enactment. But on these issues, as well as the issues that had related to slavery for more than 40 years, abolitionists were active, asking for more than most people were willing to give, condemning race prejudice and, generally, creating enough conflict within the centers of power and channels of communication to ease the decision makers into policies antagonistic to slavery. But these were always the tactics of the weak, of people whose values were much different from those of the majority and who, consequently, were unable to achieve everything they wanted, such as (specifically) confiscation of confederate estates or (more generally) justice and racial equality.[10]

THE LIMITS OF SUCCESS IN RADICALISM

This raises the question of abolitionist success. By one set of criteria abolitionists failed: slavery was not abolished peacefully through a change in public opinion, but by force and war. Neither North nor South was convinced to repudiate race prejudice; and in the end the emancipated slaves were abandoned to their former masters. Abolitionists had tried to achieve a just society—as they understood justice—but they had failed.

To put the matter in this fashion is to evaluate abolitionists by the goals that they set for themselves and by the judgments of their own rhetoric. It is to evaluate them also by assuming that they were in positions of relatively absolute power. The issue is whether it is fair or accurate to judge the weak as if they had the power of the strong, and whether to judge radicals by their own impossible standards of success. By the abolitionists' own standards of how men *ought* to behave they, of course, were not successful. But the abolitionists themselves knew that men do not behave as they should. Educated as they were in the strenuous moral theology of evangelicalism, they knew better than to expect perfection, although they believed that they had to demand it to induce a sense of guilt that could make men act in a morally acceptable way. And they were successful only as long as the major issues of each crisis in which they were involved were not those of Negro equality and slavery as a proper relationship between human beings. Their success depended on the way in which conflicting parties other than themselves could be prevailed on to follow abolitionist-inspired policies because of the necessity for using ideological explanations in times of crisis. Given these qualifica-

[10]McPherson, *Struggle. . .for Equality, passim.*

tions it is nevertheless possible to argue that the abolitionists were remarkably successful radicals.

The argument rests on relative accomplishments. When one considers the overwhelming racism of American society in the nineteenth century, the spread of antislavery sentiment before the war is remarkable, and the passage of the Thirteenth Amendment, the Fourteenth Amendment, and the Fifteenth Amendment is even more so. The education of the Negro in the South following the war, and the little interest that the North did manage to show the freedmen was the work of abolitionists and the persons who sympathized with them. The fact that the South was used as a scapegoat for the entire nation's racism was never forgotten by the abolitionists. They also knew that their success in large part rested on Northern hypocrisy and self-interest—a fact that does not lessen their accomplishment, although it helps to explain it. There is no denying that abolitionists in their weakness had to rely on the increasing contradictions in society as they developed into open antagonism; moreover, they could achieve success only in time of crisis. But that is what radicalism is all about—to persist in the purity and integrity of one's belief or ideology, to increase the pressure inherent in the contradictory characteristics of the larger society, and to seize the moment of crisis to win what one can. What abolitionists won was not enough, but it was more than society was willing to give freely. And, perhaps, the greatest success of the abolitionists is that in our times of crisis we should wish that they had been even more successful than they were.

II. DEFINING THE CAUSE

1 FROM   *William Lloyd Garrison*
          To the Public

> *Although the abolitionist movement changed in many ways from 1830 to*
> *1870, it seemed to be personified during those eventful years by William*
> *Lloyd Garrison (1805-1879), who began to popularize antislavery when he*
> *was only 26 years of age. Schooled in antipathy to slavery by the Quaker*
> *emancipationist, Benjamin Lundy, and by members of the black community,*
> *Garrison in 1831 first published The Liberator, a weekly paper popular with*
> *black Americans for its forthright attack on racism ("slaveholding prin-*
> *ciples") in the North and on slavery in the South. In the following selection,*
> *Garrison makes a distinction between gradual abolition, as proposed by many*
> *moderates, and immediatism. Gradualism was no more a definite plan of*
> *action than was the new mode which Garrison here exemplifies; instead, it*
> *was a wistful, genteel hope that the principles of Christianity would*
> *eventually convince the slaveholding South to free its slaves. Immediatism was*
> *bold, angry, and to the point, as is evident in Garrison's printed declaration*
> *"To the Public."*

SOURCE. *The Liberator*, January 1, 1831.

In the month of August, I issued proposals for publishing 'THE LIBERATOR' in Washington city; but the enterprise, though hailed in different sections of the country, was palsied by public indifference. Since that time, the removal of the Genius of Universal Emancipation to the Seat of Government has rendered less imperious the establishment of a similar periodical in that quarter.

During my recent tour for the purpose of exciting the minds of the people by a series of discourses on the subject of slavery, every place that I visited gave fresh evidence of the fact, that a greater revolution in public sentiment was to be effected in the free states—*and particularly in New-England*—than at the South. I found contempt more bitter, opposition more active, detraction more relentless, prejudice more stubborn, and apathy more frozen, than among slave owners themselves. Of course, there were individual exceptions to the contrary. This state of things afflicted, but did not dishearten me. I determined, at every hazard, to lift up the standard of emancipation in the eyes of the nation, *within sight of Bunker Hill and on the birth place of liberty.* That standard is now unfuried; and long may it float, unhurt by the applications of time or the missiles of a desperate foe—yes, till every chain be broken, and every bondsman set free! Let southern oppressors tremble—let all the enemies of the persecuted blacks tremble.

I deem the publication of my original Prospectus* unnecessary, as it has obtained a wide circulation. The principles therein inculcated will be steadily pursued in this paper, excepting that I shall not array myself as the political partisan of any man. In defending the great cause of human rights, I wish to derive the assistance of all religions and of all parties.

Assenting to the "self-evident truth" maintained in the American Declaration of Independence, "that all men are created equal, and endowed by their Creator with certain inalienable rights— among which are life, liberty and the pursuit of happiness," I shall strenuously then contend for the immediate enfranchisement of our slave population. In Park-street Church, on the Fourth of July, 1829, in an address on slavery, I unreflectingly assented to the popular but pernicious doctrine of gradual abolition. I seize this

---

*I would here offer my grateful acknowledgments to those editors who so promptly and generously inserted my Proposals. They must give me an available opportunity to repay their liberality.

opportunity to make a full and unequivocal recantation, and thus publicly to ask pardon of my God, of my country, and of my brethren the poor slaves, for having stated a sentiment so full of timidity, injustice and absurdity. A similar recantation, from my pen, was published in the Genius of Universal Emancipation of Baltimore, in September, 1829. My conscience is now satisfied.

I am aware, that many object to the severity of my language; but is there not cause for severity? I *will be* as harsh as truth, and as uncompromising as subject. On this justice, I do not wish to think, or speak, or write, with moderation. No! no! Tell a man whose house is on fire, to give a moderate alarm; tell him to moderately rescue his wife from the hands of the ravisher; tell the mother to gradually extricate her babe from the fire into which it has fallen;—but urge me not to use moderation in a cause like the present. I am in earnest—I will not equivocate—I will not excuse—I will not retreat a single inch—AND I WILL BE HEARD. The apathy of the people is enough to make every statue leap from its pedestal, and to hasten the resurrection of the dead.

It is pretended, that I am retarding the cause of emancipation by the coarseness of my invective, and the precipitancy of my measures. *The charge is not true.* On this question my influence,—humble as is,—is felt at this moment to a considerable extent, and shall be felt in coming years— not perniciously, but beneficially—not as a curse, but as a blessing; and posterity will bear testimony that I was right. I desire to thank God, that he enables me to disregard "the fear of man which bringeth a snare," and to speak his truth in its simplicity and power. And here I close with this fresh dedication:

> *"Oppression! I have seen thee, face to face,*
> *And met thy cruel eye and cloudy brow;*
> *But they soul-withering glance I fear not now—*
> *For dread to prouder feelings doth give place*
> *Of deep Abhorrence! Scorning the disgrace*
> *Of slavish knees that at the footstool bow,*
> *I also kneel—but with far other vow*
> *Do hail thee and the herd of hirelings base:—*
> *I swear, while life—blood warms my throbbing veins,*
> *Still to oppose and thwart, with heart and hand,*
> *Thy brutalising sway—till Afric's chains*

Are burst, and Freedom rules the rescued land,-
Trampling Oppression and his iron rod:
Such is the vow I take—so HELP ME GOD!"

WILLIAM LLOYD GARRISON
Boston, January 1, 1831

2. FROM   *William Lloyd Garrison*
An Address Delivered before the Old Colony Anti-Slavery
Society

"Immediatism" became a controversial issue from Garrison's first impassioned address; many opponents claimed that the intrepid editor and his ideological comrades were simply not clear. In the following two selections, however, it is quite clear that immediatism was not only an angry outburst or an intellectual perception, it was also a conscious mode of reform and agitation. The first statement is taken from a speech Garrison made to a local Massachusetts antislavery society on July 4, 1839.

Fellow Citizens:

Not for vain boasting, not for fulsome panegyric, not for noisy declamation, are we assembled together on this occasion. I take it for granted, that nothing of this kind is expected from my lips. My spirit is troubled within me, though to the great American multitude, it is a day of boisterous merriment. If I shall give clear, intelligible utterance to the emotions that swell my bosom, the ears of the people will be made to tingle: if I shall suppress them, my words will be powerless. Though I may seem to be a madman, a stirrer up of sedition, a raging incendiary, it is with me the least of all earthly considerations. The message I have received from the Lord must be delivered, without omission of a single word,

SOURCE. An address delivered before the Old Colony Anti-Slavery Society, 1839.

whether this impudent, hard-hearted, stiff necked generation will hear or forbear.

Would to God this [The Fourth of July] were truly—what it is not, though lying lips declare it to be—the JUBILEE OF FREEDOM! That jubilee cannot come, so long as one slave is left to grind in his prison-house. It will come only when liberty is proclaimed throughout ALL the land, unto ALL the inhabitants thereof. O the "fantastic tricks" which the American people are this day "playing before high heaven!" O their awful desecration of an anniversary, which should be sacred to justice, equality and brotherly love! O their profane use of the sacred name of LIBERTY! O their impious appeals to the GOD OF THE OPPRESSED, for his divine benediction, while they are making merchandize of his image!. . . Professing to be Christians,—yet withholding the Bible, the means of religious instruction, even the knowledge of the alphabet, from a benighted multitude, under terrible penalties! Boasting of your democracy,— yet determining the rights of men by the texture of their hair, and the color of their skin! Assuming to be "the land of the free and the home of the brave," —yet keeping in chains more slaves than any other nation, not excepting slave cursed Brazil! Prating of your morality and honesty,—yet denying the rites of marriage to twenty-five hundred thousand human beings, and plundering them of their hard earnings! Affecting to be horror-struck in view of the foreign slave-trade—yet eagerly pursuing a domestic traffic equally cruel and unnatural, and reducing to slavery not less than seventy thousand new victims annually! Vaunting of your freedom of speech and of the press—your matchless Constitution and your glorious Union,—yet denouncing as traitors, and treating as outlaws, those who have the courage and fidelity to plead for immediate, untrammelled, universal emancipation! Monsters that ye are! how can ye expect to escape the scorn of the world, and the wrath of heaven? Emancipate your slaves, if you would redeem your tarnished character,—if you would obtain forgiveness here and salvation hereafter! Until you do so, "there will be a stain upon your national escutcheon which all of the waters of the Atlantic cannot wash out!"

It is thus that, as a people, we are justly subjected to the reproach, the execration, the derision of mankind, and are made a proverb and a hissing among the nations. We cannot plead not guilty; every accusation that is registered against us is true; the act of violence is in our hands; the stolen property is in our possession; our fingers are stained with blood; the cup of our iniquity is full.

***

Fellow-citizens, you have done well in convening together on this occasion, to devise ways and means for the speedy abolition of American slavery. Let the hypocritical, the profligate, the thoughtless, the tyrannical, desicrate this memorable advent, if they will, by their utter forgetfulness of those who are transformed from immortal beings into four-toothed beasts and creeping things on our soil; by their swaggering airs, and senseless boasts, and vulgar hurrahs. Your patriotism is of a different stamp. Your love of country is the love of MAN–HUMANITY. . . You are not *colonizationists* but ABOLITIONISTS—not *gradualists*, but IMMEDIATISTS—a difference as great as exists between non-entities and living souls, between airy abstractions and practical realities. Your philanthropy means something more than transporting men across the Atlantic on account of their complexion, or keeping them in bondage for their good. You make no compromise with slavery, but demand immediate emancipation, "in the name of Humanity, and according to the law of the living God." Thus it becomes you, as men, as republicans, as Christians, to feel and to act. To demand less, would not be remembering those in bonds as bound with them, nor loving your neighbor as yourselves. If you deserve to be rebuked at all, it is not on account of any excess of zeal, or needless sacrifice, or superfluous effort, that you have put forth in the cause of universal liberty. It is not that you have done too much, but too little—that your ardor has been too glowing, but too moderate—that your action has been too precipitate, but too cautious. The sins of abolitionists are those of omission, rather than of commission. We do not yet reason, and feel, and act, precisely as if *our* wives and daughters were given over to the tender mercies of lewd and brutal wretches, or *our* children were liable to be sold to the slave speculators at any moment, or the chains were about to be fastened upon *our own* free limbs. They who accuse us of being uncharitable in spirit, harsh in speech, personal in denunciation, have no sympathy with the oppressed, and therefore are disqualified to sit in judgment upon our conduct. They do not regard the negro race as equal to the Anglo-Saxon; hence it is impossible for them to resent a wrong or an outrage done to a black man as they would to a white. In regard to their own rights and enjoyments, they are sensitively alive to the slightest encroachments upon them. Touch but their interest, however lightly,—conflict with their prerogatives, however gently,—injure their persons, however triflingly,—and see how they will flame, and denounce, and threaten! Such men are condemned out of their own mouths. Let no heed be given to what they say of our principles and measures. Their criticism is as false as their philanthropy is spurious. They make great pretensions to prudence—which means moral cowardice; to gentleness of spirit— which means total insensibility; to moderation—which means stonyheartedness; to candor and impartiality—which means favoritism and spleen; to evangelical piety—which means cant and bigotry. Their love for the *natives* of Africa abroad, is graduated by their prejudice against the *descendants* of Africa, who reside on our soil. The less they sympathize with the southern slave, the more they feel for the inhabitant of Guinea. The more they succeed in crushing our free colored population to the earth, the greater is their concern for the civilization and christianization of "poor benighted Africa," through the instrumentality of colored emigrants. . . .

***

The anti-slavery cause is beset by many dangers. But there is one which we have special reason to apprehend. It is, that hollow cant and senseless clamor about "hard language," will insensibly check that free utterance of thought, and close application of the truth, which have characterized abolitionists from the beginning. As that cause is becoming popular, and many may be induced to espouse it from motives of policy, rather than from any reverence for principle, let us beware how we soften our just severity of speech, or emasculate a single epithet. The whole scope of the English language is inadequate to describe the horrors and impieties of slavery, and the transcendent wickedness of those who sustain this bloody system. Instead of repudiating any of its strong terms, therefore, we rather need a new and stronger dialect. Hard language! Let us mark those who complain of its use! In ninety-nine cases out of a hundred, they will be found to be the most unscrupulous in their allegations, the most bitter in their spirit, the most vituperative in their manner of expression, when alluding to abolitionists. The cry of "hard language" has become stale in

my ears. *The faithful utterance of that language has, by the blessing of God,
made the anti-slavery cause what it is*—ample in resources, strong in
numbers, victorious in conflict. Like the handwriting upon the
wall of the palace, it has caused the knees of the American
Belshazzar to smite together in terror, and filled with dismay all
who follow in his train. Soft phrases and honied accents were tried
in vain for many a year: they had no adaptation to the subject. . . .

***

But I will not enlarge upon this point. If southern slaveholders,
and their apologists, cannot endure our rebukes, how will they be
able to bear the awful retributions of heaven which must inevitably overwhelm them, unless they speedily repent? I am ready to
make a truce with the south: if she will give up her stolen
property, I will no longer brand her as a thief; if she will desist
from driving woman into the field, like a beast, under the lash of a
brutal overseer,—from stealing infants, from trafficking in human
flesh, from keeping back the hire of the laborers by fraud, I will
agree not to call her a monster; if she will honor the marriage
institution, and sacredly respect the relations of life, and no longer
license incest, pollution and adultery, I will not represent her as
Sodomitish in spirit and practice; if she will no longer prevent the
unobstructed circulation of the holy scriptures, and the intellectual and religious education of her benighted population, I will
not stigmatize her as practically atheistical. In short, if she will
abolish her diabolical slave system, root and branch, at once and
forever, we will instantly disband all our anti-slavery societies, and
no longer agitate the land. But, until she thus act, we shall
increase instead of relaxing our effort—multiply instead of dimin-
ishing our associations—and make our rebukes more terrible than
ever!

I said that you glory in the name of abolitionists—*immediate*
abolitionists. That word "IMMEDIATE" is the sheet anchor of our
cause. If we cut loose from it, the gallant bark of Emancipation
will be wrecked inevitably. It is the motto upon our flag, which
strikes such terror into the breasts of the enemies of liberty. Let
that flag be ingloriously furled, and all will be lost. We must
conquer or perish under its broad folds. Had it not been for the
rallying cry of IMMEDIATISM, not an anti-slavery society would
have been in existence—the land would have been sleeping in the

lap of death—the consciences of the people would be seared as with a hot iron. Had it not been for that talismanic word, "IM-MEDIATE," the 800,000 ransomed bondmen in the British West India Islands, who are now standing erect, with their faces heavenward, in all the dignity of immortal men, would unquestionably be at this very hour pining in hopeless servitude, and bowed to the earth under the weight of their chains! Yes, that one word did more for the cause of African emancipation in five years, in Great Britain, than the labors of Wilberforce, Clarkson, and their coadjutors, during a half a century. *They* accomplished little or nothing toward the suppression of the slave trade or slavery, because they clung to the delusive notion, that tyranny and man-stealing must be abandoned gradually, by an almost imperceptible process. The whole anti-slavery battle in this country has turned upon the word "IMMEDIATE"—a word which has shaken the nation, from Maine to the Rocky Mountains, like a blast from the trump of the great archangel—a word which implies that slavery is accursed, that the slaveholder is a tyrant, that the negro is a man, that the right to liberty can never be alienated by the color of the skin! There are those who ask us to repudiate that word as non-essential. They might as rationally ask us to leave the negro to his fate! If they really regard it as non-essential, why are they so anxious that we whould drop it? We deem it essential to the abolition of slavery, and therefore cannot allow this "staff of accomplishment" to pass from our hands. Give it up? Why, the conscience-stricken, terrified taskmasters at the south demand nothing more at our hands. It troubles them as the presence of JESUS did the devils who possessed the Gergesenes, and they shriek out in concert, "What have we to do with thee? Art thou come hither to torment us before the time?"

It is in our power, fellow citizens, to hush all the jarring elements to repose, which now agitate the land—to regain our lost reputations—to cause every reward which has been offered for our heads to be withdrawn—to unite the North and the South in amicable companionship—to extinguish the flames of mobocracy, and to put an end to the administration of Lynch law—to recover the lost right of petition—to open every meeting-house and hall in the land, from which we are now excluded—to insure protection to every northern man who shall venture to travel beyond Mason's and Dixon's line; I say it is in our power, as abolitionists, at any moment, to effect all these changes, simply by consenting to substitute the word GRADUAL for IMMEDIATE! So important, so essential, so omnipotent does a little word sometimes become in the progress of human events, and the conflict of LIBERTY with DESPOTISM! Yes, fellow citizens, if we would only swerve one hair's breadth to public opinion—only be somewhat less tenacious of principle—only allow expediency to take the precedence of right—only concede the right of the tyrant to keep his slaves in bondage until a more convenient season—only allow an abhorrence of slavery to remain an abstraction—and instead of being regarded as the off scouring of all things, we should be hailed as sound republicans and excellent christians! But we cannot consent to lose our own souls, though we should thereby gain the whole world: and surely it would be at the peril of our souls, if we should close our ears to the cry of the slave, and strike hands in amity with the tyrant-master. Come what may—life or death, peace or war, fame or infamy—we cannot abandon his cause. To sacrifice him, that we might no longer be subjected to reproach or peril— that the "two-legged wolves" of the South might still be enabled to tear in pieces the lambs of Christ's fold, without molestation— would be the blackest perfidy. We are resolute in our determination to stand by his side, at all hazards—but not because he is a negro but a man—not on account of his complexion, but of his immortality—not because he is a representative of the colored race, but of mankind. He bears the image of God—the Saviour has died to redeem him—he is our brother by creation, affinity, redemption—in his veins flows the *one blood* of all nations of men, that dwell on all the face of the earth—he was made but a little lower than the angels, though now discrowned and sceptreless. What other, better, stronger reasons can we have or desire, why we should labor for the rescue of a being so august from the deep abyss of ruin into which he has fallen?

It is the abolition, not the mitigation of slavery, that will satisfy the demands of justice. For, in the language of a late distinguished champion of negro emancipation across the Atlantic—"Mitigate and keep down the evil as much as you can, still it is there in all its native virulence, and still it will do its work in spite of you. The improvements you have made are merely superficial. You have not reached the seat and vital spring of the mischief. You have only concealed, in some measure, and for a time, its inherent enormity. Its essence remains unchanged and untouched, and is ready to unfold itself whenever a convenient season arrives, notwithstanding all your caution and all your vigilance, in those manifold acts of injustice and inhumanity, which are its genuine and its invariable fruits. You may white-wash the sepulchre, —you may put upon it every adornment that fancy can suggest—you may cover it over with all the flowers and evergreens that the garden or the field can furnish, so that it will appear beautiful outwardly unto men. But it is a sepulchre still—full of dead men's bones and of all uncleanness. Disguise slavery as you will,—put into the cup all the pleasing and palatable ingredients which you can discover in the wide range of nature and of art,—still, it is a bitter, bitter draught, from which the understanding and the heart of every man, in whom nature works unsophisticated and un-biased, recoils with unutterable aversion and abhorrence. Slavery is the very Upas tree of the moral world, beneath whose pestiferous shade all intellect languishes, and all virtue dies. And if you would get quit of the evil, you must go more thoroughly and effectually to work than you can ever do by any or by all of those palliatives, which are included under the term *mitigation.* The foul sepulchre must be taken away. The cup of oppression must be dashed to pieces on the ground. The Pestiferous tree must be cut down and eradicated; it must be, root and branch of it, cast into the consuming fire, and its ashes scattered to the four winds of heaven. It is thus you must deal with slavery. You must annihilate it,—annihilate it now,—and annihilate it forever!"

In some bosoms, the abolition watchword, IMMEDIATE, excites terror—in others merriment. Our demand is pronounced to be impracticable, absurd, visionary. We have urged it, it is said, for the last six years, and yet the slave-system exists in all its virulence; therefore, the doctrine of immediate emancipation is proved to be false! We cannot enunciate it, before it will furnish its own refutation! The folly of all this belongs to our objectors, not to us. According to their logic, all moral obligations lose their binding power because "the whole world lieth in wickedness," and will not bow to the sceptre of the King of Zion. "God *now* commandeth all men every where to repent": but they will not repent: therefore, it is absurd to call them to immediate repen-tance! "He that believeth shall be saved, and he that believeth not shall be damned": but men will not believe: therefore, unbelief is not a crime! Slavery ought to be immediately abolished, we say: but the upholders of it will not let the oppressed go free: therefore, IMMEDIATISM, say our opponents, is an idle word! Well may logicians call such reasoning the *reductio ad absurdum*: its immorality is as glaring as its folly. What oppressors *ought* to do, and what they are *willing* to do, are separate considerations: the *ought* is not the less imperative, on acco*unt of the unwillingness.* We use the word IMMEDIATE in a common sense manner, as defining both the duty of the master and the right of the slave. "These colonies ARE, and of right OUGHT TO BE, free and independent," was the declaration of our revolutionary fathers, July 4th, 1776; but they had to fight seven long years before they secured their independence. Did they utter a falsehood, because they could not immediately obtain what was immediately their due? To declare themselves free, while they still remained in colonial vassalage, was the philosophical method to recover their liberty. In demanding equal and exact justice, we may get partial redress; in asking for the whole that is due us, we may get a part; in advocating the immediate, we may succeed in procuring the speedy abolition of slavery. But, if we demand any thing short of justice, we shall recover no damages; if we ask for a part, we shall get nothing; if we advocate gradual abolition, we shall perpetuate what we aim to destroy, and proclaim that the SELF–EVIDENT TRUTHS which are set forth in the Declaration of Independence are SELF–EVIDENT LIES! . . .

3 FROM *Wendell Phillips*
The Philosophy of the Abolition Movement

Words and images, emotions, reason, fear and hope—the abolitionists employed them all in ingenious combinations to win Americans to their cause. And if they were successful in part, abolitionists were never so persuasive as they wanted to be; they seemed to be too subversive of the peace of the Republic. That peace, abolitionists replied, was false so long as black people could not enjoy it. This insistent attack on race prejudice was combined with a strident moralism and the frequent use of harsh analogies to shock Americans into realizing the moral significance of slavery. In some way, abolitionists had to make their fellow countrymen see how slavery was a threat to them as human beings as well as a burden to the black man, an affront to republicansim and democracy. In the following excerpt from a significant speech delivered January 27, 1853, Wendell Phillips explains the problem of communication faced by reformers in a complex society made up of various communities, each with different values and frames of reference. Phillips (1811-1884) was a well-born Boston lawyer who found a sense of purpose in the antislavery cause after a period of apparent aimlessness. In the abolition movement, Phillips found many opportunities to employ his spectacular talents as an orator. A man very much at home on the public platform and well acquainted with the power and use of words and phrases, Phillips explains here, as well as anyone could, the philosophy of the abolition movement.

MR. CHAIRMAN. I have to present, from the business committee, the following resolution:

"*Resolved,* That the object of this society is now, as it has always been, to convince our countrymen, by arguments addressed to their hearts and consciences, that slaveholding is a heinous crime,

SOURCE. Wendell Phillips, *Speeches, Lectures, and Letters* (Boston, 1863).

and that the duty, safety, and interest of all concerned demand its immediate abolition without expatriation."

I wish Mr. Chairman, to notice some objections that have been made to our course ever since Mr. Garrison began his career, and which have been lately urged again. . . . The charges to which I refer are these: that in dealing with slaveholders and their apologists, we indulge in fierce denunciations, instead of appealing to their reason and common sense by plain statements and fair argument;—that we might have won the sympathies and support of the nation, if we would have submitted to argue this question with a manly patience; but instead of this, we have outraged the feelings of the community by attacks, unjust and unnecessarily severe, on its most valued institutions, and gratified our spleen by indiscriminate abuse of leading men, who were often honest in their intentions, however mistaken in their views;—that we have utterly neglected the ample means that lay around us to convert the nation, submitted to no discipline, formed no plan, been guided by no foresight, but hurried on in childish, reckless, blind, and hot headed zeal,—bigots in the narrowness of our views, and fanatics in our blind fury of invective and malignant judgment of other men's motives.

***

[On the contrary,] I claim, before you who know the true state of the case,—I claim for the antislavery movement with which this society is identified, that, looking back over its whole course, and considering the men connected with it in the mass, it has been marked by sound judgment, unerring foresight, the most sagacious adaptation of means to ends, the strictest self-discipline, the most thorough research, and an amount of patience and manly argument addressed to the conscience and intellect of the nation, such as no other cause of the kind, in England or this country, has ever offered. I claim, also that its course has been marked by a cheerful surrender of all individual claims to merit or leadership,— the most cordial welcoming of the slightest effort, of every honest attempt to lighten or to break the chain of the slave. I need not waste time by repeating the superfluous confession that we are men, and therefore do not claim to be perfect. Neither would I be understood as denying that we use denunciation, and ridicule, and every other weapon that the human mind knows. We must plead guilty, if there be guilt in not knowing how to separate the sin from the sinner. With all the fondness for abstractions attributed to us, we are not yet capable of that. We are fighting a momentous battle at desperate odds,—one against a thousand. Every weapon that ability or ignorance, wit, wealth, prejudice, or fashion can command is pointed against us. The guns are shotted to their lips. The arrows are poisoned. Fighting against such an array, we cannot afford to confine ourselves to any one weapon. The cause is not ours, so that we might rightfully, postpone or put in peril the victory by moderating our demands, stifling our convictions, or filing down our rebukes, to gratify any sickly taste of our own, or to spare the delicate nerves of our neighbors. Our clients are three millions of Christian slaves, standing dumb suppliants at the threshold of the Christian world. They have no voice but ours to utter their complaints, or to demand justice. The press, the pulpit, the wealth, the literature, the prejudices, the political arrangements, the present self-interest of the country, are all against us. God has given us no weapons but the truth, faithfully uttered and addressed, with the old prophets' directness, to the conscience of the individual sinner. The elements which control public opinion and mould the masses are against us. We can pick off here and there a man from the triumphant majority. We have facts for those who think, arguments for those who reason; but he who cannot be reasoned out of his prejudices must be laughed out of them; he who cannot be argued out of his selfishness must be shamed out of it by the mirror of his hateful self held up relentlessly before his eyes. We live in a land where every man makes broad his phylactery, inscribing thereon, "All men are created equal,"—"God hath made of one blood all nations of men." It seems to us that in such a land there must be, on this question of slavery, sluggards to be awakened, as well as doubters to be convinced. Many more, we verily believe, of the first than of the last. There are far more dead hearts to be quickened, than confused intellects to be cleared up,— more dumb dogs to be made to speak, than doubting consciences, to be enlightened. [Loud cheers] We have use, than, sometimes, for something beside argument.

What is the denunciation with which we are charged? It is endeavoring, in our faltering human speech, to declare the enormity of the sin of making merchandise of men,—of separating husband and wife,—taking the infant from its mother, and selling the daughter to prostitution,—of a professedly Christian nation denying, by statute, the Bible to every sixth man and woman of its population, and making it illegal for "two or three" to meet together, except a white man be present! What is this harsh criticism of motives with which we are charged? It is simply holding the intelligent and deliberate actor responsible for the character and consequences of his acts. Is there anything inherently wrong in such denunciation of such criticism? This we may claim,—we have never judged a man but out of his own mouth. We have seldom, if ever, held him to account, except for acts of which he and his friends were proud. All that we ask the world and thoughtful men to note are the principles and deeds on which the American pulpit and American public men plume themselves. We always allow our opponents to paint their own pictures. Our humble duty is to stand by and assure the spectators that what they would take for a knave or a hypocrite is really, in American estimation, a Doctor of Divinity or Secretary of State.

The South is one great brothel, where half a million of women are flogged to prostitution, or, worse still, are degraded to believe it honorable. The public squares of half our great cities echo to the wail of families torn asunder at the auction-block; no one of our fair rivers that has not closed over the negro seeking in death a refuge from a life too wretched to bear: thousands of fugitives skulk along our highways, afraid to tell their names, and trembling at the sight of a human being; free men kidnapped in our streets, to be plunged into the hell of slavery; and now and then one, as if by miracle, after long years, returns to make men aghast with his tale. The press says, "It is all right"; and the pulpit cries, "Amen." They print the Bible in every tongue in which man utters his prayers; and get the money to do so by agreeing never to give the book, in the language our mothers taught us, to any negro, free or bond, south of Mason and Dixon's line. The press says, "It is all right"; and the pulpit cries, "Amen." The slave lifts up his imploring eyes, and sees in every face but ours the face of an enemy. Prove to me now that harsh rebuke, indignant denunciation, scathing sarcasm, and pitiless ridicule are wholly and always unjustifiable; else we dare not, in so desperate a case, throw away any weapon which ever broke up the crust of an ignorant prejudice, roused a slumbering conscience, shamed a proud sinner, or changed, in any way, the conduct of a human being. Our aim is to alter public opinion. Did we live in a market, our talk should be of dollars and cents, and we would seek to prove only that slavery was an unprofitable investment. Were the nation one great, pure church, we would sit down and reason of "righteousness, temperance, and judgment to come." Had slavery fortified itself in a college, we would load our cannons with cold facts, and wing our arrows with arguments. But we happen to live in the world,—the world made up of thought and impulse, of self-conceit and self-interest, of weak men and wicked. To conquer, we must reach all. Our object is not to make every man a Christian or a philosopher, but to induce every one to aid in the abolition of slavery. We expect to accomplish our object long before the nation is made over into saints, or elevated into philosophers. To change public opinion, we use the very tools by which it was formed. That is all such as an honest man may touch.

4   FROM   *Charles C. Burleigh*
Slavery and the North

But what had "honest men" to do with a social system over which they had no control and for which they were presumably not responsible? Such was the response of many Americans who thought that slavery was a sectional problem and, therefore, of no concern to Northerners. Moreover, not a few Yankees feared that on emancipation the freedmen would scurry north to compete in the labor market. In response, abolitionists attempted to allay Northern fears and also to encourage resistance to slavery as an aggressive power that had the potentiality and the will to gain ever more influence in the national government to the grief of the North. The "slave power" theory, which is briefly alluded to below in the reference to "the spread of slavery," was not merely a "paranoid" perception on the part of the abolitionists. It was a way of explaining the implications of Southern actions as slaveholders responded to the spread of antislavery attitudes, a way of explaining what, in fact, was the North's interest in opposing slavery. Practical consideration of Northern interests was not the abolitionists' chief concern, however;

SOURCE. Charles C. Burleigh, "Slavery and the North," 1855.

Northerners were confronted with the facts of slavery because their section was implicated in it and because the promises of democracy would not be fulfilled until all Americans were protected in that equality to which being men entitled them. Charles C. Burleigh (1810-1878) was a pamphleteer and lecturer for the American Anti-Slavery Society and an early associate of William Lloyd Garrison. Although sometimes given to wearing his hair and clothes so as to remind one of Jesus Christ, Burleigh was no eccentric when it came to propounding abolitionist ideology. The following is a complete pamphlet published by the American Anti-Slavery society in 1855.

SLAVERY—WHAT IT DOES

The question of slavery is undeniably, for this country at least, the great question of the age. On the right decision of it depend interests too vast to be fitly set forth in words. Here are three millions of slaves in a land calling itself free; three millions of human beings robbed of every right, and, by statute and custom, among a people self-styled Christian, held as brutes. Knowledge is forbidden and religious worship, if allowed, is clogged with fetters; the sanctity of marriage is denied; and home and family and all the sacred names of kindred, which form the dialect of domestic love, are made unmeaning words. The soul is crushed, that the body may be safely coined into dollars. And not occasionally, by here and there a hardened villain, reckless alike of justice, law and public sentiment; fearing not God nor regarding man; but on system, and by the combined strength of the whole nation. Most men at the North, and many even at the South, admit that this is wrong, all wrong,—in morals, in policy every way wrong,—that it is a gross injustice to the slave, a serious evil to the master, a great calamity to the country; that it belies the nation's high professions, brings deep disgrace upon its character, and exposes it to unknown perils and disasters in the time to come.

EMANCIPATION—ITS EFFECTS

What then ought to be done? One would think a just people

need not study long upon so plain a question; that a people clear-sighted for its own welfare might soon find an answer. If slavery be wrong every way, hurtful in all its bearings, then, in the name of justice, of humanity, of self-interest even, let it be abolished at once. Give back to manhood its plundered rights; raise it up from its enforced debasement. Immediate emancipation for the slave; immediate abolition, for the system of slavery; is the least demand of right and of enlightened policy. By this is not meant, as some pretend to think, that the slaves should be "turned loose" from all restraint, to be vagabonds and thieves. Emancipation would break no bond of righteous law or moral obligation. On the contrary, it would ensure to law a readier obedience, by making it impartial, both in its benefits and its restraints. It would strengthen moral obligation, by showing that it is a *mutual* bond, henceforth to be regarded by the high no less than by the low. To emancipate, then, is not to outlaw, or cut loose from society or any of its natural relations or real duties; but it is to cease from holding men as property, and begin to treat them as men; enabling them to claim and receive the earnings of their toil; giving them a voice in the choosing of their work, their employers, their associates, abodes, and manner of life; respecting their domestic ties and rights and duties; allowing them to improve their minds with knowledge and their hearts with moral culture; and leaving them free to worship God when, where and how their consciences require.

WHO CAN OBJECT?

To what, in all this, can any one reasonably object? The master cannot justly complain of a loss of property, for what he loses was never his; but so much as the change takes from him, so much has he been wrongfully withholding from the real owner, to whom—long due—it is at last restored. Nay, if either loses, it is still the slave; for his past toils and wrongs are unrequited. He is merely to be robbed no longer;—not to have back what has been plundered from him. The state or country cannot complain of loss, for, to it, the slave was only worth what work could be forced out of him, and that is less than he will do unforced, when free. The change takes nothing from his strength or skill, but adds much to his willingness to use them. When laboring, of his own accord, with the prospect of receiving what he earns, he has a motive to be diligent and faithful, which he never had while toiling reluctantly for another's gain. Even as a mere working-tool, therefore, he is worth more for being free. And then, too, freedom makes him infinitely more than a mere working-tool. He is now a man, with all the priceless treasures of mind and soul, with all the growing powers and upward aspirations which belong to manhood; with ever-widening scope for his unfolding faculties, and nothing to forbid his progress toward any height, however lofty, of human excellence. As much as brain and muscle are worth more than muscle only; as much as moral joined to mental power is a better wealth than mere brute force; in a word, as much as *men* with human skill, contrivance and invention, with reason, affection and the sense of right, are of more account than cattle yoked, and horses trained to harness; so much will the emancipation of a nation's slaves enrich the nation. Why, then, should not our slaves go free?

SLAVES NOT UNFIT FOR FREEDOM

They are ignorant and stupid, it is said; a brutish race, not fit for freedom. True,—in part,—and partly false. No doubt the slaves are ignorant and degraded. So any race would be, if wronged as they have been, and through many generations. What else could be expected from men weighted down by ages of oppression, forbidden to use the key of knowledge,—letters,—allowed no hope of bettering their state, nor any motive to exert their minds or improve their morals? But it is not true that they are only fit for slavery; fit only to be kept under the very influences which now debase them. The bad effect is no good reason for continuing the cause, but rather shows the need of its immediate removal. What!—shall we enslave men, because slavery makes them base? Keep the burden on their backs because they stoop beneath its weight; the fetter on their limbs because their gait, with it, is awkward; their dungeon closely locked because its darkness dims their sight? Is this manly?—just?—or wise? If holding man as property would give him wisdom, virtue, manly bearing; or put

him in the way of getting them; or even fill him with a stronger
wish to have them; then ignorance and dullness, vice and degradation, might with a little better face be urged as reasons for
enslavement. But such is not its purpose nor its tendency. Its
motive is self-interest; the debasement of its subject is at once its
necessary means and its sure result. While slavery lasts the slaves
will be degraded. FREEDOM is the school which fits men to be free.
What if the black man is inferior to the white? It does not follow
that he always must be. Excel him where his chance is equal,
before you boast yourself above him. Give him his liberty, and as
strong a motive to exertion as you have;—a prospect of reward as
sure and ample; not only wages for his toil, but respect and honor
and social standing according to his worth, and see what he can
then become, before you judge him to be sunk so low that freedom
cannot lift him up and bless him. His powers have never yet been
fairly tried, for he has always had to struggle against difficulties
and discouragements which white men do not meet. When free in
name, he is denied a freeman's rights and hope and prospects, and
open field of competition, and success to match his merit. Yet how
nobly has he often proved his manhood? Throughout the United
States, spread over the broad fields of Canada, and in many
foreign countries, are thousands who are living proofs that slaves
of African descent can shake off degradation with their chains, and
win respect even from stubborn prejudice. Toussaint and Petion,
Dumas the general and Dumas the author, Placide the Cuban
poet, Wheatly, Banneker, Horton, Osborn, Jordan and Hill, are a
few among the many witnesses, that higher learning, taste, nor
talent, nor skill to rule, nor warlike prowess, nor eloquence, nor
wisdom, nor sagacity, nor any element of human greatness, is
incompatible with negro blood. What these men have achieved
may well suggest the question, "if such things can be done in the
green tree, what may be done in the dry?" If with the hindrances
of slavery and caste, the colored race has shown so many proofs of
manliness, what may it not do when these checks have been
removed. The slaves are very few, who, if set free and treated
justly, would not take better "care of themselves" than slavery has
ever taken of them. Nay, doubtless many now in bondage are
higher, both in intellect and morals, than many of the whites.
Some slaves and masters must exchange conditions, if the inferior
is to be the slave. Fix,—on your scale of mind and morals,—the

point of fitness to be free; and, high or low, it will condemn the
present practice. If high enough to doom all colored men to
slavery, it dooms a multitude of whites; if low enough to leave the
whites all free, it frees all colored men. For the lowest black is not
beneath the most degraded white.

THE JUST INFERENCE

But even if the highest blacks were lower than the lowest whites,
that would not justify enslaving them. For they are men and
brethren still, and have the sacred rights of manhood. The more
debased they are, the stronger is their claim upon the sympathy
and help of their more favored brothers. If "we who are strong
ought to bear the infirmities of the weak," our brother's weakness
is a poor excuse for making him our beast of burden. Instruction is
the right of ignorance; kind care, of helplessness; and wholesome
moral influences, of a low moral state. Slavery gives neither. They
can all be better given without it. We never offer it to the
degraded, ignorant, and helpless here among oursleves. Nay, such
an offer would be deemed an outrage on the feelings of the public,
and insulting to the very vilest of our paupers; and to urge in its
behalf that "they cannot take care of themselves," would be
thought an aggravation of the wrong. How then can we pretend to
think it suited to the case of colored men, if they are helpless,
ignorant, degraded?

"SLAVES CONTENTED"

But the slaves do not wish for freedom, we are told. Happy in
bondage, they desire no change. Prove this, and slavery needs no
heavier condemnation. If it has so utterly imbruted men that they
are *content* to be brutes,—if it has crushed out of them the very
consciousness of manhood, all hope of a higher state, and even the
wish to rise; it has wrought too fearful havoc on God's noblest
work to be borne with any longer. Let it not blight another
generation, nor sink the present still farther out of sight of
manliness, and quite beyond the reach of resurrection. If for no
other reason, it ought, for this alone, to be at once abolished.

Moreover, if the slaves desire no change, they can be freed without the slightest inconvenience to their masters, for they will serve them still, of their own accord, and all the more cheerfully and faithfully, that their free choice to do so is now made certain. The master's wife, or daughter, will not have to "black his shoes," as a distinguished statesman has foretold. Why *bind* men to the place they *choose* to stay in? Why make them chattels,—beasts,—to get the service which they *wish* to render? There is no shadow of excuse for enslaving men who are willing to serve. Nor would a generous nature,—or even a simply just—require a life-long, *willing* service with but the bare support of animal life; at most, the means of animal enjoyment; while mind and soul are starved, and manhood is, as far as may be, blotted out; or abuse an ignorant brother's unsuspecting trust, to cheat him of the common Father's richest gifts, and keep him blind to his incalculable loss. The more willingly he serves, the baser is the ingratitude of such a requital. This plea, then, would be worthless even if true.

NOT TRUE

But it is false. The slaves are not content to be in bondage. Witness the pains needed to keep them there;—the laws against their leaving home without a written pass; the penalties for helping them away or harboring them while fleeing; the nightly patrols, to watch them; the bloodhounds, trained to track their flight; the high rewards often offered for their recapture; the slaveholder's anxiety for northern aid, by legislation and otherwise, to hinder their escape; the provision of the Constitution, that they shall find no refuge in the whole land, but, wherever found, shall be given up to their pursuers; the many calls made upon northern officers and magistrates to enforce it, and the many victims torn, at its behest, from hope and freedom. Witness, too, the thousands who, in spite of all these precautions, have fled to Canada, and the multitudes scattered over the free states, or lurking in southern woods and swamps, braving unnumbered perils, toils, and hardships, rather than be slaves. How can we believe that "they would not be free if they could,"—are "better off in slavery," and choose to stay there? Why! the slaveholders themselves know better. They use enslavement as a *penalty*, and

offer freedom as the highest *rewards.* Governor Giles, of Virginia, in
his address to the legislature, in 1827, speaking of the punishing of
free blacks, by selling them as slaves, says "slavery must be
admitted to be *a punishment of the highest order,* and according to
every just rule for the apportionment of punishment to crimes, it
would seem that it ought to be applied *only to crimes of the highest
order.*" Several of the slave states permit emancipation "for
meritorious services," and for no other cause. A few years ago the
state of Georgia paid $1800 to buy freedom for a slave who, by
great exertion and at much personal risk, had saved the state-
house from being burnt. And lately the legislature of South
Carolina permitted a slave to be set free, for his valor and
devotion to his master's son,—with whom he had gone to the war,
and who fell fighting the Mexicans. Such instances show the
slaveholder's real belief as to what the slaves like best, and what is
best for them. "That our negroes will be worse off, if emancipated," says a Committee of the Synod of Kentucky, in an
address to the Presbyterians of that state, "is, we feel, but a
specious pretext for lulling our own pangs of conscience, and
answering the argument of the philanthropist. *None of us believe* that
God has so created a whole race that it is better for them to
remain in perpetual bondage."

FACTS—BRITISH WEST INDIES

For further proof that slaves love freedom and are better off for
having it, look at the British West Indies. There, as is well known,
emancipation was received with a general burst of joy and
gratitude, and its effect upon the slaves, was a great improvement
both in outward comforts, and in mind and morals. They have
more and better food and clothing and home conveniences; schools
are set up for their instruction, and are well attended by the
children and youth and often even by full grown men and women,
the churches are thronged by crowds who had no religious
teaching in the time of slavery, vice and crime are lessened,
marriage is held more sacred, beneficial societies are multiplied,
and other tokens of a better social state abound. So have testified
colonial governors, legislators, magistrates, planters, merchants,
and visiters from abroad, some of them after careful observation,

in all the principal islands, made on purpose to learn the working of freedom. One sign of the much improved outward condition of the laboring class—no longer slaves—is the great increase of imports of such articles as they use. For instance, in Jamaica, since slavery was abolished, the yearly average importation of flour, rice, corn, and bread has considerably more than doubled; of pork, about trebled; of candles, and of lumber, has increased nearly one half; and of cattle, more than four-fold. If exports have lessened, one reason is, a greater home-comsumption. The planter sends away less, for the laborer uses more, thus having not only more comforts from abroad, but also more of those produced at home. Many of the freedmen have become small landholders, and live in easy independence on their little properties. Women, to a great extent, have left field-labor, and now attend to household duties and the care of their children, formerly, of necessity, so much neglected. Self-respect and manly bearing, have, in a good degree, taken the place of that crying servility which generally marks the slave. Thus facts refute the falsehood that negroes are fit only to be slaves; and neither wish for freedom, nor would be bettered by it.

OVERRUN THE NORTH

But if freed, it is said, they will overrun the North. Ah! Wouldn't leave their masters if they could; so if allowed to do as they please, they will all run off! Sound logic, truly! And as sound morality, is the inference that therefore they must still be enslaved! If they would come north, to hinder is to wrong them. As rightfully might the West shut out the eastern emigrant, as the North shut out the southern. But there is no danger of their coming. Free them, and the motive which brings them here is gone. When they come now, it is for freedom. Let them have it at home and they will stay there. The climate of the South suits them better than ours, they are used to its employments, their habits are formed by and fitted to a southern life, there are all their attachments and associations, there the strong home-feeling binds them. There too they are needed. They do the hard work of the South, and could not be spared from its fields and shops. To employ them there at liberal wages would cost much less than to put other laborers in their places. Hence it would be for the employers' interest to keep them, and for theirs to stay. Moreover, they do stay there now, when freed; although oppressive laws—which would be repealed when the abolition of slavery had removed their cause—are now in force there against free blacks.

Of the whole South, about one man in thirty-six is free colored. And more then two-thirds of these are in the northern border slave States, when, of course, they could most easily "come north." In Virginia, there are one in twenty-five of all the people; in Maryland, nearly one in ten; in Delaware, more than one in five. Yet hardly ever does one of them remove into a free State, though slaves come often—sometimes hundreds in a year.

EFFECT ON NORTHERN LABOR

This reasoning also proves the notion false, that emancipation at the South will lower the price of labour at the North. For, instead of sending up the southern blacks to compete with the working classes here, it would both keep them at home and draw back many who were driven hither by slavery, but would gladly return when they could do so and be free. Besides, it would much enlarge the market at the South, for the fruits of northern industry and enterprise. The southern laborers, when free and paid, would buy of us many comforts and conveniences not allowed them now;—cloths, hats, shoes, furniture, household utensils, improved working-tools, a countless variety of northern manufactures, and of foreign wares, imported through the North;— the demand for which would give new activity to our shops and mills and shipping, and steadier employment, and, most likely, higher wages, to all kinds of labor here. Three million new consumers of the wares we make and sell, would add greatly to the income of the North. New shops and factories, built to meet their wants, would grow to villages and towns; and, employing many busy hands in every useful calling, create home markets for the farmers' produce; increase the worth of land and houses; put life into every branch of business; and spread the benefits of the change among all classes, over the whole country. Slavery keeps from us all these benefits, and thus, in robbing southern labor, robs also northern. Yet worse; it degrades labor; coupling it, at the South, with the lowest social debasement, and thereby lessening its respectability

at the North, till now it has become, in the esteem of many, a
positive disgrace, and the honest sons of toil are shut out of self-
styled "good society," by reason solely of their useful occupations.
Hence, doubtless is it that our hopeful youth so often flee from
field or shop, into some over-crowded "profession," and suffer in
proud poverty through life, or are corrupted and depraved by the
manifold temptations of their unwisely chosen lot. Hence, too, the
laborer, failing of the respect which he is due from others, too
often loses somewhat of his *self*-respect, grows careless of his
character and conduct, makes a little or no earnest effort to
increase in worth and rise in social standing, and perhaps *becomes*
at length, in many instances, as low as he is *rated.* Thus enslavement of labor at the South, is by no means least among the
causes which keep down labor at the North, and of course,
emancipation there would be no detriment, but a great advantage,
to the working classes here.

RIGHT TO INTERFERE—SELF DEFENCE

"But we of the North," it is often said, "have no right to meddle
with slavery; then why talk about it here? It is for the South alone
to decide whether it shall be abolished, and, if so, when and how."
Granted;—that each State has the sole right to legislate on the
subject, within its own limits. But this is far from proving northern
anti-slavery action to be wrong, or northern inaction, touching
slavery, to be right. It is our right and duty to defend ourselves
against the aggressions of the slavepower. These have been
notoriously many and gross. It has trampled on our right of
petition and free speech; demolished our free presses; plundered
our mails and burnt their contents; imprisoned and enslaved
northern colored freemen, and outraged the persons of northern
citizens, both white and colored; insulted northern States by
offering indignities to the representatives of their sovereignty;
virtually annulled that provision of the Constitution which
guaranties, to the citizens of each State, "all the privileges and
immunities of citizens in the several States;" and, in instances and
ways unnumbered, in its treatment of the North, done violence to
every dictate of justice, every principle of law, human or divine. It
has usurped, by far the greater share of all political preferments,

power and profits; controlled the action of the government in all
its branches; wasted the nation's blood and treasure in wars for its
advantage; and always shaped the most important measures of
public policy with a single eye to the promotion of its own
interests, at whatever sacrifice of northern rights or the general
welfare. Against the longer continuance of this state of things we
may and ought to labor earnestly.

OPPOSE THE SPREAD OF SLAVERY

Again; it is our right and duty to oppose the farther spread of
slavery over the national domain. For the increase of slave States
since the Union was formed, the North is justly answerable, in
common with the South. Of the seventeen new States, which
should all have been held sacred to freedom, we have yielded nine
to slavery. In getting one of these, the slave power plunged us into
murderous and costly war, and now it not only claims all it can
use of the acquisitions of that war, but, by the Nebraska bill, has
opened its way to a vast domain itself had guaranteed to freedom
forever. It grasps at Cuba, too, and Hayti, nor ever rests while
aught is unwon which can be turned into its account. And if we
still, as heretofore, hold on with it in its career of robbery and
blood, we must expect to share the ruin in which it is sure to end.
If the North has a right to shun that fate, it has, no less, a right to
use the needful means;—resistance to the spread of slavery on the
nation's territory.

NORTH SUPPORTS SLAVERY

Yet again; is it the right and duty of the North to cease
supporting slavery. We have no right to help wrong-doing. Even
on the objector's own ground, that our duty is to leave it wholly to
the South, we may no more interfere for the system than against it.
But we do interfere for it, so long as we allow a representation for
slave property in Congress; bind ourselves to give up runaway
slaves to their masters, and, at the bidding of the South, to crush
all attempts to win freedom, as our fathers did, by force; array the
laws and constitutions of the northern States against the freedom

of the slave or the rights of the free colored man; give the fellowship of our churches to slaveholders, while denying it to the doers of less flagrant wrongs; and in our social intercourse, and through all the various expressions of our public sentiment, treat slaveholding as no offense, or as a very light one. All this the North is doing now. Through Church and State and the social circle, through press and pulpit and theological seminary, it is allied with slavery. The system is not southern only; it is national. Till this alliance with it is dissolved, the North is guilty with the South. We may and must dissolve it. If we cannot abolish slavery, we can, at least, and ought ourselves to cease slaveholding, even, if need be, at the cost of separation from a slaveholding Union.

MORAL INFLUENCE—POWER OF TRUTH

And finally, it is our right and duty to exert our moral influence against slavery at the South, and—though we cannot legislate upon it there,—to change the public sentiment which governs legislation; so that they who have the *power* may also have the *will* to take from injustice the support of law, from manhood's brow the brand of chattelism, from American democracy its foul reproach, and from our country its darkest guilt and deadliest curse and greatest danger. The faithful utterance of anti-slavery truth in earnest love and untiring perseverance, will win at last this glorious result, as surely as God's promise is inviolate, that his word shall not return unto him void, but shall prosper in the thing whereto he sent it.

III. DEFINING SLAVERY

The abolitionists' analysis of slavery ranged from relatively sophisticated economic analyses to moralistic tirades. Within this range, however, abolitionists were often perceptive critics. They understood, for example, that even if slaveholders could honestly be called sinners, the latter nevertheless often exhibited all the marks of respectability and piety associated with a Christian life—a fact that made slavery an exceedingly difficult institution to destroy. The difficulty was compounded by the "peculiar institutions's" impact on persons, engaging as it did both enslaver and enslaved in a mutually crippling relationship that was enforced by the logic of the slave system. This required the constant vigilance of whites and the perpetual submission of blacks. Although abolitionists knew that affectionate relationships could develop within the slave system, they were nevertheless most conscious of slavery as a relationship between the powerful on the one hand and the powerless on the other. The quality of the power wielded by the master had to be—by the logic of the situation and the tendency of men to resent their enslavement—absolute, unmitigated, undiluted. And power checked only by ones self-interest or benevolence was not, abolitionists argued, likely to be employed for altruistic purposes or for the best interests of those who suffered its tyranny.

Abolitionists, therefore, quite naturally used vivid stories of the physical cruelty inflicted by whites on blacks to exemplify the meaning of the more subtle and devastating forms of psychological cruelty. Atrocity stories helped to "clank the chains" of slavery in the ears of sensitive Northerners, but they were meant to do more than create general revulsion at a general situation. They were also meant to make people think about what slavery would mean to them personally if they were not free. For example, stories of families' being separated made a particularly indelible impression on a generation that had been taught exceptionally well that the family was the base of civilization, the foundation of all virtue.

Nor was this all. The dignity of labor, the virtues of self-reliance and personal integrity, the freedom of education, and the hope of social mobility, all so important to the American people, were all closed to the slave—thus argued the abolitionists. Perhaps slavery differed from place to place—Kentucky slavery was thought quite rightly to be different from that in Louisiana—but the essential quality of absolute power burdened blacks everywhere and, in doing so, contradicted the American and Christian value systems.

5   FROM   *Theodore Dwight Weld*

American Slavery as It Is: Testimony of a Thousand Witnesses

The selection that follows, after rejecting commonplace apologies for the Southern social system, emphasizes the impact of slavery on persons. It is taken from one of the most widely disseminated and influential of the abolitionist tracts, American Slavery as It Is, *which was published by the American Anti-Slavery Society in 1839. The author, Theodore Dwight Weld (1803-1895), was a Presbyterian clergyman who, like many others of his generation, was dissatisfied with an ordinary parish ministry. His call to a special mission as an antislavery prophet became clear to him as the result of his association with antislavery men and of his own intellectual development. A prodigious organizer, penetrating orator, and indefatigible researcher, Weld was one of the foremost evangelical abolitionists until his voice gave out and he retired to educational experimentation. Married to Angelina Grimke, one of the foremost leaders of women's rights in the nineteenth century, Weld continued to probe the weaknesses of the American social system. But he produced nothing so complete as his early analysis of slavery which was based on newspaper reports by Southerners themselves as well as on travelers' accounts and law codes. Other abolitionists published more scholarly and dispassionate accounts of slavery, but none represents so well the juxtaposition of facts and passionate argument as* American Slavery as It Is.

SOURCE. Theodore Dwight Weld, "American Slavery As It Is: Testimony of a Thousand Witnesses," 1839.

Reader, you are empanelled as juror to try a plain case and bring in an honest verdict. The question at issue is not one of law, but of fact—"What is the actual condition of the slaves in the United States?" A plainer case never went to a jury. Look at it. *Twenty-seven hundred thousand persons* in this country, men, women, and children are in slavery. Is slavery, as a condition for human beings, good, bad, or indifferent? We submit the question without argument. You have common sense, and conscience, and a child, a father, a mother, a brother or sister—make the case your own, make it theirs, and bring in your verdict. The case of Human Rights against Slavery has been adjudicated in the court of conscience times innumerable. The same verdict has always been rendered—"Guilty;" the same sentence has always been pronounced, "Let it be accursed;" and human nature, with her million echoes, has rung it round the world in every language under heaven, "Let it be accursed. Let it be accursed." His heart is false to human nature, who will not say "Amen." There is not a man on earth who does not believe that slavery is a curse. Human beings may be inconsistent, but human NATURE is true to herself. She has uttered her testimony against slavery with a shriek ever since the monster was begotten; and till it perishes amidst the execrations of the universe, she will traverse the world on its track, dealing her bolts upon its head, and dashing against it her condemning brand. We repeat it, every man knows that slavery is a curse. Whoever denies this, his lips libel his heart. Try him; clank the chains in his ears, and tell him they are for *him*; give him an hour to prepare his wife and children for a life of slavery; bid him make haste and get ready their necks for the yoke, and their wrists for the coffle chains, then look at his pale lips and trembling knees, and you have nature's testimony against slavery.

Two million seven hundred thousand persons in these States are in this condition. They were made slaves and are held such by force, and by being put in fear, and this for no crime! Reader, what have you to say of such treatment! Is it right, just, benevolent? Suppose I should seize you, rob you of your liberty, drive you into the field, and make you work without pay as long as you live, would that be justice and kindness, or monstrous injustice and cruelty? Now, everybody knows that the slaveholders do these things to the slaves every day, and yet it is stoutly affirmed that they treat them well and kindly, and that their tender regard for their slaves restrains the masters from inflicting cruelties upon them. We shall go into no metaphysics to show the absurdity of this pretence. The man who *robs* you every day, is forsooth, quite too tenderhearted ever to cuff or kick you! True, he can snatch your money, but he does it gently lest he should hurt you. He can empty your pockets without qualms, but if your stomach is empty, it cuts him to the quick. He can make you work a life time without pay, but loves you too well to let you go hungry. He fleeces you of your *rights* with a relish, but is shocked if you work bareheaded in summer, or in winter without warm stockings. He can make you go without your liberty, but never without a shirt. He can crush, in you, all hope of bettering your condition, by vowing that you shall die his slave, but though he can cooly torture your feelings, he is too compassionate to lacerate your back—he can break your heart, but he is very tender of your skin. He can strip you of all protection and thus expose you to all outrages, but if you are exposed to the *weather*, half clad and half sheltered, how yearn his tender bowels! What! slaveholders talk of treating men well, and yet not only rob them of all they get, and as fast as they get it, but rob them of *themselves*, also; their very hands and feet, all their muscles, and limbs, and senses, their bodies and minds, their time and liberty and earnings, their free speech and rights of conscience, their right to acquire knowledge, and property, and reputation; and yet they, who plunder them of all these, would fain make us believe that their soft hearts ooze out so lovingly toward their slaves that they always keep them well housed and well clad, never push them too hard in the field, never make their dear backs smart, not let their dear stomachs get empty.

But there is no end to these absurdities. Are slaveholders dunces, or do they take all the rest of the world to be, that they think to bandage our eyes with such thin gauzes? Protecting their kind regard for those whom they hourly plunder of all they have and all they get! What! when they have seized their victims, and annihilated all their rights, still claim to be the special guardians of their happiness! Plunderers of their liberty, yet the careful suppliers of their wants! Robbers of their earnings, yet watchful sentinels round their interests, and kind providers for comfort? Filching all their time, yet granting generous donations for rest and sleep? Stealing the use of their muscles, yet thoughtful of their ease?

Putting them under *drivers,* yet careful that they are not hardpushed? Too humane forsooth to stint the stomachs of their slaves, yet force their minds to starve, and brandish over them pains and penalties, if they dare to reach forth for the smallest crumb of knowledge, even a letter of the alphabet!

It is no marvel that slaveholders are always talking of their treatment of their slaves. The only marvel is, that men of sense can be gulled by such professions. Despots always insist that they are merciful. The greatest tyrants that ever dripped with blood have assumed the titles of "most gracious," "most clement," "most merciful," &c., and have ordered their crouching vassals to accost them thus. When did not vice lay claim to those virtues which are the opposites of its habitual crimes? The guilty, according to their own showing, are always innocent, and cowards brave, and drunkards sober, and harlots chaste, and pickpockets honest to a fault. Everybody understands this. When a man's tongue grows thick, and he begins to hiccough and walk cross-legged, we expect him, as a matter of course, to protest that he is not drunk; so when a man is always singing the praises of his own honesty, we instinctively watch his movements and look out for our pocket-books. Whoever is simple enough to be hoaxed by such professions, should never be trusted in the streets without somebody to take care of him. . . .

Slaveholders, the world over, have sung the praises of their tender mercies towards the slaves. Even the wretches that plied the African slave trade, tried to rebut Clarkson's proofs of their cruelties, by speeches, affidavits, and published pamphlets, setting forth the accommodations of the "middle passage," and their kind attentions to the comfort of those whom they had stolen from their homes, and kept stowed away under hatches, during a voyage of four thousand miles. So, according to the testimony of the autocrat of the Russias, he exercises great clemency towards the Poles, though he exiled them by thousands to the snows of Siberia, and tramples them down by millions, at home. Who discredits the atrocities perpetrated by Ovando in Hispaniola, Pizarro in Peru, and Cortez in Mexico, because they filled the ears of the Spanish Court with protestations of their benignant rule? While they were yoking the enslaved nations like beasts to the draught, working them to death by thousands in their mines, hunting them with bloodhounds, torturing them on racks, and broiling them on beds of coals, their representations to the mother country teemed with eulogies of their parental sway! . . .

As slaveholders and their apologists are volunteer witnesses in their own cause, and are flooding the world with testimony that their slaves are kindly treated; that they are well fed, well clothed, well housed, well lodged, moderately worked, and bountifully provided with all things needful for their comfort, we propose. . .[to] prove that the slaves in the United States are treated with barbarous inhumanity; that they are overworked, underfed, wretchedly clad and lodged, and have insufficient sleep; that they are often kept confined in the stocks day and night for weeks together, that they are often made to wear round their necks iron collars armed with prongs, to drag heavy chains and weights at their feet while working in the field, and to wear yokes, and bells, and iron horns; made to wear gags in their mouths for hours or days, have some of their front teeth torn out or broken off, that they may be easily detected when they run away; that they are frequently flogged with terrible severity, have red pepper rubbed into their lacerated flesh, and hot brine, spirits of turpentine, &c., poured over the gashes to increase the torture; that they are often stripped naked, their backs and limbs cut with knives, bruised and mangled by scores and hundreds of blows with the paddle, and terribly torn by the claws of cats, drawn over them by their tormentors; that they are often hunted with bloodhounds and shot down like beasts, or torn in pieces by dogs; that they are often suspended by the arms and whipped and beaten till they faint, and when revived by restoratives beaten again till they faint, and sometimes till they die; that their ears are often cut off, their eyes knocked out, their bones broken, their flesh branded with red hot irons; that they are maimed, mutilated and burned to death over slow fire. All these things, more and worse, we shall prove. Reader, we know whereof we affirm, we have weighed it well; more and worse WE WILL PROVE. Mark these words, and read on; we will establish all these facts by the testimony of scores and hundreds of eye witnesses, by the testimony of slaveholders in all parts of the slave states, by slaveholding members of Congress and of state legislatures, by ambassadors to foreign courts, by judges, by doctors of divinity, and clergyman of all denominations, by merchants, mechanics, lawyers, and physicians, by presidents and professors in colleges and professional seminaries, by planters, overseers and drivers. We shall show, not merely that such deeds are committed, but that they are frequent; not done in corners, but before the sun; not in one of the slave states, but in all of them; not perpetrated by brutal overseers and drivers merely, but by magistrates, by legislators, by professors of religion, by preachers of the gospel, by governors of states, by "gentle men of property and standing," and by delicate females moving in the "highest circles of society." We know, full well, the outcry that will be made by multitudes, at these declarations; the multiform cavils, the flat denials, the charges of "exaggeration" and "falsehood" so often bandied, the sneers of affected contempt at the credulity that can believe such things, and the rage and imprecations against those who give them currency. We know, too, the threadbare sophistries by which slaveholders and their apologists seek to evade such testimony. If they admit that such deeds are committed, they tell us that they are exceedingly rare, and therefore furnish no grounds for judging of the general treatment of slaves. . . .

They tell us, also that the slaveholders of the South are proverbially hospitable, kind, and generous, and it is incredible that they can perpetrate such enormities upon human beings; further, that it is absurd to suppose that they would thus injure their own property, that self interest would prompt them to treat their slaves with kindness, as none but fools and madmen wantonly destroy their own property; further, that Northern visitors at the South came back testifying to the kind treatment of the slaves, and that the slaves themselves corroborated such representations. All these pleas, and scores of others are bruited in every corner of the free States; and who that hath eyes to see, has not sickened at the blindness that saw not, at the palsy of heart that felt not, or at the cowardice and sycophancy that dared not expose such shallow fallacies. We are not to be turned from our purpose by such rapid babblings.

"TESTIMONY OF A CLERGYMAN"

The following letter was written to Mr. *Arthur Tappan*, of *New York*, in the summer of 1833. As the name of the writer cannot be published with safety to himself, it is withheld.

* * *

The following testimonials, from *Mr. Tappan*, Professor *Wright*, and *Thomas Ritter*, M.D. of New York, establish the trust-worthiness and high respectability of the writer.

"I have received the following letters from the south during the year 1833. They were written by a gentleman who had then resided some years in the slave states. Not being at liberty to give the writer's name, I cheerfully certify that he is a gentleman of established character, a graduate of Yale College, and a respected minister of the gospel.

Arthur Tappan."

"My acquaintance with the writer of the following letter commenced, I believe, in 1823, from which time we were fellow students in Yale College till 1826. I have occasionally seem him since. His character, so far as it has come within my knowledge, has been that of an upright and remarkably CANDID man. I place great confidence both in his habits of careful and unprejudiced observation and his veracity.

E. Wright, jun."

"New York, April 13, 1839.

I have been acquainted with the writer of the following letter about twelve years, and know him to be a gentleman of high respectability, integrity, and piety. We were fellow students in Yale College, and my opportunities for judging of his character, both at that time and since our graduation, have been such, that I feel myself fully warranted in making the above unequivocal declaration.

Thomas Ritter.
104 Cherry-street, New York."

"Natchez, 1833.

It has been almost four years since I came to the south-west; and although I have been told, from month to month, that I should soon wear off my northern prejudices, and probably have slaves of my own, yet my judgment in regard to oppression, or my prejudices, if they are pleased so to call them, remain with me still. I judge still from those principles which were fixed in my mind at the north; and a residence at the south has not enabled me so to pervert truth, as to make injustice appear justice.

"I have studied the state of things here, now for years, coolly and deliberately, with the eye of an uninterested looker on; and hence I may not be altogether unprepared to state to you some facts, and to draw conclusions from them.

"Permit me then to relate what I have seen; and do not imagine that these are all exceptions to the general treatment, but rather believe that thousands of cruelties are practiced in this Christian land, every year, which no eye that ever shed a tear of pity could look upon.

"Soon after my arrival I made an excursion into the country, to the distance of some twenty miles. And as I was passing by a cotton field, where about fifty negroes were at work, I was inclined to stop by the road side to view a scene which was then new to me. While I was, in my mind comparing this mode of labor with that of my own native place, I heard the driver, with a rough oath, order one that was near him, who seemed to be laboring to the extent of his power, to "lie down". In a moment he was obeyed; and he commenced whipping the offender upon his naked back, and continued, to the amount of about twenty lashes, with a heavy raw-hide whip, the crack of which might have been heard more than half a mile. Nor did the females escape; for although I stopped scarcely fifteen minutes, no less than three were whipped in the same manner, and that so severely, I was strongly inclined to interfere.

"You may be assured, sir, that I remained not unmoved: I could no longer look on such cruelty, but turned away and rode on while the echoes of the lash were reverberating in the woods around me. Such scenes have long since become familiar to me. But then the full effect was not lost; and I shall never forget, to my latest day, the mingled feelings of pity, horror, and indignation that took possession of my mind. I involuntarily exclaimed, O God of my fathers, how dost thou permit such things to defile our land! Be merciful to us! and visit us not in justice, for all our iniquities and the iniquities of our fathers!

"As I passed on I soon found that I had escaped from one horrible scene only to witness another. A planter with whom I was well acquainted, had caught a negro without a pass. And at the moment I was passing by, he was in the act of fastening his feet and hands to the trees, having previously made him take off all his clothing except his trowsers. When he had sufficiently secured this poor creature, he beat him for several minutes with a green switch more than six feet long; while he was writhing with anguish, endeavoring in vain to break the cords with which he was bound, and incessantly crying out, 'Lord, master! do pardon me this time! do master, have mercy!' These expressions have recurred to me a thousand times since, and although they came from one that is not considered among the sons of men, yet I think they are well worthy of remembrance, as they might lead a wise man to consider whether such shall receive mercy from the righteous Judge, as never showed mercy to their fellow men.

"At length I arrived at the dwelling of a planter of my acquaintance, with whom I passed the night. At about eight o'clock in the evening I heard the barking of several dogs, mingled with the most agonizing cries that I ever heard from any human being. Soon after the gentleman came in, and he began to apologize, by saying that two of his runaway slaves had just been brought home; and as he had previously tried every species of punishment upon them without effect, he knew not what else to add, except to set his blood hounds upon them. 'And,' continued he, 'one of them has been so badly bitten that he has been trying to die. I am only sorry that he did not; for then I should not have been further troubled with him. If he lives I intend to send him to Natchez or to New Orleans, to work with the ball and chain.'

"From this last remark I understood that private individuals have the right of thus subjecting their unmanageable slaves. I have since seen numbers of these 'ball and chain' men, both in Natchez and New Orleans, but I do not know whether there were any among them except the state convicts.

"As the summer was drawing towards a close, and the yellow fever beginning to prevail in town, I went to reside some months in the country. This was cotton picking season, during which the planters say, there is a greater necessity for flogging than at any other time. And I can assure you, that as I have sat in my window night after night, while the cotton was being weighed, I have heard the crack of the whip, without much intermission, for a whole hour, from no less than three plantations, some of which were a full mile distant.

"I found that the slaves were kept in the field from daylight until dark; and then, if they had not gathered what the master or overseer thought sufficient, they were subjected to the lash.

"Many by such treatment are induced to run away and take up their lodging in the woods. I do not say that all who run away are thus closely pressed, but I do know that many are; and I have known no less than a dozen desert at a time from the same plantation, in consequence of the overseer's forcing them to work to the extent of their power, and then whipping them for not having done more.

"But suppose that they run away—what is to become of them in the forest? If they cannot steal they must perish of hunger if the nights are cold, their feet will be frozen; for if they make a fire they may be discovered, and be shot at. If they attempt to leave the country, their chance of success is about nothing. They must return, be whipped—if old offenders, wear the collar, perhaps be branded, and fare worse than before.

"Do you believe it, sir, not six months since, I saw a number of my CHRISTIAN neighbors packing up provisions as I supposed for a deer hunt; but as I was about offering myself to the party, I learned that their powder and balls were destined to a very different purpose: it was, in short, the design of the party to bring on home a number of runaway slaves, or to shoot them if they should not be able to get possession of them in any other way.

"You will ask, is not this murder? Call it, sir, by what name you please, such are the facts:—many are shot every year and that too while the masters say they treat their slaves well.

"But let me turn your attention to another species of cruelty. About a year since I knew a certain slave who had deserted his master, to be caught, and for the first time fastened to stocks. In those same stocks, from which at midnight I have heard cries of distress, while the master slept, and was dreaming perhaps, of drinking wine and of discussing the price of cotton. On the next morning he was chained in an immovable posture, and branded in both cheeks with red hot stamps of iron. Such are the tender mercies of men who love wealth, and are determined to obtain it at any price.

"Suffer me to add another to the list of enormities, and I will not offend you with more.

"There was, some time since, brought to trial in this town a planter residing about fifteen miles distant, for whipping his slave to death. You will suppose, of course, that he was punished. No, sir, he was acquitted, although there could be no doubt of the fact. I heard the tale of murder from a man who was acquainted with all the circumstances. 'I was,' said he, 'passing along the road near the burying ground of the plantation, about nine o'clock at night, when I saw several lights gleaming through the woods; and as I approached, in order to see what was doing, I beheld the coroner of Natchez, with a number of men standing around the body of a young female, which by the torches seemed almost perfectly white. On the inquiry I learned that the master had so unmercifully beaten this girl that she died under the operation: and that also he had so severely punished another of his slaves that he was but just alive.' "

We here rest the case for the present, so far as respects of the presentation of facts showing the condition of the slaves, and proceed to consider the main objections which are usually employed to weaken such testimony, or wholly to set it aside. But before we enter upon the examination of specific objections, and introductory to them, we remark,—

1. That the system of slavery must be a system of horrible cruelty, follows of necessity, from the fact that two million seven hundred thousand human beings are *held by force*, and used as articles of property. Nothing but a heavy yoke, and an iron one, could possibly keep so many necks in the dust. That must be a constant and mighty pressure which holds so still such a vast army; nothing could do it but the daily experience of severities, and the ceaseless dread and certainty of the most terrible inflictions if they should dare to toss in their chains.

2. Were there nothing else to prove it a system of monstrous cruelty, the fact that *fear* is the only motive with which the slave is plied during his whole existence, would be sufficient to brand it with exercration as the grand tormentor of man. The slave's *susceptibility of pain* is the sole fulcrum on which slavery works the lever that moves him. In this it plants all its strings; here it sinks its hot irons; cuts its deep gashes; flings its burning embers, and dashes its boiling brine and liquid fire: into this it strikes its cold flesh hooks, grappling irons, and instruments of nameless torture; and by it drags him shrieking to the end of his pilgrimage. The fact that the master inflicts pain upon the slave not merely as an end to gratify passion, but constantly as a *means* of extorting labor,

is enough of itself to show that the system of slavery is unmixed cruelty.

3. That the slaves must suffer frequent and terrible inflictions, follows inevitably from the *character of those who direct their labor.* Whatever may be the character of the slaveholders themselves, all agree that the overseers are as a class most abandoned, brutal, and desperate men. This is so well known and believed that any testimony to probe it seems needless. The testimony of *Mr. Wirt,* late Attorney General of the United States, a Virginian and a slaveholder, is as follows. In his life of Patrick Henry, p. 36, speaking of the different classes of society in Virginia, he says,—

"Last and lowest, a feculum of beings called 'overseers'—the most abject, degraded, unprincipled race, always cap in hand to the dons who employ them, and furnishing materials for the exercise of their pride, insolence, and spirit of domination."

That the overseers are, as a body, sensual, brutal, and violent men is *proverbial.* The tender mercies of such men *must be cruel.*

4. The *ownership* of human beings necessarily presupposes an utter disregard of their happiness. He who assumes it monopolizes their whole *capital,* leaves them no stock on which to trade, and out of which to make happiness. Whatever is the master's gain is the slave's loss, a loss wrested from him by the master, for the express purpose of making it *his own gain;* this is the master's constant employment—forcing the slave to toil—violently wringing from him all he has and all he gets, and using it as his own;—like the vile bird that never builds its nest from materials of its own gathering, but either drives other birds from theirs and takes possession of them, or tears them in pieces to get the means of constructing their own. This daily practice of forcibly robbing others, and habitually living on the plunder, cannot but beget in the mind of the *habit* of regarding the interests and happiness of those whom it robs, as of no sort of consequence in comparison with its own; consequently whenever those interests and this happiness are in the way of its own gratification, they will be sacrifices without scruple. He who cannot see this would be unable to *feel* it, if it were seen.

OBJECTIONS CONSIDERED
OBJECTION I.—"SUCH CRUELTIES ARE INCREDIBLE"

The enormities inflicted by slaveholders upon their slaves will never be discredited except by those who overlook the simple fact, that he who holds human beings as his bona fide property, *regards* them as property, and not as *persons*; this is his permanent state of mind toward them. He does not contemplate slaves as human beings, consequently does not *treat* them as such; and with entire indifference sees them suffer privations and writhe under blows, which, if inflected upon whites would fill him with horror and indignation. He regards that as good treatment of slaves, which would seem to him insufferable abuse if practiced upon others; and would denounce that as a monstrous outrage and horrible cruelty, if perpertated upon white men and women, which he sees every day meted out to black slaves, without perhaps ever thinking it cruel. Accustomed all his life to regard them rather as domestic animals, to hear them stormed at, and to see them cuffed and caned; and being himself in the constant habit of treating them thus, such practices have become to him a mere matter of course, and make no impression on his mind. True, it is incredible that men should treat as *chattels* those whom they truly regard as human beings but that they should treat as chattels and working animals those whom they *regard* as such, is no marvel. The common treatment of dogs, when they are in the way, is to kick them out of it; we see them every day kicked off the sidewalks, and out of shops, and on Sabbaths out of churches,—yet, as they are but dogs, these do not strike us outrages; yet it we were to see men, women, and children—our neighbors and friends, kicked out of stores by merchants, or out of churches by the deacons and sexton, we should call the perpetrators inhuman wretches.

We have said that slaveholders regard their slaves not as human beings, but as mere working animals, or merchandise. The whole vocabulary of slaveholders, their usages, and their entire treatment of their slaves fully establish this. The same terms are applied to slaves that are given to cattle. They are called "stock." So when the children of slaves are spoken of prospectively, they are called their "increase"; the same term that is applied to flocks and herds. So the female slaves that are mothers, are called "breeders" till past child bearing; and often the same terms are applied to the different sexes that are applied to the males and females among cattle. Those who compel the labor of slaves and cattle have the same appellation, "drivers": the names which they call them are the same and similar to those given to their horses and oxen. The laws of slave states make them property, equally with goats and swine; they are levied upon for debt in the same way; they are included in the same advertisements of public sales with cattle, swine, and asses; when moved from one part of the country to another, they are herded in droves like cattle, and like them urged on by drivers; their labor is compelled in the same way. They are bought and sold, and separated like cattle: when exposed for sale, their good qualities are described as jockies show off the good points of their horses; their strength, activity, skill, power of endurance &c. are lauded, and those who bid upon them examine their persons, just as purchasers inspect horses and oxen; they open their mouths to see if their teeth are sound; strip their backs to see if they are badly scarred, and handle their limbs and muscles to see if they are firmly knit. Like horses, they are warranted to be "sound," or to be returned to the owner if "unsound." A father gives his sons a horse and a *slave*: by his will he distributes among them his race-horse, hounds, game-cocks, and *slaves*. We leave the reader to carry out the parallel which we have only begun. Its details would cover many pages.

* * *

Whoever disbelieves . . . statements of cruelities, on the ground of their enormity, proclaims his own ignorance of the nature and history of man. What is incredulous about the atrocities perpetrated by those who hold human beings as property, to be used for their pleasure, when history herself has done little else in recording human deeds, than to dip her blank chart in the blood shed by arbitrary power, and unfold to human gaze the great red scroll? That cruelty is the natural effect of arbitrary power has been the result of all experience, and the voice of universal testimony since the world began. Shall human nature's axioms, six thousand years old, go for nothing? Are the combined product of human experience, and the concurrent records of human character, to be set down as "old wives" fables? To disbelieve that arbitrary power naturally and habitually perpetrates cruelties, where it can do it with impunity, is not only ignorance of man, but of *things*. It is to be blind to innumerable proofs which are before every man's eyes; proofs that are stereotyped in the very words and phrases that are

on everyone's lips. Take for example the words *despot and despotic.*
Despot, signifies etymologically, merely one who *possesses* arbitrary
power, and at first, it was used to designate those alone who
possessed unlimited power over human beings, entirely irrespective
of the way in which they exercised it, whether mercifully or
cruelly. But the fact, that those who possessed such power, made
their subjects their *victims,* has wrought a total change in the
popular meaning of the word. It now signifies, in common
parlance, not one who possesses unlimited power over others, but
one who exercises the power that he has, whether little or much,
cruelly. So *despotic,* instead of meaning what it once did, something
pertaining to the possession of unlimited power, signifies something
pertaining to the *capricious, unmerciful and relentless exercise* of such
power.

* * *

Arbitrary power is to the mind what alcohol is to the body; it
intoxicates. Man loves power. It is perhaps the strongest human
passion; and the more absolute the power, the stronger the desire
for it; and the more it is desired, the more its exercise is enjoyed:
this enjoyment is to human nature a fearful temptation—generally
an overmatch for it. Hence it is true, with hardly an exception,
that arbitrary power is abused in proportion as it is desired. The
fact that a person intensely desires power over others, without
restraint, shows the absolute necessity of restraint. What woman
would marry a man who made it a condition that he should have
the power to divorce her whenever he pleased? Oh! he might never
wish to exercise it, but the power he would have! No woman, not
stark mad, would trust her happiness in such hands.

Would a father apprentice his son to a master who insisted that
his power over the lad should be *absolute?* The master might
perhaps, never wish to commit a battery upon the boy, but if he
should, he insists upon having full swing! He who would leave his
son in the clutches of such a wretch, would be bled and blistered
for a lunatic as sons of his friends could get their hands upon him.

The possession of power, even when greatly restrained, is such a
fiery stimulant, that its lodgement in human hands is always
perilous. Give men the handling of immense sums of money—and
all the eyes of Argus and the hands of Briareus can hardly prevent
embezzlement.

The mutual and ceaseless accusations of the two great political parties in this country, show the universal belief that this tendency of human nature to abuse power, is so strong, that even the most powerful legal restraints are insufficient for its safe custody. From congress and state legislatures down to grog-shop caucuses and streetwranglings, each party keeps up an incessant din about *abuses of power.* Hardly an officer, either of the general or state governments, from the President down to the ten thousand postmasters, and from governors to the fifty thousand constables, escapes the charge of "*abuse of power.*" "Oppression," "Extortion," "Venality," "Bribery," "Corruption," "Perjury," "Misrule," "Spoils," "Defalcation," stand on every newspaper. Now without any estimate of the lies told in these mutual charges, there is truth enough to make each party ready to believe of the other, and *of their best men* too, nay abuse of power, however monstrous. As is the State, so is the Church. From General Conferences to circuit preachers; and from General Assemblies to church sessions, abuses of power spring up as weeds from the dunghill.

All legal restraints are framed upon the presumption, that men will abuse their power if not hemmed in by them. This lies at the bottom of all those checks and balances contrived for keeping governments upon their centres. If there is among human convictions one that is invariable and universal, it is, that when men possess unrestrained power over others, over their time, choice, conscience, persons, votes, or means of subsistence, they are under great temptations to abuse it; and that the intensity with which such power is desired, generally measures the certainty and the degree of its abuse.

That American slaveholders possess a power over their slaves which is virtually absolute, none will deny.* That they desire this absolute power, is shown from the fact of their holding and exercising it, and making laws to confirm and enlarge it. That the *desire* to possess this power, every title of it is *intense,* is proved by

---

*The following extracts from the laws of slave-states are proofs sufficient.

"The slave is *entirely* subject to the *will* of his master."—

Louisiana Civil Code, Art. 272.

"Slaves shall be deemed, sold, taken, reputed, and adjudged in law to be *chattels personal,* in the hands of their owners and possessors, and their executors, administrators and assigns, *to all intents, constructions, and purposes, whatsoever.*"—Laws of South Carolina, 2 Brev. Dig. 229; Prince's Digest, 446, &c

the fact, that slaveholders cling to it with such obstinate tenacity, as well as by all their doings and sayings, their threats, cursings and gnashings against all who denounce the exercise of such power as usurpation and outrage, and counsel its immediate abrogation.

From the nature of the case—from the laws of mind, such power, so intensely desired, gripped with such a death-clutch, and with such fierce spurnings of all curtailment of restraint, *cannot but be abused.* Privations and inflictions must be its natural, habitual products, with ever and anon, terror, torture, and despair let loose to do their worst upon the helpless victims.

Though power over others is in every case liable to be used to their injury, yet, in almost all cases, the subject individual is shielded from great outrages by strong safeguards. If he had talents, or learning, or wealth, or office, or personal respectability, or influential friends, these with the protection of law and the rights of citizenship, stand round him as a body guard: and even if he lacked all these, yet had he the same color, features, form, dialect, habits, and associations with the privileged caste of society, he would find in *them* a shield from many injuries, which would be *invited,* if in these respects he differed widely from the rest of the community, and was on that account regarded with disgust and aversion. This is the condition of the slave; not only is he deprived of the artificial safeguards of the law, but has none of those *natural* safeguards enumerated above, which are a protection to others. But not only is the slave destitute of those peculiarities, habits, tastes, and acquisitions, which by assimilating the possessor to the rest of the community, excite their interest in him, and thus, in a measure, secure for him their protection; but he possesses those peculiarities of bodily organization which are looked upon with deep disgust, contempt, prejudice, and aversion. Besides this, constant contact with the ignorance and stupidity of the slaves, their filth, rags, and nakedness; their cowering air, servile employments, repulsive food, and squalid hovels, their purchase, and sale, use as brutes—all these associations, constantly mingling and circulating in the minds of slaveholders, and inveterated by the hourly irritations which must assail all who use human beings as things, produce in them a permanent state of feeling toward the slave, made up of repulsion and settled ill-will. When we add to this the corrosions produced by the petty thefts of slaves, the necessity of constant watching, their reluctant service, and indifference to their master's interests, their ill-concealed aversion to him, and spurning of his authority; and finally, that fact, as old as human nature, that men always hate those whom they oppress, and oppress those whom they hate, thus oppression and hatred mutually begetting and perpetuating each other—and we have a raging compound of fiery elements and disturbing forces, so stimulating and inflaming the mind of the slaveholder against the slave, that it CANNOT BUT BREAK FORTH UPON HIM WITH DESOLATING FURY.

To deny that cruelty is the spontaneous and uniform product of arbitrary power, and that the natural and controlling tendency of such power is to make its possessor cruel, oppressive, and revengeful towards those who are subjected to his control, is, we repeat, to set at nought the combined experience of the human race, to invalidate its testimony, and to reverse its decisions from time immemorial.

* * *

OBJECTION V.—"IT IS FOR THE INTEREST OF THE MASTERS TO TREAT THEIR SLAVES WELL."

So it is for the interest of the drunkard to quit his cups; for the glutton to curb his appetite; for the debauchee to bridle his lust; for the sluggard to be up betimes; for all sinners to stop sinning. Even if it were for the interest of masters to treat their slaves well, he must be a novice who thinks that a proof that the slaves are well treated. The whole history of man is a record of real interest sacrificed to present gratification. If all men's actions were consistent with their best interest, folly and sin would be words without meaning.

If the objector means that it is for the *pecuniary* interests of masters to treat their slaves well, and thence infers their good treatment, we reply, that though the love of money is strong, yet appetite and lust, pride, anger and revenge, the love of power and honor, are each an overmatch for it; and when either of them is roused by a sudden stimulant, the love of money is worsted in the grapple with it. Look at the hourly lavish outlays of money to procure a momentary gratification for those passions and appetites. As the desire for money is, in the main, merely a desire for the means of gratifying other desires, or rather for one of the means, it must be the *servant* not the sovereign of those desires, to whose gratification its only use is to minister. But even if the love of money were the strongest human passion, who is simple enough to believe that it is all the time so powerfully excited, that no other passion or appetite can get the mastery over it? Who does not know that gusts of rage, revenge, jealousy and lust drive it before them as a tempest tosses a feather?

The objector has forgotten his first lessons; they taught him that it is human nature to gratify the *uppermost* passion: and is *prudence* the uppermost passion with slaveholders, and self-restraint their great characteristic? The strongest feeling of any moment is the sovereign of that moment and rules. Is a propensity to practice *economy* the predominant feeling with slaveholders? Ridiculous! Every northerner knows that slaveholders are proverbial for lavish expenditures, never higgling about the *price* of a gratification. Human passions have not, like the tides, regular ebbs and flows, with their stationary, high and low water marks. They are a dominion convulsed with revolutions; coronations and dethronements in ceaseless succession—each ruler a usurper and despot. Love of money gets a snatch at the sceptre as well as the rest, not by hereditary right, but because, in the fluctuations of human feelings a chance wave washes him up to the throne and the next perhaps washes him off, without time to nominate his successor. Since, then, as a matter of fact, a host of appetites and passions do hourly get the better of love of money, what protection does the slave find in his master's *interest*, against the sweep of his passions and appetites? Besides, a master can inflict upon his slave horrible cruelties without perceptibly injuring his health, or taking time from his labor, or lessening his value as property. Blows with a small stick give more acute pain, than with a large one. A club bruises, and benumbs the nerves, while a *switch*, neither breaking nor bruising the flesh instead of blunting the sense of feeling, wakes up and stings to torture all the susceptibilities of pain. By this kind of infliction, more actual cruelty can be perpetrated in the giving of pain at the instant, than by the most horrible bruisings and lacerations; and that, too, with little comparative hazard to the slave's health, or to his value as property, and without loss of time from labor. Even giving to the objection all the force claimed for it, what protection is it to the slave? It *professes* to shield the slave from such treatment alone, as would either lay him aside from labor, or injure his health, and thus lessen his value as a working animal, making him a damaged article in the market. Now, is nothing *bad treatment* of a human being except that which produces these effects? Does the fact that a man's constitution is not actually shattered, and his life shortened by his treatment, prove that he is treated well? Is no treatment cruel except what sprains muscles, or cuts sinews, or bursts blood vessels, or breaks bones, and thus lessens a man's value as a working animal?

A slave may get blows and kicks every hour in the day, without having his constitution broken, or without suffering sensibly in his health, or flesh, or appetite, or power to labor. Therefore, beaten and kicked as he is, he must be treated *well*, according to the objector, since the master's *interest* does not suffer thereby.

Finally, the objector virtually maintains that all possible privations and inflictions suffered by slaves, that do not actually cripple their power to labor, and make them "damaged merchandize," are to be set down as "good treatment," and that nothing is *bad* treatment except what produces these effects.

Thus we see that even if the slave were effectually shielded from all those inflictions, which by lessening his value as property, would injure the interests of his master, he would still have no protection against numberless and terrible cruelties. But we go further, and maintain that in respect to large classes of slaves, it is for the interest of their masters to treat them with barbarous inhumanity.

* * *

OBJECTION VIII.—"PUBLIC OPINION IS A PROTECTION
TO THE SLAVE"

ANSWER. It was public opinion that *made him a slave.* In a republican government the people make the laws, and those laws are merely public opinion in *legal forms.* We repeat it,—public opinion made them slaves, and keeps them slaves; in other words, it sunk them from men to chattels, and now, forsooth, this same public opinion will see to it, that these *chattels* are treated like *men!*

By looking a little into this matter, and finding out how this "public opinion" (law) protects the slaves in some particulars, we can judge of the amount of its protection in others.

1. It protects the slaves from *robbery*, by declaring that those who robbed their mothers may rob them and their children. "All negroes, mulattoes, or mestizoes who now are, or shall hereafter be in this province, and all their offspring, are hereby declared to be, and shall remain, forever, hereafter, absolute slaves, and shall follow the condition of the mother,"—Law of South Carolina, 2 Brevard's Digest, 229. Others of the slave states have similar laws.

2. It protects their *persons*, by giving their master a right to flog, wound, and beat them when he pleases. See Deveraux's North Carolina Reports, 263—Case of the State vs. Mann, 1829; in which the Supreme Court decided, that a master who SHOT at a female slave and wounded her, because she got loose from him when he was flogging her, and started to run from him, had violated *no law, and could not be indicted.* It has been decided by the highest courts of the slave states generally, that assault and battery upon a slave is not indictable as a criminal offence.

The following decision on this point was made by the Supreme Court of South Carolina in the case of the State vs. Cheetwood, 2 Hill's Reports, 459.

"Protection of slaves.—The criminal offence of the assault and battery cannot, at common law, be committed on the person of a slave. For, notwithstanding for some purposes a slave is regarded in law as a person, yet generally he is a mere chattel personal, and his right of personal protection belongs to his master, who can maintain an action of trespass for the battery of his slave.

"There can be therefore no offence against the state for a mere beating of a slave, unaccompanied by any circumstances of cruelty, or an attempt to kill and murder. The peace of the state is not thereby broken; for a slave is not generally regarded as legally capable of being within the peace of the state. He is not a citizen, and is not in that character entitled to her protection."

This "public opinion" protects the *persons* of the slaves by depriving them of Jury trial*; their *consciences*, by forbidding them to assemble for worship, unless their oppressors are present; their *characters*, by branding them as liars, in denying them their oath in law; their *modesty*, by leaving their master to clothe, or let them go naked, as he pleases; and their *health*, by leaving him to feed or starve them, to work them, wet or dry, with or without sleep, to lodge them, with or without covering, as the whim takes him; and their liberty, marriage relations, parental authority, and filial obligations, by *annihilating* the whole. This is the protection which "*public opinion*" in the form of *law*, affords to the slaves; this is the chivalrous knight, always in stirrups, with lance in rest, to champion the cause of the slaves.

Public opinion, protection to the slave! Brazen effrontery, hypocrisy, and falsehood! We have in the laws cited and referred to above, the formal testimony of the Legislatures of the slave states that, "public opinion" does pertinaciously *refuse* to protect the slaves; not only so, but that it does itself persecute and plunder them all: that it originally planned, and now presides over, sanctions, executes and perpetuates the whole system or robbery, torture and outrage under which they groan.

In all the slave states, this "public opinion" has taken away from the slave his *liberty*; it has robbed him of his right to his own body, of his right to improve his mind, of his right to read the Bible, of his right to worship God according to his conscience, of his right to receive and enjoy what he earns, of his right to live with his wife and children, of his right to better his condition, of his right to eat when he is hungry, to rest when he is tired, to sleep when he needs it, and to cover his nakedness with clothing: this "public opinion" makes the slave a prisoner for life on the plantation, except when his jailor pleases to let him out with a

---

*Law of South Carolina. James' Digest, 392-3. Law of Louisiana. Martin's Digest, 642. Law of Virginia. Rev. Code, 429.

Miss. Rev. Code, 390. Similar laws exist in the slave states generally.

"A slave cannot be a witness against a white person, either in a civil or criminal cause." Stroud's Sketch of the Laws of Slavery, 65.

Stroud's Sketch of the Slave Laws. 132.

Stroud's Sketch, 26-32.

Stroud's Sketch, 22-24.

"pass," or sells him, and transfers him in irons to another jail-yard: this "public opinion" traverses the country, buying up men, women, children—chaining them in coffles and driving them forever from their nearest friends; it sets them on the auction table, to be handled, scrutinized, knocked off to the highest bidder; it proclaims that they shall not have their liberty; and, if their masters give it them, "public opinion" seizes and throws them back into slavery. This same "public opinion" has formally attached the following legal penalties to the following acts of slaves.

If more than seven slaves are found together in any road, without a white person, *twenty lashes a piece*; for visiting a plantation without a written pass, *ten lashes*; for letting loose a boat from where it is made fast, *thirty-nine lashes for the first offence*; and for the second, "*shall have cut off from his head one ear*"; for keeping or carrying a club, *thirty-nine lashes*; for having any article for sale, without a ticket from his master, *ten lashes*; for traveling in any other than "the most usual and accustomed road," when going alone to any place, *forty lashes*; for traveling in the night, without a pass, *forty lashes*; for being found in another person's negro-quarters, *forty lashes*; for hunting with dogs in the woods, *thirty lashes*; for being on horseback without the written permission of his master, *twenty-five lashes*; for riding or going abroad in the night, or riding horses in the day time, without leave, a slave may be whipped, cropped, or branded *in the cheek* with the letter R, or otherwise punished, *nor extending to life*, or so as to render him *unfit for labor.* The laws referred to may be found by consulting 2 Brevard's Digest, 228, 243, 246; Haywood's Manual, 78, chap. 13, pp. 518, 529; I Virginia Revised Code, 722-3; Prince's Digest, 454; 2 Missouri Laws, 741; Mississippi Revised Code, 371. Laws similar to these exist throughout the southern slave code. Extracts enough to fill a volume might be made from these laws, showing that the protection which "public opinion" grants to the slaves, is hunger, nakedness, terror, bereavements, robbery, imprisonment, the stocks, iron collars, hunting and worrying them with dogs and guns, mutilating their bodies, and murdering them.

Having already drawn so largely on the reader's patience, in illustrating southern "public opinion" by the slave laws, instead of additional illustrations of the same point from another class of those laws, as was our design, we will group together a few particulars, which the reader can take in at a glance, showing that the "public opinion" of slaveholders towards their slaves, which exists at the south, in the form of law, tramples on all those fundamental principles of right, justice, and equity, which are recognized as sacred by all civilized nations, and receive the homage even of barbarians.

1. One of these principles is, that the *benefits* of law to the subject should overbalance its burdens—its protection more than compensate for its restraints and exactions—and its blessings altogether outweigh its inconveniences and evils—the former being numerous, positive, and permanent, the latter few, negative, and incidental. Totally the reverse of all this is true in the case of the slave. Law is to him all exaction and no protection: instead of lightening his *natural* burdens, it crushes him under a multitude of artificial ones; instead of a friend to succor him, it is his deadliest foe, transfixing him at every step from the cradle to the grave. Law has been beautifully defined to be "benevolence acting by rule"; to the American slave it is malevolence torturing by system. It is an old truth that *responsibility* increases with *capacity*; but those same laws which make the slave a "chattel," require of him *more* than of *men*. The same law which makes him a thing incapable of obligation, loads him with obligations superhuman—while sinking him below the level of a brute in dispensing its *benefits*, it lays upon him burdens which would break down an angel.

2. *Innocence is entitled to the protection of law.* Slaveholders make innocence free plunder; this is their daily employment; their laws assail it, make it their victim, inflict upon it all, and, in some respects, more than all the penalties of the greatest guilt. To other innocent persons, law is a blessing, to the slave it is a curse, only a curse and that continually.

3. *Deprivation of liberty is one of the highest punishments of crime;* and in proportion to its justice when inflicted on the innocent; this terrible penalty is inflicted on two million seven hundred thousand, innocent persons in the Southern states.

4. *Self-preservation and self-defence,* are universally regarded as the most sacred of human rights, yet the laws of slave states punish the slave with *death* for exercising these rights in that way, which in others is pronounced worthy of the highest praise.

5. *The safe-guards of law are most needed where natural safeguards are weakest.* Every principle of justice and equity requires, that, those

who are totally unprotected by birth, station, wealth, friends, influence, and popular favor, and especially those who are the innocent objects of public contempt and prejudice, should be more vigilantly protected by law, than those who are so fortified by defence, that they have far less need for *legal* protection; yet the poor slave who is fortified by *none* of these *personal* bulwarks, is denied the protection of law, while the master surrounded by them all, is panoplied in the mail of legal protection, even to the hair of his head; yea, his very shoe-tie and coat-button are legal protegees.

6. The grand object of law is to *protect men's natural rights, but instead of protecting the natural rights* of the slaves, it gives slaveholders license to wrest them from the weak by violence, protects them in holding their plunder, and KILL the rightful owner if he attempt to recover it.

* * *

Having drawn out this topic to so great a length, we waive all comments and only say to the reader, in conclusion, *ponder these things,* and lay it to heart, that slaveholding "is justified of her children." Verily, they have their reward! "With what measure ye mete withal it shall be measured to you again." Those who combine to trample on others, will trample on *each other.* The habit of trampling upon one, begets a state of mind that will trample upon *all* . Accustomed to wreak their vengeance on their slaves, indulgence of passion becomes with slaveholders a second law of nature, and when excited even by their equals, their hot blood brooks neither restraint nor delay; *gratification* is the first thought— prudence generally comes too late, and the slaves see their masters fall a prey to each other, the victims of those very passions which have been engendered and infuriated by the practice of arbitrary rule over *them.* Surely it need not be added, that those who thus tread down their equals, must trample as in a wine-press their defenceless vassals. If, when in passion, they seize those who are *on their own level,* and dash them under their feet, with what a crushing vengeance will they leap upon those who are always under their feet?

IV. CONFRONTING SOCIETY

6   FROM   *Stephen S. Foster*
The Brotherhood of Thieves, or, a True Picture of the
American Church and Clergy

*In a very real sense, abolitionists confronted society in everything they said.
That is, they tried to shock the American people into seeing the moral
implications of actions and customs by reducing them to their simplest forms:
slavetrading was theft, the dehumanizing qualities of slavery were murder, the
violation of the slave family was prostitution. Annoying as this simplification
was, it was not so annoying as the abolitionists' tendency to judge American
institutions by one standard: whether or not they opposed slavery. Since most
American institutions had adjusted to slavery, they were found to be imperfect,
unworthy of loyalty and, therefore, subject to the most searching kinds of
criticism. Thus, the political parties and the churches found themselves
accused of justifying theft, murder, and prostitution.*

*One of the most stinging denunciations came from the acerbic pen of
Stephen Symonds Foster (1809-1881) who in 1843 published The
Brotherhood of Thieves: or, a True Picture of the American Church and
Clergy. Through 20 editions this pamphlet ripped away at the "hypocrit-
ical" respectability of churches that pretended to support morality and pure
religion while in truth, according to Foster, they perpetuated immorality and*

SOURCE. Stephen S. Foster, "The Brotherhood of Thieves, or, a True Picture of
the American Church and Clergy," 1843.

sin. Foster became involved in the abolition movement while still a student at Dartmouth College; later he left Union Theological Seminary of New York to become an agent for the American Anti-Slavery Society. Throughout a life of reform activity he supported penal reform, temperance, and women's rights, often with the same kind of devotion that led him to disrupt church services on behalf of the slave, to refuse to pay taxes to a government that denied women the right to vote, or go to jail to protest the requirement of militia duty. The bluntness of his actions was matched by his words, as is shown in the following selection. Here Foster employs a method that was quite popular among abolitionist speakers and writers. He engages the attention of his audience by accusations that may, at first, appear to be outrageous, perhaps, even irrational, and certainly dramatic. The next step is to explain how these simplified accusations can really be true, outrageous as they may have appeared at first. Although this method invited the kind of riotous counter-measures mentioned in the first part of Foster's introduction, it also invited prospective abolitionists to view the meaning of institutional action in terms of the voluntaristic, personal morality of evangelical Protestantism. The concepts employed are not especially sophisticated, but they are not meant to be reasoned analysis so much as declarations of the moral meaning of African slavery. To evaluate their impact, the reader must try to imagine himself as a Northern Protestant evangelical of the nineteenth century whose moral world was relatively simple and who understood the meaning of theft, murder, or piracy far better than involved theories about the impact of slavery on personality. To be sure, the language is harsh and provocative; it was meant to be. The meaning of compromise with slavery, abolitionists argued, is harsh too. This is not to say that all abolitionists suggested Foster's methods or applauded his language—they did not; but Foster's pamphlet is nevertheless an excellent example of one type of abolitionist progaganda.

LETTER

ESTEEMED FRIEND

In the early part of last autumn, I received a letter from you requesting me to prepare an article for the press in vindication of the strong language of denunciation of the American church and clergy, which I employed at the late Anti-Slavery Convention on your island [Nantucket], and which was the occasion of the disgraceful mob, which disturbed and broke up that meeting. In my answer, I gave you assurance of prompt compliance with your request; but, for reasons satisfactory to myself, I have failed to fulfill my promise up to the present time. The novelty of the occasion has now passed away; the deep and malignant passions which were stirred in the bosoms of no inconsiderable portion of your people, have, doubtless, subsided; but the important facts connected with it are yet fresh in the memories of all; and, as the occasion was one of general, not local, interest, and the spirit which was there exhibited was a fair specimen of the general temper and feeling of our country towards the advocates of equal rights and impartial justice, I trust it will not be deemed amiss in me to make it a subject of public notice, even at this late period.

* * *

The remarks which I made at your Convention were of a most grave and startling character. They strike at the very foundation of all our popular ecclesiastical institutions, and exhibit them to the world as the apologists and supporters of the most atrocious system of oppression and wrong, beneath which humanity was ever groaned. They reflect on the church the deepest possible odium, by disclosing to public view the chains and handcuffs, the whips and branding-irons, the rifles and bloodhounds, with which her ministers and deacons bind the limbs and lacerate the flesh of innocent and defenceless women. They cast upon the clergy the same dark shade which Jesus threw over the ministers of his day, when he tore away the veil beneath which they had successfully concealed their diabolical schemes of personal aggrandizement and power, and denounced them before all the people as a "den of thieves," as "fools and blind," "white sepulchres," "blind guides, which strain at a gnat, and swallow a camel," "hypocrites, who devour widows houses, and for a pretence make long prayers," "liars," "adulterers," "serpents," "a generation of vipers," who could not "escape the damnation of hell." But, appalling and ominous as they were, I am not aware that I gave the parties accused, or their mobocratic friends, any just cause of complaint. They were all spoken in public, in a free meeting, where all who dissented from me were not only invited, but warmly urged to reply. . . .

In exposing the deep and fathomless abominations of those *pious* thieves, who gain their livelihood by preaching sermons and stealing babies, I am not at liberty to yield to any intimidations, however imposing the source from whence they come. The right of speech—the liberty to utter our own convictions *freely*, at all times and in all places, at discretion, unawed by fear, unembarrassed by force—is the gift of God to every member of the family of man, and should be preserved inviolate; and for one, I can consent to surrender it to no power on earth, but with the loss of life itself. Let not the petty tyrants of our land, in church or state, think to escape the censures which their crimes deserve, by hedging themselves about with the frightful penalties of human law, or the more frightful violence of a drunken and murderous mob. . . .

The fact that my charges against the religious sects of our country were met with violence and outrage, instead of sound arguments and invalidating testimony, is strong presumptive evidence of their truth. The innocent never find occasion to resort to this disgraceful mode of defence. If our clergy and church were the ministers and church of Christ, would their reputation be defended by drunken and murderous mobs? Are brickbats and rotten eggs the weapons of truth and Christianity?. . . But I rest not on presumptive evidence, however strong and conclusive, to sustain my allegations against the American church and clergy. The proof of their identity with slavery, and of their consequent deep and unparalleled criminality, is positive and overwhelming, and is fully adequate to sustain the gravest charges, and to justify the most denunciatory language that has ever fallen from the lips of their most inveterate opponents.

I said at your meeting, among other things, that the American church and clergy, as a body, were thieves, adulterers, man-stealers, pirates, and murderers; that the Methodist Episcopal church was more corrupt and profliigate than any house of ill-fame in the city of New York; that the Southern ministers of that body were desirous of perpetuating slavery for the purpose of supplying themselves with concubines from among its hapless victims; and that many of our clergymen were guilty of enormities that would disgrace an Algerine pirate!! These sentiments called forth a burst of holy indignation from the *pious* and *dutiful* advocates of the church and clergy, which overwhelmed the meeting with repeated showers of stones and rotten eggs, and eventually compelled me to leave your island, to prevent the shedding of human blood. But whence this violence and personal abuse, not only of the author of these obnoxious sentiments, but also of your own inoffending wives and daughters, whose faces and dresses, you will recollect, were covered with the most loathsome filth? It is reported of the ancient Pharisees and their adherents, that they stoned Stephen to death for preaching doctrines at war with the popular religion of their times, and charging them with murder of the Son of God; but their successors of the modern church, it would seem, have discovered some new principle in theology, by which it is made their duty not only to stone the heretic himself, but all those also who have at any time been found listening to his discourse without a permit from their priest. . . .

You will agree with me, I think, that slaveholding involves the commission of all the crimes specified in my first charge, viz., theft, adultery, man-stealing, piracy, and murder. But should you have any doubts on this subject, they will be easily removed by analyzing this atrocious outrage on the laws of God, and the rights and happiness of man, and examining separately the elements of which it is composed. Wesley, the celebrated founder of the Methodists, once denounced it as the "sum of *all* villanies." Whether it is the sum of *all* villanies, or not, I will not here express an opinion; but that it is the sum of at least *five*, and those by no means the least atrocious in the catalogue of human aberrations, will require but a small tax on your patience to prove.

1. Theft. To steal, is to take that which belongs to another, without his consent. Theft and robberty are, *morally*, the same act, different only in form. Both are included under the command, "Thou shalt not steal;" that is, thou shalt not take thy neighbor's property. Whoever, therefore, either secretly or by force possesses himself of the property of another, is a thief. Now, no proposition is plainer than that every man owns his own industry. He who tills the soil has a right to its products, and cannot be deprived of them by an act of felony. This principle furnishes the only solid basis for the right of private or individual property; and he who denies it, either in theory or practice, denies that right, also. But every slaveholder takes the entire industry of his slaves, from infancy to gray hairs; they dig the soil, but he receives its products. No matter how kind or humane the master may be, he lives by plunder. He is emphatically a freebooter; and, as such, he is as

much more despicable a character than the common horse-thief, as his depredations are more extensive.

2. Adultery. This crime is disregard for the requisitions of marriage. The conjugal relation has its foundation deeply laid in man's nature, and its strict observance is essential to his happiness. Hence, Jesus Christ has thrown around it the sacred sanction of his written law, and expressly declared that the man who violates it, even by a lustful eye, is an adulterer. But does the slaveholder respect this sacred relation? Is he cautious never to tread upon forbidden ground? No! His very position makes him the minister of unbridled lust. By converting woman into a commodity to be bought and sold, and used by claimant as his avarice or lust may dictate, he totally annihilates the marriage institution, and transforms the wife into what he very significantly terms a "BREEDER," and her children into "STOCK."

This change in woman's condition, from a free moral agent to a chattel, places her domestic relations entirely beyond her own control, and makes her a mere instrument for the gratification of another's desires. The master claims her body as his property, and, of course, employs it for such purposes as best suit his inclinations,—demanding free access to her bed; nor can she resist his demands but at the peril of her life. Thus is her chasity left entirely unprotected, and she is made the lawful prey of every pale-faced libertine who may choose to prostitute her! To place woman in this situation, or to retain her in it when placed there by another, is the highest insult any one could possibly offer to the dignity and purity of her nature; and the wretch who is guilty of it deserves an epithet compared with which adultery is spotless innocence. *Rape* is his crime! death his desert,—if death be ever due to criminals! Am I too severe? Let the offence be done to a sister or daughter of yours; nay, let the Rev. Dr. Witherspoon, or some other *ordained* miscreant from the South lay his vile hands on your own bosom companion, and do to her what he has done to the companion of another, and what Prof. Stuart and Dr. Fisk say he may do, "without violating the Christian faith,"—and I fear not your reply. None but a moral monster ever consented to the enslavement of his own daughter, and none but fiends incarnate ever enslave the daughter of another. Indeed, I think the demons in hell would be ashamed to do to their fellow-demons what many of our clergy do to their own church memebers.

3. Man-Stealing. What is it to steal a man? Is it not to claim him as your property?—to call him yours? God has given to every man an inalienable right to himself,—a right of which no conceivable circumstance of birth, or forms of law, can divest him; and he who interferes with the free and unrestricted exercise of that right, who, not content with the proprietorship of his own body, claims the body of his neighbor, is a man-stealer. This truth is self-evident. Every man, idiots and the insane only excepted, knows that he has no possible right to another's body; and he who persists, for a moment, in claiming it, incurs the guilt of man-stealing. The plea of the slave-claimant, that he has bought, or inherited his slaves, is of no avail. What right had he, I ask, to purchase, or to inherit, his neighbors? The purchase, or inheritance of them as a legacy, was itself a crime of no less enormity than the original act of kidnapping. But every slaveholder, whatever his profession or standing in society may be, lays his felonious hands on the body and soul of his equal brother, robs him of himself, converts him into an article of merchandise, and leaves him a mere chattel personal in the hands of his claimants. Hence he is a kidnapper, or manthief.

4. Piracy. The American people, by an act of solemn legislation, have declared the enslaving of human beings on the coast of Africa to be piracy, and have affixed to this crime the penalty of death. And can the same act be piracy in Africa, and not be piracy in America? Does crime change its character by changing longitude? Is killing, with malice aforethought, no murder, where there is no human enactment against it? Or can it be less piratical and Heavendaring to enslave our own native countrymen, than to enslave the heathen sons of a foreign enslaver? Slaveholding loses none of its enormity by a voyage across the Atlantic, nor by baptism into the Christian name. It is piracy in Africa; it is piracy in America; it is piracy the wide world over; and the American slaveholder, though he possess all the sanctity of the ancient Pharisees, and make prayers as numerous and long, is a *pirate* still; a base, profligate adulterer, and wicked contemner of the holy institution of marriage; identical in moral character with the African slave-trader, and guilty of a crime which, if committed on a foreign coast, he must expiate on the gallows.

5. Murder. Murder is an act of the mind, and not of the hand.

"Whosoever hateth his brother is a murderer." A man may kill,—
that is his hand may inflict a mortal blow,—without committing
murder. On the other hand, he may commit murder without
actually taking life. The intention constitutes the crime. He who,
with a pistol at my breast, demands my pocket-book or my life, is
a murderer, whichever I may choose to part with. And is not he a
murderer, who, with the same deadly weapon, demands the
surrender of what to me is of infinitely more value than my pocket-
book, nay, than life itself—my liberty—my self—my wife and
children—all that I possess on earth, or can hope for in heaven?
But this is the crime of which every slaveholder is guilty. He
maintains his ascendency over his victims, extorting their unrequited labor, and sundering the dearest ties of kindred, only by
the threat of extermination. With the slave, as every intelligent
person knows, there is no alternative. It is submission or death, or,
more frequently, protracted torture more horrible than death.
Indeed, the South never sleeps, but on dirks, and pistols, and
bowie knives, with a troop of bloodhounds standing sentry at
every door! What, I ask, means this splendid enginery of death,
which gilds the palace of the tyrant master? It tells the story of his
guilt. The burnished steel which waits beneath his slumbering
pillow, to drink the life-blood of outraged innocence, brands him
as a murderer. It proves, beyond dispute, that the submission of
his victims is the only reason he has not already shed their blood.

By this brief analysis of slavery, we stamp upon the forehead of
the slaveholder, with a brand deeper than that which marks the
victim of his wrongs, the infamy of theft, adultery, manstealing,
piracy and murder. We demonstrate, beyond the possibility of
doubt, that he who enslaves another—that is, robs him of his right
to himself, to his own hands, and head, and feet, and transforms
him from a free moral agent into a mere *brute*, to obey, not the
commands of God, but his claimant—is guilty of every one of these
atrocious crimes. And in doing this, we have only demonstrated
what, to every reflecting mind, is self-evident. Every man, if he
would but make the case of the slave his own, would feel in his
inmost soul the truth and justice of this charge. But these are the
crimes which I have alleged against the American church and
clergy. Hence, to sustain my charge against them, it only remains
for me to show that they are slaveholders. That they are slaveholders—party to a conspiracy against the liberty of more than two

millions of our countrymen, and as such, are guilty of the crimes of which they stand accused—I affirm, and will now proceed to prove.

It is a common but mistaken opinion, that, to constitute one a slaveholder, he must be the claimant of slaves. That title belongs alike to the slave-claimant, and all those who, by their countenance or otherwise, lend their influence to support the slave system. If I aid or countenance another in stealing, I am a thief, though he receiive all the booty. . . .Hence all who, through their political or ecclesiastical connections, aid or countenance the master in his work of death, are slaveholders, and, as such, are stained with all the moral turpitude which attaches to the man who, by their sanction, wields the bloody lash over the heads of his trembling victims, and buries it deep in their quivering flesh. Nay, the human *hounds* which guard the plantation, ever eager to bark on the track of the flying fugitive, are objects of deeper indignation and abhorrence than even its lordly proprietor.

* * *

It is to this union and pledge of protection from the North, that the slave system owes its perpetuity to the present time. Such, at least, is the opinion of the slave-claimants themselves. Hence they shriek out in dismay at the first proposition of the abolitionists to dissolve the Union, and leave them alone in the enjoyment of their peculiar institutions. Such, too, is the opinion of every man of sense who knows anything of the past history or present condition of our slave population. The North, as he very well knows, are emphatically the slave-*holders*. They are the soldiers who *level the musket*, as the South gives the word of command. . . .

* * *

The consciousness that, in a controversy with their masters, [the slaves] must meet the combined forces, military and naval, of the whole country alone deters them from [rebellion]. It is not the lilyfingered aristocracy of the South that they fear, as the South herself tells us, but the "white slaves" of the North, who have basely sold themselves for scullions to the slave power, and who are always ready to do the bidding of their haughty proprietors, whatever service they may require at their hands. The slaves know too well, that, should they unfurl the banner of freedom, and demand the recognition of their liberty and rights at the point of the bayonet, the *Northern* pulpit, aghast with holy horror at the incendiary measure, would raise the maddening cry of *insurrection*— the *Northern* church, animated by a kindred spirit, and echoing the infamous libel, would pour forth her sons in countless hordes, and a mighty avalanche of *Northern* soldiery, well disciplined for their work of death by long experience in *Northern* mobs, would rush down upon them from our *Northern* hills in exterminating wrath, and sweep away, in its desolating ruins, the last vestige of their present "forlorn hope!" Do I misrepresent the church and clergy? No! You, at least, know that this would be to redeem their plighted faith. They stand before the world and before high Heaven sworn to protect every slave-breeder in the land in his *lawful* business of rearing men and women for the market; nor have they, as a body, ever shown any symptoms of intention to violate the requirements of their oath. They preach and practice allegience to a government which is based upon the bones and sinews, and cemented with the blood, of millions of their countrymen, and hold themselves in readiness to execute its every decree, at the point of the bayonet. Thus emphatically are they holders of the slaves—the bulwarks of the bloody slave system—and as such, at their hands, if there by any truth in Christianity, will God require the blood of every slave in our land. And, for one, so long as they continue in their present position, I deem it the duty of every friend of humanity to brand them as a Brotherhood of thieves, adulterers, manstealers, pirates, and murderers, and to prove to the world that, in sustaining the slave system, they do actually commit all these atrocious crimes.

* * *

There is another view of this subject, which presents the guilt of the Northern church and clergy in a still more glaring light. It is this: To legalize crime, and throw around it the sanction of statutory enactments, is undeniably, an act of much greater wickedness than to perpetuate it after it has been made lawful. Thus the members of a legislative body, which should enact a law authorizing theft or murder, would more deserve the penitentiary, or gallows, than the man who merely steals, or, in a fit of anger, takes his neighbor's life. The former justify crime, and make it honorable, and thus obliterate all distinction between virtue and vice; the latter merely commits it, when legalized, but attempts no justification of his offence. But the religious professions of the country have legalized slavery, and the infernal slave trade, in the District of Columbia, and in the Territory of Florida! They have made their national capital one of the greatest slave marts on the globe; and they now hold in slavery, by direct legislation, more than thirty thousand human beings, whom they have sternly refused to emancipate. No sect can claim exemption from this charge. In whatever else they differ, they have all united, without exception, by the most unanimous voice of their members, in opposing the abolition of slavery in those places where they have the power to emancipate, and have declared to the world, by their vote (the most effective way in which they could speak on the subject), that it was their sovereign will and pleasure that the traffic in human beings, which they have branded as piracy on the coast of Africa, should be lawful and honorable commerce in the United States. . . .

* * *

There are in our country more than twenty thousand [ministers], scattered over every part of the land, and at the same time so united in national and local associations as to act in perfect harmony, whenever concert is required. They constitute what may properly be termed a *religious aristocracy*. Among the exclusive privileges which they claim and enjoy, is the right to administer the ordinances of religion, and to lead in all our religious services. The ear of the nation is open to them every seventh day of the week, when they pour into it just such sentiments as they choose. And not only are they in direct and constant contact with the people in their public ministrations, but in their parochial visits, at the sick bed, at weddings, and at funerals, all of which are occasions when the mind is peculiarly tender, and susceptible of deep and lasting impressions. Amply supported by the contributions of the church, their whole time is devoted to the work of moulding and giving character to public sentiment; and with the advantages which they enjoy over all other classes of society, of leisure, the sanctity of their office, and direct and constant contact with their people as their "spiritual guides," their power has become all-controlling. It is in a *finite* sense omnipresent in every section of the country, and is absolutely *irresistible*, wherever their claims are allowed. Hence, what they countenance, it will be next to an impossibility to overthrow, at least till their order itself be

overthrown; and whatever system of evil they oppose, must melt
away like snow beneath the warm rays of an April sun.

* * *

But it is not in their political capacity that the influence of the
church and clergy has been most prejudicial to the cause of
emancipation. True, they have rivalled the infidel and nothingar-
ian in their support of pro-slavery parties; and their recreancy at
the ballot-box has been such as to merit the severest epithets
which I have ever bestowed upon them. But in their ecclesiastical
character, *they have publicly defended the slave system as an innocent and
Heaven-ordained institution, and have thrown the sacred sanctions of religion
around it, by introducing it into the pulpit, and to the communion table!* At
the South, nearly the entire body of the clergy publicly advocate
the perpetuity of slavery, and denounce the abolitionists as
fanatics, incendiaries, and cut-throats; and the churches and
clergy of the North still fellowship them, and palm them off upon
the world as the ministers of Christ. I know it will be said that
there are exceptions to this charge; but if there be any, I have yet
to learn of them. I know not of a single ecclesiastical body in the
country which has excommunicated any of its members for the
crime of slaveholding, since the commencement of the anti-slavery
enterprise, though most of them have cast out the true and faithful
abolitionists from their communion.

I might, with great propriety, pursue these general remarks, and
indulge in a somewhat severer strain, but to understand the true
character of the American church and clergy, and the full extent
of their atrocities, you must hear them speak in their own
language. Should I tell you the whole truth respecting them, and
tell it in my own words, I fear you would. . .think me guilty of
falsehood. I will therefore introduce several of the leading sects,
and let them speak for themselves, through the resolves of their
respective ecclesiastical bodies, and the published sentiments of
their accredited ministers; and although you may not believe me,
should I tell you that they have "no wish or intention" to abolish
slavery, yet you will believe them, I trust, when you hear the
declaration from their own lips.

[There follow forty pages of statements from each of the major
Christian denominations in the United States, begining with the
Methodist Episcopal church. Ministers of that body in 1836 had

resolved that they were "decidedly opposed to modern abolitionism, and [did] wholly disclaim any right, wish, or intention to
interfere in the civil and political relation between master and
slave, as it exists in the slaveholding states of the Union."
Ministers of all the major communions were quoted as denying
that slaveholding was a sin, and some were bold to say that some
men should become slaveholders on principle in order to civilize
and to Christianize the blacks. The statements and actions of the
American clergy, charged Foster, stained and darkened "almost
every page of the modern history of the American church; and if
generally known, they would render that church a stench in the
nostrils of the heathen of every realm on the globe!" He concluded
with the following statement:]

My task is done. My pledge is redeemed. I have here drawn a
true but painful picture of the American church and clergy. I have
proved them to be a BROTHERHOOD OF THIEVES! I have shown
that multitudes of them subsist by ROBBERY and make THEFT
their trade!—that they plunder the cradle of its precious contents,
and rob the youthful lover of his bride!—that they steal "from
principle," and teach their people that slavery "is not opposed to
the will of God," but "IS A MERCIFUL VISITATION"!--that they
excite the mob to deeds of violence, and advocate LYNCH LAW for
the suppression of the sacred right of speech!—I have shown that
they sell their own sisters in the church for the SERAGLIO, and invest
the proceeds of their sales in BIBLES for the heathen!—that they rob the
forlorn and despairing mother of her babe, and barter away that
babe to the vintner for wine for the Lord's supper! I have shown
that nearly all of them *legalize* slavery, with all its barbarous,
bitter, burning wrongs, and make PIRACY lawful and honorable
commerce; and that they dignify slave-holding, and render it
popular, by placing MAN-STEALERS in the Presidential chair! I
have shown that those who themselves abstain from these enormities, are in church fellowship with those who perpetrate them;
and that, by this connection, they countenance the wrong, and
strengthen the hands of the oppressor! I have shown that while
with their lips they profess to believe that LIBERTY is God's free
and impartial gift to all, and that it is "*inalienable,*" they hold
2,500,000 of their own countrymen in the most abject bondage;
thus proving to the world, that they are not *Infidels* merely, but
blank ATHEISTS—disbelievers in the existence of a God who will

hold them accountable for their actions! These allegations are all supported by evidence which none can controvert, and which no impartial mind can doubt. The truth of them is seen on every page of our country's history; and it is deeply *felt* by more than two millions of our enchained countrymen, who now demand their plundered rights at our hands. In making this heart-rending and appalling disclosure of their hypocrisy and crimes, I have spoken with great severity; but it is the severity of truth and love. I have said that *only* which I could not in kindness withhold! and in discharging the painful duty which devolved upon me in this regard, I have had but a single object in view—the redemption of the oppressor from his *guilt*, and the oppressed from his *chains*. To this darling object of my heart, this letter is now dedicated. As it goes out through you, to the public, a voice of terrible warning, and admonition to the guilty oppressor, but of consolation, as I trust, to the despairing slave, I only ask for it, that it may be received with the same kindness, and read with the same candor, in which it has been written.

> With great respect and affection,
> Your Sincere friend,
> S. S. FOSTER

Canterbury, N.H., July 1843

7 FROM

Gerrit Smith
On the Character, Scope and
Duties of the Liberty Party

Political as well as religious life was affected by abolitionist controversy. The Whig and Democratic parties were attacked for their "temporizing" on the issue of black servitude; and some abolitionists simply refused to have anything to do with politics. Others, however, attempted to make politicians take stands on matters such as slavery in the District of Columbia, the interstate slave trade, and eventually the Compromise of 1850. By 1840, however, the tactics of questioning politicians of the two major parties was considered by some as incapable of producing good results. The decision was then made to organize a new, antislavery party, which proceeded to do very poorly at the polls. Many of the issues that were to plague the new party are discussed in the following selection— whether to be a universal reform party, whether to follow politically wise but morally "lax" policies, whether to accept "Wilmot Proviso men" as legitimate antislavery allies. The latter were identified with the opposition to extending slave territory. David Wilmot, a Pennsylvania Democrat in the House of Representatives, spoke for a faction of his party that had become alienated from President James K. Polk and his expansionist and pro-Southern policies. To embarrass the President and to capture rising antislavery feeling in the North for the Democratic party, Wilmot suggested a "proviso" to a House appropriations bill during the Mexican War in August of 1846. The provision was that the money to be appropriated would not be used to acquire land from Mexico if it were to become "slave territory." Obviously this measure (which never passed both houses of Congress) was not an abolitionist tactic, since it opposed the extension of slavery instead of proposing its outright abolition. Such a "pragmatic" approach to politics did not satisfy many Liberty Party men, among them, Gerrit Smith, who published one of his speeches on the matter in 1847.

Smith (1797-1874) was associated with reform efforts all of his life: temperance, women's rights, prison reform, peace, as well as abolition. A wealthy man who gave lavishly to benevolent enterprises, Smith was also

SOURCE. Gerrit Smith, "On the Character, Scope, and Duties of the Liberty Party," 1847.

*interested in politics even before he helped to organize the Liberty party in
1840 and ran as that party's gubernatorial candidate in New York the same
year. In 1852 he was elected to Congress as an independent; in 1858 he
again ran for governor and, when the war came, moved rather easily into the
Republican party where he supported suffrage for the freedmen. So sure was
he of the rightness of his opposition to slavery that he supported with money
as well as prayers the efforts of the New England Emigrant Aid Society in
Kansas. In the following selection, Smith demonstrates the consistency that
directed most abolitionist thought: the efficacy of all institutions is to be
judged by how well they support righteousness, justice, and equality.*

Gerrit Smith offered the following Resolution of the National
Liberty Party Convention, held in Buffalo, October 20th, 1847:

"Whereas, the Liberty party, whether it was, or was not,
organized for the one purpose of engaging in a contest with
slavery; and whether it was, or was not, organized with the
expectation, that the great political parties would very speedily
espouse that contest, and leave the Liberty party to disband; is
now, because the corruption of these great political parties is seen
to be past all cure, and their reformation beyond all hope, to be
regarded as a permanent party:—and, whereas, every political
party, which looks upon itself to be a permanent party, is
therefore, bound to acquaint itself, so far as it can, with the
important duties of that Government, which it aspires to control
and administer:—and, whereas, this is peculiarly and emphatically
the duty of the Liberty party, inasmuch, as from the first moment
of its existence, the equal rights of all men—equal justice to all
men—has been its acknowledged and boasted principle of action;

"Resolved, therefore, that, in the light of these premises, the
Liberty party should no longer delay to be studying and inculcat-
ing all the duties, which are justly called for at the hands of the
Government of the United States—all the duties, which if it shall
not prove false to its confessed principle of action, it will itself
discharge, when that Government shall come into its hands."

Whether the Convention would have adopted this Resolution is
not known. Those members of the Convention, who alone had the

right to participate in nominating candidates, gave 26 votes for it and 103 against it. Probably, not a small share of such members felt themselves bound by the views of those, who deputed them, not only to vote for Mr. Hale, but to vote against the positions and doctrines of this Resolution. The gentleman, who gave the first of the aforesaid 129 votes, arose, when his name was called, and said, that, as a man and a member of the Convention, he wished to vote for the Resolution; but, that, as one of those, appointed to nominate, he felt bound to vote against it.

Mr. Smith advocated the Resolution in the following speech:

"January 29th, 1840, it was solemnly resolved, after a two days' discussion of the subject in a large Convention held in Arcade, Wyoming county, State of New York, to organize a new political party. The object of this party, in the esteem of some, was universal political reform; in the esteem of more, but the overthrow of slavery.

"This new party, which was rightly named the Liberty party, sprung from the conviction, that the great political parties were not to be trusted on the subject of slavery; and that the continued interrogation of their candidates on this subject, or any other reliance on these parties for aiding the cause of the slave, would, as ever hitherto, end but in disappointment and vanity. I said, that the Liberty party sprang from the conviction of the untrustworthiness of the great political parties on the subject of slavery. But this conviction, although deep and abiding in the breasts of many Liberty party men, has not proved to be so in the breasts of all of them. This was manifest at the very first general Election, after the Liberty party was organized. Many, who had enrolled themselves in the Liberty party, listened to the cunning phrase, that the Whig party is "the more favorable party," and voted for Harrison and Tyler. And such were the seductive representations of the Whig party, four years afterwards, when thousands upon thousands quit the Liberty party to vote for Henry Clay, as to threaten the very existence of the Liberty party. It was fondly hoped, that. . .Whig devices. . .for drawing away our votes would forever cure Liberty party men of the delusion of looking upon the Whigs to be a class of Abolitionists, or to be, at least, as much as half-brothers of the Abolitionists. But, alas, there has been many a subsequent occurrence to prove how groundless was this hope! We have seen Liberty party men of New Hampshire elect the Whig candidate for Governor: and we have seen nearly the whole Liberty party press silently consenting to, or openly justifying, this outrage upon—this very tearing up of—the foundation principles of the Liberty party—this very repealing of the law of its existence. We have also seen, and within the last few months too, Liberty party men of this same State, New Hampshire, helping in great numbers, to elect to Congress that notorious Whig, General Wilson:—and, this too, notwithstanding the General had so recently manifested his great impatience to go to Mexico, that there, under the banner of slavery, he might shed innocent blood. And, here again, scarce a Liberty party paper uttered a word of remonstrance. We have seen Liberty party men of Massachusetts desert that accomplished, tried, and able friend of the slave, James G. Carter, to help elect to Congress John G. Palfrey, who, whatever his merits, is an unrepenting voter for Henry Clay. What other Liberty party papers, besides the Bangor Gazette, justified this infidelity to Liberty party principles, I cannot, at this moment, say. Sure I am, that very few Liberty party papers protested against it. We have seen Liberty men, by hundreds and thousands, voting pro-slavery tickets, that they might thereby aid the cause of temperance. Not to mention any other of the very numerous instances, in which Liberty men have expressed a measure of confidence in Whigs and Democrats, (almost always in the former,) it is as painful, as it is fresh, in our recollections, that, only the last year, the vast majority of the Liberty men of this great State were eager to entrust the Whig party with the high and holy work of framing the fundamental and organic laws of the State. And I cannot forget, that almost the whole Liberty press of the nation advocated this suicidal policy."

Mr. Smith here adverted to the fact, that the Liberty party press held him up as the calumniator of the Liberty party for having said, a couple of months ago, that in his judgment, more than half of the editors and members of the Liberty party might be induced to vote for pro-slavery voters. He kindly put it to the candor of the Convention, whether, judging in the light of the past, he had done injustice to his brethren. He bade them remember, that he had never impeached their motives; and, that he, had always, cheerfully admitted, that, in casting their votes for pro-slavery voters, they were prompted by the desire of aiding some good cause—generally, the cause of the slave. He had not referred to instances of their casting votes for pro-slavery voters, that he might thereby prove, that Liberty men were, all, or any of them, wanting in heart for the slave. It was for quite another purpose that he had referred to them—for the purpose of constituting therefrom, and establishing the basis fact of the speech he is now making. THIS BASIC FACT IS, THAT MANY LIBERTY MEN REPOSE A MEASURE OF CONFIDENCE IN THE PRO-SLAVERY PARTIES; AND THEREBY HINDER THEMSELVES FROM RIGHTLY DECIDING WHAT SHOULD BE THE CHARACTER AND WORK OF THE LIBERTY PARTY.

Mr. Smith had spoken on one personal matter—on one matter affecting himself. Will the Convention bear with the egotism of his speaking on another? An attempt is made to read me out of the Liberty party, because I have called the Liberty League a "better party." Why did I call it a "better party?" Because, it surpasses the Liberty party, in that it discerns more, and commits itself to more, of the bearings of their common principle of action—the equal rights of all men. But, I am asked, why if I think the Liberty League better than the Liberty party, I do not quit the latter to join the former? Must I, however, because there is a family in my neighborhood better governed than my own, break mine up to join that? Is not my duty rather to profit by the example before me, and to elevate the standard of discipline under my own roof? So, too, we need not quit the Liberty party to join the Liberty League. But, wherein the latter is superior to the former, "let us walk by the same rule—let us mind the same thing"—whatever foolish pride, or dirty jealousy, or any other wicked spirit, may counsel to the contrary.

But, to return from this digression—I was adverting to a few of the numerous instances, in which Liberty men have shown a degree of confidence in the pro-slavery parties. Even to this day, they continue to show it. Else what means this desire on the part of so many of them to postpone the making of our Presidential nomination until the pro-slavery parties have made theirs? This desire must stand connected with the hope of good to the cause of the slave at the hands of these parties. A postponement of our nomination, I admit, may be proper:—but not with any reference to the nominations of the pro-slavery parties.

Many Liberty men are eager to vote for a Wilmot Proviso Whig, or a Wilmot Proviso Democrat—for a Thomas Corwin, or for some one, who shall be found in the Democratic ranks to supply the place of the lamented Silas Wright. Indeed, it is only a few weeks, since I saw the name of Thomas Corwin flying from the mast-head of the Liberty party paper of Rhode Island. And it is only a few days, since I read in the National Era, that, in the New Hampshire Convention, which appointed delegates to this Convention, George Barstow, Esq., spoke of his readiness to vote for Thomas Corwin. The writer of the account of that Convention added, that Mr. Barstow spoke, on this point, the sense of the Convention generally. But, I trust, he did not ["He did not," from many voices.] I rejoice to learn, that he did not.

A Wilmot Proviso man! A Wilmot Proviso man! Even, Abolitionists are wont to praise the Wilmot Proviso man. But, who is the Wilmot Proviso man? He is the man, who, under the most favorable representation of him, is willing to let slavery live, where it now lives—but no where else. King Canute, you remember, told the sea, how far it might come, and no farther. But, the sea wouldn't mind him. The Wilmot Proviso man tells slavery, how far it may come, and no farther:—but, will it mind him? A farmer sees a huge and venomous serpent in one of his fields. He is afraid it will crawl into his other fields—into his garden—into his house. What shall he do? Shall he build a high and close fence around the field, in which the serpent is? Oh, no! The only adequate security against the serpent is to kill it. So too, if you would arrest the progress of slavery—that hugest and most venomous of all serpents—you must kill it. A license to slavery to live any where, is a license to it to live everywhere. Call you the Wilmot Proviso man an anti-slavery man? He is a pro-slavery man, who will consent, that slavery live any where. Call you him a temperance man, who opposes but the multiplication beyond their present number of distilleries and dramshops? As well, may you do so, as to call him an anti-slavery man, who opposes but the extension of slavery.

But, I turn away from the soulless creature, who calls himself a Wilmot Proviso man; and repeat, that there are still many Liberty men, who are disposed to go down to Egypt for help; and to rely on the pro-slavery parties to aid the slave. There are still many of them, who indulge, at least, occasional hopes, that, ere long, one or both of the great pro-slavery parties will stand forth the friend of the slave; and, thus, permit the Liberty party to disband and to dissolve into its original elements. But, can such hopes be indulged any longer?

These parties are destroying a poor, weak, distracted, unoffending nation, to make more room for slavery. If the Democratic party be the louder in the boast of having done most to produce the Mexican war, the Whig party, nevertheless, is the louder in the boast of having done most toward its vigorous prosecution. Indeed, it is the especial boast of the Whig party, that the most distinguished butchers in the war—Scott, Taylor, &c.—are Whigs. Now, whatever right we may, once, have had to look for mercy to the slave at the hands of these parties; and, however, we might, once, have been excused from believing, that they could ever sink into their present depths of wickedness; I ask, whether we can, any longer, entertain hopes for the cause of freedom from these parties. Would, that an emphatic "No" might sound out from this whole Convention! [An overwhelming "No."] Are all Liberty men, at last, prepared to take the solemn vow upon their souls, never more to think of re-uniting with those parties, which they forsook?—nevermore, in Bible language, to be mindful of the country, whence they came out? [A thundering "Yes"—"They are."] Cortez, the invader and conqueror of Mexico, burnt his ships, shortly after landing. He did this to the end, that his little band might feel themselves cut off from the possibility of retreating to the country, whence they came out; to the end, that they might feel themselves shut up to the necessity of conquering, or being conquered—to the necessity to do or die. And, now, all Liberty men ready to resolve, by the inflexible, iron, holiest, purposes of their deepest souls, to cut themselves off from all re-union, and desire of re-union, with the parties, whence they came out? ["They are—They are"—from innumerable voices.] Have Liberty men all done with placing dependence on these incorrigibly besotted and corrupted parties? In the language of the auctioneers—"Gentlemen, have you all done? ["We have—we have"—came loud and deep from every part of the Convention.]

Are all Liberty men, at last, prepared to say, that the Liberty party is a permanent party? ["They are—they are"—seemed to be a well-nigh universal shout.] Are they all, at last, prepared to say, that its business is no longer to wait upon the other parties, and to regard itself as of a short or conditional existence:—but, that its business is to break up those other parties, and to press its way to power and to the possession of the reins of government? [A most cheering cry of "They are—they are."] My whole heart rejoices in your replies. We are, then, a permanent party. We have not only run our colors up —but we have nailed them up.

Here, then, the Liberty party stands forth a permanent party. And, now, what is its duty in the light of this, its acknowledged character? What less than to look after all the political interests of the country; and to qualify itself to wield those powers of government which it expects to possess? Whilst the Liberty party regarded itself as a temporary party, and but an instrument to bring the pro-slavery political parties to the ground of anti-slavery, there was consistency in confining its regards to the one subject of slavery. But, to say, that, now, in its altered circumstances—that, now, since it is of necessity to regard itself as a permanent party—to say, that, now, its only duty is to qualify itself to dispose of slavery—is, virtually, to say, that the abolition of slavery is the only political want of the nation, and that nothing else is due from its government. What, however, when the Liberty party shall have come into power, will be its answer to inquiries touching its policy on commerical restrictions, land-monopoly, war, &c.? Shall its answer be "Mill-post—mill-post—mill-post?" This, says the Liberty party press, should be its answer now to such inquiries: and, if now, ere it be in power, it may refuse to listen to such inquiries, why, in the name of consistency, may it not also refuse to listen to them, after it shall have come into power? But, the Liberty party will not refuse then—and it will no longer refuse now:—for, it is no longer to be regarded as a mere anti-slavery party—as a party for colored men only—but as a party for all men—as a party both for the whole, and of the whole—as a party, not for one political reform—but for universal political reform.

But, we must pass on, to glance at the objections to the proposed extension of the scope of the Liberty party.

It is said, that this extension is needless, for the reason, that the Liberty party will, when in power, (as a matter of course, and because it is an anti-slavery party,) do justice to all classes and conditions of men. It is said, that the party, which undertakes to go right on the subject of slavery, will go right on every other subject. Not so, however, if it shall refuse to look at the claims of every other subject. The party, which shall thus refuse, whilst on its way to power, will act but consistently, if it shall continue to do so, after it shall get into power. Great Britain, almost as one man, abolished chattel-slavery. Nevertheless, she continues to cling to innumerable forms of oppression.

But, can a party ever get into power, which pursues this policy of turning its back on the claims of every other subject, whilst endeavoring to do justice to the claims of only one subject? May we not as well expect, that a wagon will make progress by the process of turning one of its wheels, and leaving the other three to stand still?

It is, also, said, that, if we extend the scope of the Liberty party, the slave, who had hitherto received our concentrated and exclusive attention, will then, being but a sharer with other objects in that attention, be comparatively neglected. Not so, however. The pre-eminent wrongs of the slave will still continue to receive our first and incomparably highest attention. And I contend, that he will have all the stronger hold upon our hearts from the fact, that we have permitted other objects to share in their pity. Who is he, that is foremost in pitying the class of greatest sufferers? Is it he, who neglects every other class of sufferers? Oh, no! It is he, who allows his sympathies to travel most freely among all the forms of wrong and wretchedness and ruin. To limit the objects of our sympathies is to kill other sympathies—whereas to multiply them is to invigorate them, and preserve them in a healthy tone. His is but a sickly and ineffective sympathy, which looks after the poor black man only, and not after the poor red and white man also. He, who sets out to have a heart for but one thing, will find, in the end, that he has a heart for no thing. Does he cultivate the deepest abhorrence of murder, who neglects all other crimes? Sofar from this, even murder itself will, in the end, cease to move him, who undertakes to restrict his sensibilities to it.

Another objection. It is claimed, that, in the success of Bible, Missionary, Tract, Temperance, and other voluntary Associations, we have conclusive proof of the propriety and advantage of their each confining themselves to one object. Admitted—at least for the sake of the argument. But, does it follow, that a political party may also confine itself to one object? Far from it. By the instrumentality of voluntary Associations, a man may, simultaneously, aid several objects—because he can belong simultaneously, to several such Associations. But, if he would be, simultaneously, aiding several objects, by political action, and through the ballot-box; he must belong to a political party, which goes for those several objects:—and this, necessarily from the fact, that he can belong to but one political party, at a time. He cannot vote at the same Election with the Liberty party against slavery, and with the Whig party for a high Tariff, and with the Democratic party for a lower one:—for he has but one vote to cast.

I have, for some time, felt the need of a political party, in which I could serve all the great political interests of my country. The loud-speaking and instructive events of the last year or two (prominently among these is the Irish famine,) have greatly increased my sense of this need. For many years, I have advocated the beautiful, truthful, and Christian doctrine of absolute Free trade; and, I confess, that, for the last two or three years, my impatience to vote for it has run high. For several years, I have advocated the no less beautiful, truthful, and Christian doctrine of Anti-land-monopoly; and, I confess, that, for the last two or three years, my impatience to vote for *it* also has run high. What shall I do? What shall I do? My heart, in respect to these subjects is, to use a Bible figure, like a cart pressed with sheaves. I cannot refrain from uttering my sentiments—my deep convictions upon them:— and, how can I longer refrain from voting in consonance with those sentiments and convictions? Again, I ask—what shall I do?— what shall I do? Do you tell me, that I must postpone acting on these subjects, until chattel-slavery is abolished? But, that may not take place in less than twenty years:—and, ere then, I shall, probably, be numbered with the dead:—and, if I shall have listened to the counsels of some of you, I shall have gone to my final account with the heavy sin upon my soul of never having testified through the ballot-box against such giant iniquities as Tariffs and Land-monopolies. Moreover, as an Abolitionist, I am impatient to vote against these iniquities—for I regard them, as among the strongest props of American slavery. The death of Tariffs and Land-monopolies would work the speedy death of American slavery.

Tell me, Mr. President—tell me, where in logic, or morals, or religion, I can find a license, not only to postpone, but to oppose, the claims of righteous objects?—and such do I, manifestly, not only postpone, but oppose, when, for the sake of voting for a man, who is right on Slavery, I vote for a man, who is wrong on the subjects of War, and Temperance, and Land-monopoly and

Tariffs. I have referred to my deep interest in several questions. Why do not Liberty men generally feel as deeply upon them? For the simple reason, that these questions are not brought before their minds. Liberty party meetings and Liberty party papers will not discuss them. I have in my own poor way, and other Liberty men have in their own good way, written on these questions. But, the Liberty party press will print nothing of it. Not only does it not let us speak for ourselves through its columns on these questions; but it misrepresents us (unintentionally, I have no doubt,) by calling these questions, to which we have yielded our hearts, mere dollars and cents questions! You remember the story of the Lion and the picture. The picture represented a man in the act of killing a lion. "Ah!" said the lion, "if we lions were painters, we would make very different pictures from that." So, too, if we free traders, and anti-land-monopolists, and anti-war men had the privilege of the columns of the Liberty party press, we would make very different representations of these questions from what are now made in those columns. I say it in sorrow—that I have more access to the minds of Whigs and Democrats on these questions than I have to the minds of my own party;—for many Whig and Democratic papers do print a part of what I write on these questions. I do not say, that they print it to commend it to their readers. Some of them print what I write against Land-monopoly, but for the purpose of showing what a great hypocrite a man must be, who can so write, and yet, at the same time, hold great tracts of land.

Mere dollars and cents questions! Is War a mere dollars and cents question? It is surely, something more than this to him, who falls in battle, and to her, whom it reduces to widowhood and orphanage. And is Land-monopoly a mere dollars and cents question? Is it a mere dollars and cents question, whether one, born into the world, shall be allowed light, air and water? But, why needs he not as absolute and as unquestioned a title to land, as to those other elements? Alas that so many millions of our brothers and sisters should have no acknowledged standing-place on the earth, save by the road-side! And the Tariff-system—is that too but a mere dollars and cents question? I admit, that one of its aspects is a dollars and cents aspect:—and a most terrific aspect it is:—for, I venture to affirm, that, under this system, one-fifth of the wealth of the nation pays more than the remaining four-fifths toward the cost of the Government. Or, in other words—they, who own but one-fifth of this wealth, pay more than they do, who own the remaining four-fifths of it. But, the Tariff-system is most to be condemned for its inhumanity and its violation of the Divinely-appointed brotherhood and unity of our race. That system interposes to prevent my sending my spare barrel of flour to feed the starving family of my fellow man; and to prevent his sending his spare roll of cloth to cover my naked and shivering family, if but a National line pass between us. And that system, in imposing restraints on commerce, keeps millions in estrangement from each other, who else would be enlightening and blessing each other.

Do you blame me for feeling on these subjects? Blame me not. Blame yourselves. You have but yourselves to blame for it. It is you, who made me an abolitionist,—And it is because I am an abolitionist, that I feel on these subjects. I had but little feeling on them until I became an abolitionist. I am, what I have become in your abolition school. And, now, for you, who gave me my education, to be thus rudely repressing its legitimate and necessary tendencies:—and, now, for you, who gave me my impetus, to be thus jerking me back—is indeed, most unreasonable and cruel. It was in your abolition-school, that I learned, as I never before had learned, the brotherhood and oneness of the human race. It was there, that I learned, as I never before had learned, to love an Englishman, a Frenchman, aye, and a Mexican too, as a man:—and to look upon an American to be but a man. It was there, that I learned, as I never before had learned, what a compound of selfishness, folly, wickedness, madness, is that thing called patriotism—that thing, which generates Tariffs and wars.

Can *you* then, who gave me my abolition heart, be guilty of throwing back upon it the floods of feeling, which rush from it, and demand outlets in the direction of free trade, free soil, peace, &c. Will you keep pouring into the fountain-head, and then complain of the streams, that burst forth from it? Will you be so unreasonable, as to dig around the roots of the tree, and prune its branches, and then quarrel with the fair fruit, which you have caused it to produce?

Oh, Sir, if you would stop me, and the rapidly multiplying thousands, who, along with me, are considering the claims of the poor to their shares of this goodly green earth, which our Common Father has given equally to us all:—oh, Sir, if you would stop us from considering the claims of the poor to the benefits of free-trade:—oh, Sir, if you would stop us from looking with compassion on the poor, who can no longer afford to pay for war, or to perish in war:—oh, Sir, if you would stop all this, you must, first, stop your abolition—for that is the great begetting cause of these our uncontrollable feelings:—you must, first, stop your abolition-press; and break up your abolition-societies, and your Liberty party; and burn up your abolition libraries; and roll back upon us a dead sea of pro-slavery influence, upon whose leaden waters the strongest gales of Liberty cannot so much, as raise one ripple, and beneath whose leaden waters every sentiment of humanity expires.

But, to return. I was glancing at the objections to the proposed extension of the scope of the Liberty party.

It is said, that the Whig and Democratic parties aim at universal political reform;—and, yet, fail to accomplish it:—and it is asked, whether the Liberty party would, by the like extension of its scope, succeed any better. I answer, that, should the Liberty party take the ground of doing justice to all classes and conditions of men, my reliance, that it would do it, would, under God, be on its admitted principle of action—the principle of the equal rights of all men. But, it is said, that this is the principle of action with the Whig and Democratic parties also. I admit, that it is their professed—but it is not their real principle—of action. The Liberty party, however, actually takes the ground of the political and social equality of all men. He is not a Liberty party man, who makes political rights turn on physical peculiarities: and he is not a Liberty party man, who does not as warmly welcome a colored man, as a white man, to his dinner table. But Whigs and Democrats (speaking of them as parties) exclude colored men both from political and social equality: and, thereby, stamp with hypocrisy their professed devotion to the doctrine of equal rights. Argue not then, that the Liberty party would, if in power, fail, as the other parties have done, to reform Civil Government, and make it a blessing to the world. It would not so fail: for in the profession of the doctrine of equal rights, it is as sincere, as the other parties are hypocritical. It would not so fail:—for in its career, as a permanent and comprehensive party, it would faithfully apply this doctrine, not only to the overthrow of slavery, but to the correction of every other political evil.

Again. It is said, that, in arguing for an extension of the scope of the Liberty party, I am proposing new tests of membership in the Liberty party. But, I am not. I am but asking, that the Liberty party shall conform itself to its now admitted character of a permanent and comprehensive party; and shall fairly render what is fairly due from a political party of such a character. I am but asking, that the Liberty party shall qualify itself for the high trust of administering the Government of the United States, by honestly inquiring, and, as far as it can, by honestly deciding, what will be its various duties, when it shall have come into the possession of that trust.

I am not calling on the Liberty party to commit itself to this, or that view of trade—to this, or that view of Land-reform—to this, or that view of oath-bound secret societies. I am but asking, that it shall, frankly and immediately, declare, that it stands ready to espouse every political truth. And, moreover, I leave it with itself to decide what is, and what is not, a political truth. I am free to practice this liberality, because I am confident, that the political party, which, have, for its heartily embraced principle of action, the principle of the equal rights of all men, sets out, in the light of that principle, and by the faithful application of it, to learn political truths, will learn them. I AM ENTIRELY WILLING TO RUN THE RISK OF THE FUTURE CHARACTER AND POLICY OF THE LIB-ERTY PARTY, ONLY LET IT UNDERTAKE TO FORM THAT CHARAC-TER AND POLICY IN THE LIGHT OF ITS ADMITTED PRINCIPLE OF ACTION, AND BY THE FAITHFUL APPLICATION OF THAT PRINCIPLE TO THE WHOLE RANGE OF POLITICAL DUTIES.

But, I must bring my remarks to a close. Civil Government is now, and the history of the world shows, that, in every age, it has been a heavy and horrible curse. Why should it be so? Is it because this is its legitimate—its necessary, character? Oh, no! It is, because of its perversions—of its perversion from the care of the poor, to the crushing of the poor—of its perversion from the protection of human rights to the prostration of human rights. Let the Liberty party now undertake with an honest and an earnest heart, to recover Civil Government from its perversions, and to restore it to its Heaven-intended uses, and Civil Government will then begin to be the precious, priceless, blessing to the world, which God designed, that it always, and every where, should be; but, which, with scarce an exception it, never and no where, has been.

The mission of the Liberty party, if such, indeed, it once were, is no longer but to overthrow slavery. It is the unspeakably more important one of reducing to practice the true and divine idea of Civil Government. In proportion, as this idea is realized and made practical, slavery and every other political oppression will disappear;—for God gave Civil Government, chiefly for the purpose of providing protection therein for those who are too poor, and ignorant, and weak, to protect themselves. To prevent, and punish, and put an end to, oppression, is the work, that God has assigned to Civil Government. No other party is summoned to this high and holy service, which is the mission of the Liberty party—for no other party is capable of rendering it. No other party has even begun to imbibe the true idea of Civil Government. But the Liberty party has gone far in imbibing it. And, now, shall the Liberty party be guilty of holding the truth in unrighteousness, and of hiding its light under a bushel? I trust not. .

Should the Liberty party listen to unwise counsels—and resolve to confine its opposition to one form of oppression, instead of extending it to all;—then, in my humble judgment, its doom is sealed. It will dwindle, and dwindle, and dwindle, until it shall finally, and, that too, very speedily, expire in its own disgrace, and its light go out forever. But should the Liberty party, listening to wise counsels, and taking for its motto those words of the Lord Jesus: "FULFILL ALL RIGHTEOUSNESS"—"FULFILL ALL RIGHTEOUSNESS"—resolve to do manful battle, not only with slavery, THAT CRIME OF CRIMES, but with land-monopolies, commercial restrictions, oath-bound secret societies, and every other iniquity in the field of politics:—then, indeed, would it make rapid progress to victory, and the possession of the reins of Government:—then, indeed, would it speedily become, the world over, the attractive model of a political party, and the praise, not only of this, but of every other land.

8 FROM *Board of Managers of the Massachusetts Anti-Slavery Society*
The Fugitive Slave Bill

If parties were to be judged by whether or not they furthered justice and equality, so were laws. And the law that came under the most determined abolitionist attack was the Fugitive Slave Act. Part of the Compromise of 1850, the law became a rallying point for antislavery men who did not share the abolitionists' radical convictions about racial equality. The implied bribe in the law to give "slavecatchers" their quarry, the lack of provision for trial by jury, the use of federal power for what even the South at one time had claimed was a sectional institution seemed to be too much for many Northerners to accept. Abolitionists, of course, were particularly disturbed and appealed to a "higher law" than the Constitution to annul the act. Such annulment, announced abolitionists, was possible because the Fugitive Slave Act was "contrary to the moral sense of the community." The confidence inherent in these words was only partially justified; but the spread of antislavery ideas and the growing perception on the part of many Northerners that the South was, indeed, a threat to the natural development of American democracy was facilitated by the passage of the act and by the subsequent attempts to enforce it. The call to refuse to obey a law that offended conscience and human dignity is clear in the following selection, which was an address from the Board of Managers of the Massachusetts Anti-Slavery Society.

ADDRESS TO THE PEOPLE OF MASSACHUSETTS, BY THE BOARD OF MANAGERS OF THE MASSACHUSETTS ANTI-SLAVERY SOCIETY

Massachusetts Freemen and Women! Politicians and worldly

SOURCE. Board of Managers of Massachusetts Anti-Slavery Society, "The Fugitive Slave Bill," *The Liberator*, September 27, 1850.

men are just congratulating themselves that the much vexed question of slavery is at rest, and that a compromise which is satisfactory to the moderate men of both sections of the country has been effected. They do not know, or have forgotten, that the law of the eternal God is right and truth. They do not know, or have forgotten, that any question, in order to be really settled, must be settled right. No abiding compromise can possibly be made between right and wrong—between truth and falsehood—between slavery and freedom. Right and Truth and Freedom *must* prevail, as surely as God's law is right and true.

The Constitution of the United States (Art. 4, sect. 2) provides that "No person, held to service or labor in one State, under the laws thereof, escaping into another, shall, in consequence of any law or regulation therein, be discharged from such service or labor; but shall be delivered up on claim of the party to whom such service or labor may be due!" This the is only clause which provides for the return of fugitive slaves.

Two things must be established, before any one can be surrendered under this clause. (1) It must appear that he owes service, or is a slave; and, (2) that it is his master or his agent who claims him. The first opens the whole question, whether the man is legally a slave or not. The second, implying that he is a slave of some one, simply relates to the question, whether the right master claims him. Obviously, there is nothing in all this, which prevents Congress from allowing the alleged fugitive to prove his freedom, or test the legality of the claim by a jury trial, where witnesses can be introduced on both sides and the evidence most carefully sifted. Congress most manifestly has the power, would that it had the will, to surround the person of the alleged fugitive with all those safeguards to liberty of that special individual which having approved themselves to the experience of centuries, are justly considered invaluable. Not only this, but a compliance with the spirit, at least, of other parts of the Constitution should oblige Congress to provide these safeguards. "In all *criminal* prosecutions," says the Constitution. . ." the accused shall enjoy the right to a speedy and public trial, by an impartial jury." "To be confronted with the witnesses against him: to have compulsory process for obtaining witnesses in his favor: and to have the assistance of counsel for his defence; and in suits at common law, where the value in controversy shall exceed twenty dollars, the right to trial by jury shall be preserved." "The privilege of the writ of habeas corpus shall not be suspended, unless when in case of rebellion or treason the public safety may require it." (Art. 1, sec. 9) Congress, therefore, not only has the power, but in order to come up to the spirit of the constitutional provision, it is bound to enact that if a party claim another as his slave, the legality of that claim shall be tested by a jury of twelve men, under all the formalities and guards which it is possible to throw around the liberty of the subject, before the alleged fugitive shall be surrendered. Most manifestly, the same security ought to be given to a person who is claimed only as a slave, which is extended to the vilest of criminals. The guiding principle should be, it is far better that ninety and nine persons who are really fugitive slaves shall escape than that one freeman, however, humble his condition, shall be put in jeopardy.

But the Fugitive Slave Bill has become a law. Do you fully realize how entirely these fundamental safeguards of liberty, which the Constitution thus points out, are disregarded in its enactment? Are you fully aware how completely the rights and liberties of our own free citizens are placed at the mercy of the slavehunters?

At the South, if two slaveholders disagree as to the ownership of a slave, a jury must pass upon the question, so sacred is deemed the right of property! But if the man claimed on Massachusetts soil as a slave, protests that he owns himself may, even if he is really a free citizen of the Old Bay State, and legally capable of holding any office under its Constitution or laws: still, under the provisions of this act of Congress, he is denied the right of a trial by jury to establish his freedom!—If the man's *horse* is claimed, the *Constitution* requires that a jury shall be summoned to decide the question of property, because twenty dollars is at stake; but if the owner of the horse is claimed, Congress declares that this question is not of sufficient magnitude to call for a jury trial; for only a man's body and soul are at stake! In the estimation of Congress, the right of a freeman to own himself, to sit unmolested by his own fireside, surrounded by his wife and children, is of less consequence, and to be less carefully guarded, than the right to own a horse, a cow, or a pig, worth twenty dollars!

The law provides that the Judge of the U. States Circuit and District Courts, and those commissioners appointed by the Circuit Court who have authority to arrest, imprison, or bail offenders against the laws of the U. States, shall have jurisdiction under the act. And it is made the duty of the Circuit Court from time to time to *enlarge* the number of commissioners, with a view to afford *reasonable facilities* to reclaim fugitives from labor, and to the *prompt discharge* of the duties imposed by this act! And it would seem to be the intention of Congress, that one or more of these commissioners should be appointed in each county, because the law requires claimants who take out a warrant to arrest a fugitive, to procure it from the judge or commissioner of the *proper* circuit, district, or county, and also authorizes the commissioners, "within their *respective counties,*" to do certain acts. From these latter provisions, as well as from the nature of the service required, it is manifest that the chief, if not the whole duty of administering this law will, in practice, fall upon these commissioners. Some of those who are commissioners have been appointed from family and others from political and private considerations, moving the circuit judge. Having no fixed salary, they all depend upon the amount of fees they receive for their compensation, and in many instances, doubtless, for their entire support. When the number of these officers becomes so materially enlarged as contemplated by this act, it is difficult to avoid the conclusion, that many corrupt persons will be able to secure an appointment.

The law makes either of these judges, or any one of these commissioners, the sole and final arbiter of the freedom of any man, white* or black, who shall happen to be brought before him, and claimed as a slave; and, in order, as would seem, more fully to qualify these commissioners to administer this law in its true spirit, their fee is fixed at ten dollars, if the slaveholder is successful, and a certificate to that effect is granted him, whilst only five dollars is allowed them, if they fail to see sufficient proof!—Truly, it will be next to a miracle if, from such a class, not a few are found willing to become the tools of the oppressor.

The marshal and deputy marshals are obliged, under a penalty of $1000, to receive and use all proper means diligently to execute all warrants and precepts directed to them; and if any fugitive,

---

*There are slaves at the South who have as white, clear complexions, and as straight hair, as any Northern man or woman possesses. Ellen Craft passed easily for a white planter when making her escape.

after being arrested, shall escape from the custody of the marshal or his deputy, no matter whether with or without their assent, the marshal may be compelled to pay the value of the slave by a suit on his official bond. And the better to enable the commissioners to execute their duties faithfully and efficiently—they are authorized, from time to time, to appoint as many persons to execute their warrants as they see fit to, with authority, if need be, "to summon and call to their aid the by-standers or posse comitatus," when necessary to insure a faithful observance of the law; and efficient execution of the law, whenever their services may be required.

Any slaveholder, or his agent or attorney, may legally, either with or without any warrant, as he may see fit, seize any citizen, or other person found in this State, and take him before any one of these commissioners, in any county, whom for any reason he may please to select, and claim the man as his slave. It then becomes the duty of the commissioner "to hear and determine the case of such claimant in a *summary* manner," by a person who has more pecuniary interest to make him out a slave than he has to find him a freeman! And in order to simplify the matter as much as possible, the law declares that the testimony of the alleged fugitive shall in no case be admitted, but at the same time points out a way in which the claimant can, by his own oath, or that of his agent, most easily fabricate *conclusive* evidence in support of his claim.

To obtain this evidence, a slaveholder may go before the judge of any court of record in his own State, and by *ex parte* testimony "make satisfactory proof" to that judge of the escape of his slave; and thereupon a record is made of the matter so proved, "and also a general description of the person so escaping with such convenient certainty as may be, and a transcript of such record, authenticated by the attestation of the clerk and of the seal of said court being produced" in Massachusetts, and exhibited to any of the above named judge or commissioners, "shall be held and taken to be full and *conclusive* evidence, of the fact of escape, and that the service or labor of the persons escaping is due to the party in such record mentioned. And upon the production by the said party of other, and further evidence, if *necessary*, either oral or by affidavit, in addition to what is contained in the said record of the identity of the person escaping, he or she shall be delivered up to the claimant."

The result of this provision, in nearly every case, must be: that the slaveholder, by his own oath, or, what is the same thing, that of his agents, taken wholly *ex parte*, and without being subjected to any close examination, may through the process of a court record in his own State, prepare for use against citizens and residents here, *conclusive* evidence of the fact that a person of such a size, shape, and personal appearance, is his fugitive slave. But the daily experience of every reader must have already convinced him how frequently even entire strangers are mistaken for one another, even by intimate acquaintances of one of the parties. . . .

Now, what security have we, under this law, if the slaveholder's agent, with authenticated record in his pocket, seizes the wrong man? Very little indeed—almost none! Suppose he meets a man in the street, whose appearance tallies, he thinks, with the description given in the record. He seizes him, and hurries him before that commissioner whose perceptions are most likely to be quickened by the difference in his fees. If terror does not, the law does, close the mouth of the poor colored man. He may be an entire stranger in the place, and consequently unable to prove his freedom. He may, it is true, protest, on oath, before the commissioner, that he is a freeman, but the law pays no heed to his oath, though it fabricates conclusive proof out of that of the claimant. If the commissioner also thinks that the description in the record agrees with the appearance of the man before him, he may adjudge the production of any further proof of identity unnecessary, and grant the claimant a certificate that the man is his slave. He may, if he pleases, even refuse to hear a particle of evidence in favor of the victim, supposing the latter so be in a situation where he can procure any, which frequently must happen not to be the case. This certificate, no *matter how corruptly procured,* cannot possibly be legally impeached or set aside in any way. The law declares that it shall be *conclusive* evidence of the right of the claimant to remove the alleged slave, and shall prevent all molestation of the claimant "by any process issued by any court, judge, magistrate or other persons whomsoever." The writ of habeas corpus—the writ of personal replevin—the right of trial by jury—all fall powerless before this "certificate," thus "summarily" procured. The State is bound to protect its citizens, and yet there is no process known to the law which can avail the victim. Thus completely is the liberty of any citizen of this State placed at the mercy of any one corrupt or careless commissioner!

Suppose one of the many colored seamen and stewards (our own freeborn citizens) who have been, agreeably to Southern law, sold into slavery for life in Charleston and other Southern ports, for venturing to exercise the right guaranteed to them by the Constitution, should escape from slavery, and once more breathe the free air of Massachusetts. There is not sufficient power in all the commonwealth legally to prevent that man from being torn from the very spot of his birth, under the provisions of this law, and taken back to slavery! The master would come here with the authenticated record which would constitute *conclusive* evidence of his slavery and escape, and not even the testimony of the mother who bore him, of his wife and children, singly or combined, would shake in the slightest degree the conclusive character of the record. The identity of the man would be beyond doubt. It would be beyond all doubt that he was really a freeman. Even the commissioner might believe him to have been a native of this State; and yet, under the provisions of this law, we could not protect him from being carried back to slavery! Our laws would be powerless! Whoever had the manliness to endeavor to aid him to escape, would expose himself to a fine of $1,000 and six months imprisonment, and perhaps to a further claim of $1,000, by way of civil damages to the claimant. It is possible that public opinion might be powerful enough to avail him, but it would avail him only, by trampling the law under foot. And this is not the kind of protection or the liberty of the citizen, which our State Constitution speaks of when it declares that each individual has a right to be protected by society in the enjoyment of his liberty, according to standing laws. Even this kind of protection, which public opinion might offer, the law of Congress guards against, as far as possible. In case the claimant makes affidavit that he has reason to apprehend a rescue by force, before he can take the fugitive beyond the limits of the State in which the arrest is made, it is made the duty of the officer to retain custody of the fugitive, and remove him to the State from whence he fled; and to do this, he is authorised to employ at the expense of the United States, such a number of men as will be sufficient to overcome any rescuing force which may be brought.

Such are some of the legal objections which may be brought

against this law. As we have seen, a regard for the fundamental principles of the Constitution, for the self-evident truths of the Declaration of Independence, required Congress, when enacting a law on this subject, jealously to guard the rights of citizens of the free States. Not only has Congress not done this, but it has passed a law, which places at the sole discretion of any one of a number of interested men, the liberty of any man in the Commonwealth, and which deprives the Commonwealth of all power to protect, in any way except by force of arms, the liberty of its own admitted citizens; a law which tramples under foot long acknowledged and fundamental principles of civil liberty, and those legal rules of evidence, the application of which the experience of centuries has demonstrated to be necessary to protect the personal rights of the individual.

But there are other and far higher and more important objections to this law, and the clause of the Constitution under which it is framed, than any or all of those which have been alluded to. Even if we could be perfectly sure that none but those who are legally slaves would be returned to bondage—even if it was capable of demonstration, that under this law and constitutional provision, the rights of every free citizen would be protected—still, it would be morally wrong to support these laws. Slaveholding is always wrong. It is wrong to hold any man in slavery. It is wrong to return or aid in returning a fugitive slave. These things are wrong—the Constitution of the United States and law of 1850 to the contrary notwithstanding. Not all the constitutions and laws of the universe can make wrong in the slightest degree right. No one hesitates to deny the right of any one to hold us in slavery. Every one admits that if we were slaves, it would be right to escape if we could, and wrong for any one to force us back into slavery. But if it is wrong for any one to enslave us, or to force us back into slavery, it is just as great a wrong for us to enslave any one else, or to aid in returning any one else to slavery. The soul of each man responds to the laws of God—"Do unto others as ye would have them do unto you"—"Thou shalt love thy neighbor as thyself"—and the slave who is toiling on a Southern plantation, and the slave who has manfully compassed his escape, are no less our neighbors than the friend whom we have known and loved from boyhood. God is the common Father of us all. All men, black as well as white, are brethren.

We cannot bring ourselves to believe that the Old Bay State is to become a hunting-ground for slaves. We will not believe that Massachusetts freemen will lend their aid to this monstrous inhumanity, until sad experience has demonstrated the fact. Who is there who is so heartless as not to be willing to succor and assist the fugitives, William and Ellen Craft? Where shall we find the man with soul so dead as to be willing to seize the heroic woman, Betsey Blakeley, who, concealed on board ship, escaped from Wilmington, North Carolina. Whose house and purse would not be opened to afford her shelter and protection against the slavehunter? No! The law cannot be enforced in Massachusetts! It is contrary to the moral sense of the community, and the community will repudiate it. "Pass enactments," says the earnest-souled Henry Ward Beecher, "enough to fill all the archives of the Senate, and your slave-catcher shall not budge an inch faster than he now does in the North. Every village will spurn him. Every yeoman along the valleys will run the slave, and trip the shameless hunter. Bread and shelter, protection and direction will be the slave's portion north of Mason and Dixon's line, with more certainty and effect every year that elapses until the day of emancipation." "It will be so, because, since the world began, the sympathies of common men have been with the weak and oppressed. In that sympathy, they have conformed to the fundamental law of humanity, which lies deeper in the consciousness of honest men than any national compact, can ever go. Man cannot plant parchments in deep as God plants principles. The Senate of the United States is august; and such men as lead her counsels are men of might. But no man, and no Senate of men, when once the eyes of a community are open to a question of humanity, can reason and enact them back again to a state of indifference, and still less can they enlist them along with the remorseless hunters of human flesh. And of all the very men who will justify Mr. Webster's adhesion to the South, if a trembling woman, far spent with travel and want, holding her babe to her bare bosom, true in her utmost misery to motherhood, should timidly beg a morsel of bread, a place to sleep, or a night's hiding-place from a swift pursuer—is there one of them all who would hesitate what to do? Is there a New England village that would not vomit out the wretch that should dare harm the slave mother? There are thousands of merchants who will say Mr. Webster is right, who

the next moment will give a fugitive slave a dollar to speed on
with! There are thousands who will say we ought to stick to the
Constitution, who, when the case comes, would sooner cut their
right hand off than be a party to a slave's recovery."

We cannot refrain from quoting one other extract from the same
writer:—

"If the compromises of the Constitution include requisitions
which violate Humanity, I will not be bound by them. Not even
the Constitution shall make me unjust. If my patriotic sires
confederated in my behalf, that I should maintain that instrument
so I will, to the utmost bounds of Right. But who, with power
which even God, denies to Himself, shall by compact foreordain
me to the commission of inhumanity and injustice? I disown the
act. I repudiate the obligation. Never while I have breath will I
help any official miscreant in his base errand of recapturing a
fellow-man for bondage. And may my foot palsy, and my right
hand forget her cunning. If I ever become so untrue to mercy and
to religion as not, by all the means in my power, to give aid and
succor to every man whose courageous fight tells me that he is
worthy of liberty! If asked, what then becomes of the Constitution,
I reply by asking what becomes of God's Constitution of Humanity, if you give back a slave to the remorseless man of servitude. I
put Constitution against Constitution—God's against man's.
Where they agree, they are doubly sacred. Where they differ, my
reply to all questioners—but especially to all timid Christian
scruples—is in the language of Peter: "Whether it be right, in the
sight of God, to hearken unto you, more than unto God, judge
ye!"

Freemen of Massachusetts! Followers of Christ, the Redeemer!
Believe in a higher law than that of man, even the unchangeable
law of God! The hour has come to prove your unfaltering
attachment to liberty—the sincerity of your religious profession—
that you are not atheistical in heart! As citizens, it is your
prerogative to question the constitutionality of any enactment of
Congress, and, in case you are convinced of its illegality, to contest
it, as such, till a final decision be made by the rightful judicatory.
As moral and religious men, you cannot obey an immoral and
irreligious statute, whether it be constitutional or otherwise,
without forfeiting your character, and committing gross impiety.

The edict of Nebuchadnezzar setting up the golden image to be worshipped, on pain of the rebellious being cast into the den of lions, was just as obligatory as is the fugitive slave law of Congress. This law is to be denounced, resisted, disobeyed, at all hazards. Its denunciation on Massachusetts soil must be so emphatic and universal, that no slave hunter will dare to make his appearance among us, and no officer of the government presume to give any heed to it. The religious or political journal that refuses to record its protest against the law must be marked, exposed, and held up to popular abhorrence. In every city, town, and village, the clergy, of all denominations, should be respectfully requested by deputation or letter, to arraign the law from the pulpit as inhuman and immoral, and therefore null and void; and, should any shrink from the performance of a duty so clearly obligatory, let their names be published to the world, and handed down to posterity. Let a vigilance committee be appointed in every place, whose duty it shall be to succor and help in every way, the fugitive slave. Let those who exercise the elective franchise send up such senators and respresentatives to the next Legislature as will be ready to give official expression to the deep detestation of the law of Congress which pervades the Commonwealth. But in mind, that laws which are contrary to public opinion are dead, though living on the statue book.

To his undying infamy, one of the representatives in Congress from this State SAMUEL A. ELIOT, of Boston—voted for this cruel, illegal, unchristian enactment! It was the vote of one recreant to justice, humanity, and honor; and however, a proud, corrupt, heartless aristocracy in the city may seek to screen him from condemnation, the people of the Commonwealth will never forget his base servility to the Slave Power.

In conclusion—though at the present session of Congress, the cause of liberty has been most shamefully betrayed, there is no real ground for. . .dismay or discouragement. "The triumphing of the wicked is short." The revolution which has for twenty years been steadily going on, is not to be stayed by a fictitious victory or specious compromise, but shall actively accomplish its work in due time. . . .

9 FROM   *Wendell Phillips*
Under the Flag, 1861

Although abolitionists opposed civil authority at the beginning of the 1850's, by the end of the decade they were beginning to perceive signs of hope for the slave even from trends in political life. And with the election of Abraham Lincoln, the secession of the South, and the eventual call to arms, abolitionists found themselves in a strange position. They now did not so much oppose public authority as prod it to do more, with some expectation of mild success. There was a genuine sense of accomplishment, perhaps, even of victory, as they began to realize that the South's rash move for independence to keep its slaves could be transformed into a crusade by the North to free them. Wendell Phillips in this selection reveals the abolitionists' knowledge of the way in which civil "convulsions" had been and could still be used to achieve advances in civil rights. This speech was delivered in Boston's Music Hall, April 21, 1861 from a platform adorned with the American flag, an identification with national symbols that radical abolitionists were willing to make only after the South seceded. It seemed to them that finally the United States could truly say it stood for justice and liberty.

Therefore thus saith the Lord: Ye have not hearkened unto me in pro claiming liberty every one to his brother, and every man to his neighbor: behold, I proclaim a liberty for you, saith the Lord, to the sword, to the pestilence, and to the famine. Jer. XXXIV. . .17.

Many times this winter, here and elsewhere, I have counselled peace, urged, as well as I knew how, the expediency of acknowledging a Southern Confederacy, and the peaceful separation of these thirty-four States. One of the journals announces to you that I come here this morning to retract those opinions. No, not one of them! [Applause.] I need them all,—every word I have spoken this winter,—every act of twenty-five years of my life, to

SOURCE. Wendell Phillips, *Speeches, Lectures and Letters,* Boston, 1894.

make the welcome I give this war hearty and hot. Civil war is a momentous evil. It needs the soundest, most solemn justification. I rejoice before God to-day for every word that I have spoken counselling peace; but I rejoice also with an especially profound gratitude, that now, the first time in my antislavery life, I speak under the stars and stripes, and welcome the tread of Massachusetts men marshalled for war. [Enthusiastic cheering.] No matter what the past has been or said; to-day the slave asks God for a sight of this banner, and counts it the pledge of his redemption. [Applause.] Hitherto it may have meant what you thought, or what I did; to-day it represents sovereignty and justice. [Renewed applause.] The only mistake that I have made, was in supposing Massachusetts wholly choked with cotton-dust and cankered with gold. [Loud cheering.] The South thought her patience and generous willingness for peace were cowardice; to-day shows the mistake. She has been sleeping on her arms since '83, and the first cannon-shot brings her to her feet with the war-cry of the Revolution on her lips. [Loud cheers.] Any man who loves either liberty or manhood must rejoice at such an hour. [Applause.]

. Let me tell you the path by which I at least have trod my way up to this conclusion. I do not acknowledge the motto, in its full significance, "Our country, right or wrong." If you let it trespass on the domain of morals it is knavish. But there is a full, broad sphere for loyalty; and no war-cry ever stirred a generous people that had not in it much of truth and right. It is sublime, this rally of a great people to the defence of what they think their national honor! A "noble and puissant nation rousing herself like a strong man from sleep, and shaking her invincible locks." Just now, we saw her "reposing, peaceful and motionless; but at the call of patriotism, she ruffles, as it were, her swelling plumage, collects her dormant thunders."

But how do we justify this last appeal to the God of battles? Let me tell you how I do. I have always believed in the sincerity of Abraham Lincoln. You have heard me express my confidence in it every time I have spoken from this desk. I only doubted sometimes whether he were really the head of the government. To-day he is at any rate Commander-in-chief.

The delay in the action of government has doubtless been necessity, but policy also. Traitors within and without made it hesitate to move till it had tried the machine of government just given it. But delay was wise, as it matured a public opinion definite, decisive, and ready to keep step to the music of the government march. The very postponement of another session of Congress till July 4th plainly invites discussion,—evidently contemplates the ripening of public opinion in the interval. Fairly to examine public affairs, and prepare a community wise to co-operate with the government, is the duty of every pulpit and every press.

Plain words, therefore, now, before the nation goes mad with excitement, is every man's duty. Every public meeting in Athens was opened with a curse on any one who should not speak what he really thought. "I have never defiled my conscience from fear or favor to my superiors," was part of the oath every Egyptian soul was supposed to utter in the Judgment-Hall of Osiris, before admission to heaven. Let us show to-day a Christian spirit as sincere and fearless. No mobs in this hour of victory, to silence those whom events have not converted. We are strong enough to tolerate dissent. That flag which floats over press or mansion at the bidding of a mob, disgraces both victor and victim.

All winter long, I have acted with that party which cried for peace. The antislavery enterprise to which I belong started with peace written on its banner. We imagined that the age of bullets was over; that the age of ideas had come; that thirty millions of people were able to take a great question, and decide it by the conflict of opinions; that, without letting the ship of state founder, we could lift four millions of men into Liberty and Justice. We thought that if your statesmen would throw away personal ambition and party watchwords, and devote themselves to the great issue, this might be accomplished. To a certain extent it has been. The North has answered to the call. Year after year, event by event, has indicated the rising education of the people,—the readiness for a higher moral life, the calm, self-poised confidence in our own convictions that patiently waits—like master for a pupil— for a neighbor's conversion. The North has responded to the call of that peaceful, moral intellectual agitation which the antislavery idea has initiated. Our mistake, if any, has been that we counted too much on the intelligence of the masses, on the honesty and wisdom of statesmen as a class. Perhaps we did not give weight enough to the fact we saw, that this nation is made up of different ages; not homogeneous, but a mixed mass of different centuries. The North *thinks*,—can appreciate argument,—is the nineteenth century,—hardly any struggle left in it but that between the working class and the money-kings. The South *dreams*,—it is the thirteenth and fourteenth century,—baron and serf,—noble and slave. Jack Cade and Wat Tyler loom over its horizon, and the serf, rising, calls for another Thierry to record his struggle. There the fagot still burns which the Doctors of the Sorbonne called, ages ago, "the best light to guide the erring." There men are tortured for opinions, the only punishment the Jesuits were willing their pupils should look on. This is, perhaps, too flattering a picture of the South. Better call her, as Sumner does, "the Barbarous States." Our struggle, therefore, is between barbarism and civilization. Such can only be settled by arms. [Prolonged cheering.] The government has waited until its best friends almost suspected its courage or its integrity; but the cannon shot against Fort Sumter has opened the only door out of this hour. There were but two. One was compromise; the other was battle. The integrity of the North closed the first; the generous forbearance of nineteen States closed the other. The South opened this with cannon-shot, and Lincoln shows himself at the door. [Prolonged and enthusiastic cheering.] The war, then, is not aggressive, but in self defence, and Washington has become the Thermopylae of Liberty and Justice. [Applause.] Rather than surrender that Capital, cover every square foot of it with a living body [loud cheers]; crowd it with a million of men, and empty every bank vault at the North to pay the cost. [Renewed cheering.] Teach the world once for all, that North America belongs to the Stars and Stripes, and under them no man shall wear a chain.[Enthusiastic cheering.] In the whole of this conflict, I have looked only at Liberty,—only at the slave. Perry entered the battle of the Lakes with "DON'T GIVE UP THE SHIP!" floating from the masthead of the Lawrence. When with his fighting flag he left her crippled, heading north, and, mounting the deck of the Niagara, turned her bows due west, he did all for one all the same purpose,—to rake the decks of the foe. Steer north or west, acknowledge secession or cannonade it, I care not which; but "Proclaim liberty throughout all the land unto all the inhabitants thereof." [Loud cheers.]

I said, civil war needs momentous and solemn justification. Europe, the world, may claim of us, that, before we blot the nineteenth century by an appeal to arms, we shall exhaust every concession, try every means to keep the peace; otherwise, an appeal to the God of battles is an insult to the civilization of our age; it is confession that our culture and our religion are superficial, if not a failure. I think that the history of the nation and of the government both is an ample justification to our own times and to history for this appeal to arms. I think the South is all wrong, and the administration is all right. [Prolonged cheering.] Let me tell you why. For thirty years the North has exhausted conciliation and compromise. They have tried every expedient, they have relinquished every right, they have sacrificed every interest, they have smothered keen sensibility to national honor, and Northern weight and supremacy in the Union; have forgotten they were the majority in numbers and in wealth, in education and strength; have left the helm of government and the dictation of policy to the Southern States. For all this, the conflict waxed closer and hotter. The administration which preceded this was full of traitors and thieves. It allowed the arms, ships, money, military stores of the North to be stolen with impunity. Mr. Lincoln took office, robbed of all the means to defend the Constitutional rights of the government. He offered to withdraw from the walls of Sumter everything but the flag. He allowed secession to surround it with the strongest forts which military science could build. The North offered to meet in convention her sister States, and arrange the terms of peaceful separation. Strength and right yielded everything,—they folded their hands, waited the returning reason of the mad insurgents. Week after week elapsed, month after month went by, waiting for the sober second-thought of two millions and a half of people. The world saw the sublime sight of nineteen millions of wealthy, powerful, united citizens, allowing their flag to be insulted, their rights assailed, their sovereignty defied and broken in pieces, and yet waiting, with patient, brotherly, magnanimous kindness, until insurrection, having spent its fury, should reach out its hand for a peace arrangement. Men began to call it cowardice, on the one hand; and we, who watched closely the crisis, feared that this effort to be magnanimous would demoralize the conscience and the courage of the North. We were afraid that, as the hour went by, the virtue of the people, white-heat as it stood on the fourth day of March, would be cooled by the temptations, by the suspense, by the want and suffering which it was feared would stalk from the Atlantic to the valley of the Mississippi. We were afraid the government would wait too long, and find at last, that instead of a united people, they were deserted, and left alone to meet the foe.

All this time, the South knew, recognized, by her own knowledge of Constitutional questions, that the government could not advance one inch toward acknowledging secession; that when Abraham Lincoln swore to support the Constitution and laws of the United States, he was bound to die under the flag on Fort Sumter, if necessary. [Loud applause.] They knew, therefore, that the call on the administration to acknowledge the Commissioners of the Confederacy was a delusion and a swindle. I know the whole argument for secession. Up to a certain extent, I accede to it. But no administration that is not traitor can acknowledge secession until we are hopelessly beaten in fair fight. [Cheers.] The right of a State to secede, under the Constitution of the United States,—it is an absurdity; and Abraham Lincoln knows nothing, has a right to know nothing, but the Constitution of the United States. [Loud cheers.] The right of a State to secede, as a revolutionary right, is undeniable; but it is the nation which is to recognize that; and the nation offered, at the suggestion of Kentucky, to meet the question in full convention. The offer was declined. The government and the nation, therefore, are all right. [Applause.] They are right on constitutional law; they are right on the principles of the Declaration of Independence. [Cheers.]

Let me explain this more fully, for this reason; because—and I thank God for it, every American should be proud of it—you cannot maintain a war in the United States of America against a constitutional or a revolutionary right. The people of these States have too large brains and too many ideas to fight blindly,—to lock horns like a couple of beasts in the sight of the world. [Applause.] Cannon think in this nineteenth century; and you must put the North in the right,—wholly, undeniably, inside of the Constitution and out of it,—before you can justify her in the face of the world; before you can pour Massachusetts like an avalanche through the streets of Baltimore, [great cheering] and carry Lexington on the 19th of April south of Mason and Dixon's line. [Renewed cheering.] Let us take an honest pride in the fact that our Sixth Regiment made a way for itself through Baltimore, and were first to reach the threatened Capital. In this war Massachusetts has a right to be the first in the field.

I said I knew the whole argument for secession. Very briefly let me state the points. No government provides for its own death; therefore there can be no constitutional right to secede. But there is a revolutionary right. The Declaration of Independence establishes, what the heart of every American acknowledges, that the people—mark you THE PEOPLE!—have always an inherent, paramount, inalienable right to change their governments, whenever they think—whenever *they* think—that it will minister to their happiness. That is a revolutionary right. Now, how did South Carolina and Massachusetts come into the Union? They came into it by a convention representing the people. South Carolina alleges that she has gone out by convention. So far, right. She says that when the *people* take the State rightfully out of the Union, the right to forts and national property goes with it. Granted. She says, also, that it is no matter that we bought Louisiana of France, and Florida of Spain. No bargain made, no money paid, betwixt us and France or Spain, could rob Florida or Louisiana of her right to remodel her government whenever the people found it would be for their happiness. So far, right. THE PEOPLE,—Mark you! South Carolina presents herself to the administration at Washington, and says "There is a vote of my convention, that I go out of the Union." "I cannot see you," says Abraham Lincoln. [Loud cheers.] "As President, I have no eyes but constitutional eyes; I cannot see you." [Renewed cheers.] He could only say, like Speaker Lenthal before Charles the First, "I have neither eyes to see nor tongue to speak but as the Constitution is pleased to direct me, whose servant I am." He was right. But Madison said, Hamilton said, the Fathers said, in 1789, "No man but an enemy of liberty will ever stand on technicalities and forms, when the essence is in question." Abraham Lincoln could not see the Commissioners of South Carolina, but the North could; the nation could; and the nation responded, "If you want a Constitutional secession, such as you claim, but which I repudiate, I will waive forms: let us meet in convention, and we will arrange it." [Applause.] Surely, while one claims a right within the Constitution, he may, without dishonor or inconsistency, meet in convention, even if finally refusing to be bound by it. To decline doing so is only evidence of intention to provoke war. Everything under the instrument may be changed by a national convention. The South says, "No!" She says, "If you don't allow me the Constitutional right, I claim the revolutionary right." The North responds, "When you have torn the Constitution into fragments, I recognize the right of The People of South Carolina to model their government. Yes, I recognize the right of the three hundred and eighty-four thousand white men, and four hundred and eighty-four thousand black men to model their Constitution. Show me one that they have adopted, and I will recognize the revolution. [Cheers.] But the moment you tread outside of the Constitution, the black man is not three fifths of a man—he is a whole one." [Loud cheering.], Yes, the South has the right of revolution; the South has a right to model her government; and the moment she shows us four million of black votes thrown even against it, and balanced by five million of other votes, I will acknowledge the Declaration of Independence is complied with [loud applause],—that the PEOPLE south of Mason and Dixon's line have remodelled their government to suit themselves; and our function is only to recognize it.

Further than this, we should have the right to remind them, in the words of our Declaration of Independence, that "government long established are not to be changed for light and transient causes," and that, so long as government fulfils the purposes for which it was made,—the liberty and happiness of the people,—no one section has the right capriciously to make changes which destroy joint interests, advantages bought by common toil and sacrifice, and which division necessarily destroys. Indeed, we should have the right to remind them that no faction, in what has been recognized as one nation, can claim, by any law, the right of revolution to set up or to preserve a system which the common conscience of mankind stamps as wicked and infamous. The law of nations is only another name for the common sense and average conscience of mankind. It does not allow itself, like a county court, to be hookwinked by parchments or confused by technicalities. In its vocabulary, the right of revolution means the right of the people to protect themselves, not the privilege of tyrants to tread under foot good laws, and claim the world's sympathy in riveting weakened chains.

I say the North had a right to assume these positions. She did not. She had a right to ignore revolution until these conditions were complied with; but she did not. She waived it. In obedience to the advice of Madison, to the long history of her country's forbearance, to the magnamimity of nineteen States, she waited; she advised the government to wait. Mr. Lincoln, in his inaugural, indicated that this would be the wise course. Mr. Seward hinted it in his speech in New York. The London Times bade us remember the useless war of 1776, and take warning against resisting the principles of popular sovereignty. The Tribune, whose unflinching fidelity and matchless ability make it in this fight "the white plume of Navarre," has again and again avowed its readiness to waive forms and go into convention. We have waited. We said, "Anything for peace." We obeyed the magnanimous statesmanship of John Quincy Adams. Let me read you his advice, given at the "Jubilee of the Constitution," to the New York Historical Society, in the year 1839. He says, recognizing this right of the *people* of a State,—mark you, not a State: the Constitution in this matter knows no States; the right of revolution knows no States: it knows only THE PEOPLE. Mr. Adams says;—

"The PEOPLE of each State in the Union have a right to secede from the confederated Union itself.

"Thus stands the RIGHT. But the indissoluble link of union between the people of the several States of this confederated nation is, after all, not in the *right,* but in the *heart.*

"If the day should ever come (may Heaven avert it!) when the affections of the people of these States shall be alienated from each other, when the fraternal spirit shall give way to cold indifference, or collisions of interest shall fester into hatred, the bands of political association will not long hold together parties no longer attracted by the magnetism of conciliated interests and kindly sympathies; and far better will it be for the people of the disunited States to part in friendship from each other, than to be held together by constraint. Then will be the time for reverting to the precedents which occurred at the formation and adoption of the Constitution, to form again a more perfect union, by dissolving that which could no longer bind; and to leave the separated parts to be reunited by the law of political gravitation to the centre."

The North said "Amen" to every word of it. They waited. They begged the States to meet them. They were silent when the cannon-shot pierced the flag of the Star of the West. They said

"Amen" when the government offered to let nothing but the bunting cover Fort Sumter. They said "Amen" when Lincoln stood alone, without arms, in a defenseless Capital, and trusted himself to the loyalty and forbearance of thirty-four States.

The South, if the truth be told, *cannot* wait. Like all usurpers, they dare not give time for the people to criticise their power. War and tumult must conceal the irregularity of their civil course, and smother discontent and criticism at the same time. Besides, bankruptcy at home can live out its short term of possible existence only by conquest on land and piracy at sea. And, further, only by war, by appeal to popular frenzy, can they hope to delude the Border States to join them. War is the breath of their life.

To-day, therefore, the question is, by the voice of the South, "Shall Washington or Montgomery own the continent?" And the North says, "From the Gulf to the Pole, the Stars and Stripes shall atone to four millions of negroes whom we have forgotten for seventy years; and, before you break the Union, we will see that justice is done to the slave." [Enthusiastic and long-continued cheer.]

There is only one thing those cannon-shot in the harbors of Charleston settled,—that there never can be a compromise. [Loud applause.] We Abolitionists have doubted whether this Union really meant justice and liberty. We have doubted the intention of nineteen millions of people. They have said, in answer to our criticism: "We believe that the Fathers meant to establish justice. We believe that there are hidden in the armory of the Constitution weapons strong enough to secure it. We are willing yet to try the experiment. Grant us time." We have doubted, derided the pretence, as we supposed. During these long and weary weeks we have waited to hear the Northern conscience assert its purpose. It comes at last. [An impressive pause.] Massachusetts blood has consecrated the pavements of Baltimore, and those stones are now too sacred to be trodden by slaves. [Loud cheers.]

You and I owe it to those young martyrs, you and I owe it, that their blood shall be the seed of no mere empty triumph, but that the negro shall teach his children to bless them for centuries to come. [Applause.] When Massachusetts goes down to that Carolina fort to put the Stars and Stripes again over its blackened walls [enthusiasm], she will sweep from its neighborhood every institution which hazards their ever bowing again to the palmetto.

[Loud cheers.] All of you may not mean it now. Our fathers did not think in 1775 of the Declaration of Independence. The Long Parliament never thought of the scaffold of Charles the First, when they entered on the struggle; but having begun, they made thorough work. [Cheers.] It is an attribute of the Yankee blood,—slow to fight, and fight once. [Renewed cheers.] It was a holy war, that for Independence: this is a holier and the last,—that for LIBERTY. [Loud applause.]

I hear a great deal about Constitutional liberty. The mouths of Concord and Lexington guns have room only for one word, and that is LIBERTY. You might as well ask Niagara to chant the Chicago Platform, as to say how far war shall go. War and Niagara thunder to a music of their own. God alone can launch the lightnings, that they may go and say, Here we are. The thunderbolts of His throne always abase the proud, lift up the lowly, and execute justice between man and man.

Now let me turn one moment to another consideration. What should the government do? I said, "thorough" should be its maxim. When we fight, we are fighting for justice and an idea. A short war and a rigid one is the maxim. Ten thousand men in Washington! it is only a bloody fight. Five hundred thousand men in Washington, and none dare come there but from the North. [Loud cheers.] Occupy St. Louis with the millions of the West, and say to Missouri, "You cannot go out!" [Applause.] Cover Maryland with a million of the friends of the administration, and say: "We must have our capital within reach. [Cheers.] If you need compensation for slaves taken from you in the convulsion of battle, here it is. [Cheers.] Government is engaged in the fearful struggle to show that '89 meant justice, and there is something better than life, holier than even real and just property, in such an hour as this." And again, we must remember another thing,—the complication of such a struggle as this. Bear with me a moment. We put five hundred thousand men on the banks of the Potomac. Virginia is held by two races, white and black. Suppose those black men flare in our faces the Declaration of Independence. What are we to say? Are we to send Northern bayonets to keep slaves under the feet of Jefferson Davis? [Many voices, "No!" "Never!"] In 1842, Governor Wise of Virginia, the symbol of the South, entered into argument with Quincy Adams, who carried Plymouth Rock to Washington. [Applause.] It was when Joshua Giddings offered his resolution stating his constitutional doctrine that Congress had no right to interfere, in any event, in any way, with the slavery of the Southern States. Plymouth Rock refused to vote for it. Mr. Adams said (substantially): "If foreign war comes, if civil war comes, if insurrection comes, is this beleaguered capital, is this besieged government, to see millions of its subjects in arms, and have no right to break the fetters which they are forging into swords? No; the war power of the government can sweep this institution into the Gulf." [Cheers.] Ever since 1842, that statesman-like claim and warning of the North has been on record, spoken by the lips of her wisest son. [Applause.]

When the South cannonaded Fort Sumter the bones of Adams stirred in his coffin. [Cheers.] And you might have heard him, from that granite grave at Quincy, proclaim to the nation: "The hour has struck! Seize the thunderbolt God has forged for you, and annihilate the system which has troubled your peace for seventy years!" [Cheers.] Do not say this is a cold-blooded suggestion. I hardly ever knew slavery go down in any other circumstances. Only once, in the broad sweep of the world's history, was any nation lifted so high that she could stretch her imperial hand across the Atlantic, and lift by one peaceful word a million of slaves into liberty. God granted that glory only to our mother-land.

You heedlessly expected, and we Abolitionists hoped, that such would be our course. Sometimes it really seemed so, and said confidently, the age of bullets is over. At others the sky lowered so darkly that we felt our only exodus would be one of blood; that, like other nations, our Bastile would fall only before revolution. Ten years ago I asked you, How did French slavery go down? How did the French slave-trade go down? When Napoleon came back from Elba, when his fare hung trembling in the balance, and he wished to gather around him the sympathies of the liberals of Europe, he no sooner set foot in the Tuileries than he signed the edict abolishing the slave-trade, against which the Abolitionists of England and France had protested for twenty years in vain. And the trade went down, because Napoleon felt he must do something to gild the darkening hour of his second attempt to clutch the sceptre of France. How did the slave system go down? When, in 1848, the Provisional Government found itself in the Hotel de Ville, obliged to do something to draw to itself the sympathy and liberal feeling of the French nation, they signed an edict—it was the first from the rising republic—abolishing the death-penalty and slavery. The storm which rocked the vessel of state almost to foundering snapped forever the chain of the French slave. Look, too, at the history of Mexican and South American emancipation; you will find that it was in every instance, I think, the child of convulsion.

That hour has come to us. So stand we to-day. The Abolitionist who will not now cry, when the moment serves, "Up, boys, and at them!" is false to liberty. [Great cheering. A voice, "So is every other man."] Yes, to-day Abolitionist is merged in citizen—in American. Say not it is a hard lesson. Let him who fully knows his own heart and strength, and feels, as he looks down into his child's cradle, that he could stand and see that little nestling borne to slavery, and submit,—let him cast the first stone. But all you, whose blood is wont to stir over Naseby and Bunker Hill, will hold your peace, unless you are ready to cry with me,—*Sic semper tyrannis!* "So may it ever be with tyrants!" [Loud applause.]

Why, Americans, I believe in the might of nineteen millions of people. Yes, I know that what sewing-machines and reaping-machines and ideas and types and school-houses cannot do, the muskets of Illinois and Massachusetts can finish up. [Cheers.] Blame me not that I make everything turn on liberty and the slave. I believe in Massachusetts. I know that free speech, free toil, school-houses, and ballot-boxes are a pyramid on its broadest base. Nothing that does not sunder the solid globe can disturb it. We defy the world to disturb us. [Cheers.] The little errors that dwell upon our surface, we have medicine in our institutions to cure them all. [Applause.]

Therefore there is nothing left for a New England man, nothing but that he shall wipe away the stain which hangs about the toleration of human bondage. As Webster said at Rochester, years and years ago: "If I thought that there was a stain upon the remotest hem of the garment of my country, I would devote my utmost labor to wipe it off." [Cheers.] To-day that call is made upon Massachusetts. That is the reason why I dwell so much on the slavery question. I said I believed in the power of the North to conquer; but where does she get it. I do not believe in the power of the North to subdue two millions and a half of Southernmen, unless she summons justice, the negro, and God to her side [cheers]; and in that battle we are sure of this,—we are sure to rebuild the Union down to the Gulf. [Renewed cheering.] In that battle, with what watchword, with those allies, the thirteen States, and their children will survive,—in the light of the world, a nation which has vindicated the sincerity of the Fathers of '87, that they bore children, and not pedlers, to represent them in the nineteenth century. [Repeated cheers.] But without that,—without that, I know also we shall conquer. Sumter annihilated compromise. Nothing but victory will blot from history that sight of the Stars and Stripes giving place to the palmetto. But without justice for inspiration, without God for our ally, we shall break the Union asunder; we shall be a confederacy, and so will they. This war means one of two things,—Emancipation or Disunion. [Cheers.] Out of the smoke of the conflict there comes that,—nothing else. It is impossible there should come anything else. Now, I believe in the future and permanent union of the races that cover this continent from the pole down to the Gulf. One in race, one in history, one in religion, one in industry, one in thought, we never can be permanently separated. Your path, if you forget the black race, will be over the gulf of Disunion,—years of unsettled, turbulent, Mexican and South American civilization, back through that desert of forty years to the Union which is sure to come.

But I believe in a deeper conscience, I believe in a North more educated than that. I divide you into four sections. The first is the ordinary mass, rushing from mere enthusiasm to

> *A battle whose great aim and scope*
> *They little care to know,*
> *Content, like men-at-arms, to cope*
> *Each with his fronting foe.*

Behind that class stands another, whose only idea in this controversy is sovereignty and the flag. The seaboard, the wealth, the just-converted hunkerism of the country, fill that class. Next to it stands the third element, the people; the cordwainers of Lynn, the farmers of Worcester, the dwellers on the prairie,—Iowa and Wisconsin, Ohio, and Maine,—the broad surface of the people who have no leisure for technicalities, who never studied law, who never had time to read any further into the Constitution than the first two lines,—"Establish *Justice* and secure *Liberty.*" They have waited long enough; they have eaten dirt enough; they have apologized for bankrupt statesmen enough; they have quieted their consciences enough; they have split logic with their Abolition neighbors long enough; they are tired of trying to find a place between the forty-ninth and forth-eighth corner of a constitutional hair [laughter]; and now that they have got their hand on the neck of a rebellious aristocracy, in the name of the PEOPLE, they mean to strangle it. That I believe is the body of the people itself. Side by side with them stands a fourth class,—small active,—the Abolitionists, who thank God, that he has let them see his salvation before they die. [Cheers.]

The noise and dust of the conflict may hide the real question at issue. Europe may think, some of us may, that we are fighting for forms and parchments, for sovereignty and a flag. But really the war is one of opinions: it is Civilization against Barbarism: it is Freedom against Slavery. The cannon-shot against Fort Sumter was the yell of pirates against the DECLARATION OF INDEPEND-ENCE, the war-cry of the North is the echo of that sublime pledge. The South, defying Christianity, clutches its victim. The North offers its wealth and blood in glad atonement for the selfishness of seventy years. The result is as sure as the throne of God. I believe in the possibility of justice, in the certainty of union. Years hence, when the smoke of this conflict clears away, the world will see under our banner all tongues, all creeds, all races,—one brother-hood,—and on the banks of the Potomac, the Genius of Liberty, robed in light, four and thirty stars for her diadem, broken chains under feet, and an olive-branch in her right hand. [Great applause.]

V. Freedom for the Black Man

Freedom for the black man required the freeing of white people from race prejudice. This, the abolitionists attempted to do throughout their entire career. They condemned segregation in public facilities, churches, and schools; they attacked laws that did not allow black Americans to be full citizens; they worked to repeal legislation that made pariahs of blacks; and during the Civil War they prodded public officials into allowing blacks to take up arms to free their enslaved brothers in the South. In the following selections is evidence of the original and continuing concern about the racism that seemed to be so deeply rooted in American life. And yet, also, much effort is not required to discover the stereotypical thinking, the lack of sympathy, the patronizing air, and the ignorance about black people that abolitionists often shared with their opponents. It would be too much to expect of these early reformers that they could suddenly slough off the cultural conditioning that required whites to look on the black man as an inferior human being. The abolitionists were not perfect; they shared many of the prejudices of their society. But they did not believe that the black man should be victimized even by the prejudice of his friends. And it is this determination to fight prejudice that set them apart from their fellow Americans.

10 FROM *Lydia Maria Francis Child*
An Appeal in Favor of That Class of Americans Called Africans

Lydia Maria Francis Child (1802-1880) was a novelist, journalist, and woman of letters who first employed her eloquent pen in the antislavery crusade in 1833. Her husband, David, an abolitionist editor and lawyer, was only one of America's foremost antislavery authors. She read widely and thoroughly before articulating the ideas that formed An Appeal in Favor of That Class of Americans Called Africans. Although not an especially strident statement, the Appeal's reasonableness was not apparent to many of its readers because it was offered in behalf of Africans. For this very reason, many of her friends and associates began to avoid her. A trustee of the Boston Atheneum warned her against presuming to visit the library again; and so many subscriptions to her magazine, The Miscellany, were cancelled that she was forced to quit publishing it. Other readers were more favorably impressed; Wendell Phillips considered the Appeal one of the important influences in his conversion to abolitionism. The following selection is from Chapter VIII of the book, and demonstrates abolitionist opposition to Northern race prejudice as well as to Southern slavery.

VIII. PREJUDICES AGAINST PEOPLE OF COLOR, AND OUR DUTIES IN RELATION TO THIS

While we bestow our earnest disapprobation of the system of slavery, let us not flatter ourselves that we are in reality any better than our brethren of the South. Thanks to our soil and climate, and the early exertions of the Quakers, the *form* of slavery does not exist among us; but the very *spirit* of the hateful and mischievous thing is here in all its strength. The manner in which we use what power we have, gives us ample reason to be grateful that the

SOURCE. Lydia Maria Francis Child, "An Appeal in Favor of That Class of Americans Called Africans," 1833.

nature of our institutions does not intrust us with more. Our prejudice against colored people is even more inveterate than it is at the South. The planter is often attached to his negroes, and lavishes caresses and kind words upon them, as he would on a favorite hound; but our cold-hearted, ignoble prejudice admits of no exception—no intermission.

The Southerners have long continued habit, apparent interest and dreaded danger, to palliate the wrong they do; but we stand without excuse. They tell us that Northern ships and Northern capital have been engaged in this wicked business and the reproach is true. Several fortunes in this city have been made by the sale of negro blood. If these criminal transactions are still carried on, they are done in silence and secrecy, because public opinion has made them disgraceful. But if the free states wished to cherish the system of slavery forever, they could not take a more direct course than they now do. Those who are kind and liberal on all other subjects, unite with the selfish and the proud in their unrelenting efforts to keep the colored population in the lowest state of degradation; and the influence they unconsciously exert over children early infuses into their innocent minds the same strong feelings of contempt.

The intelligent and well-informed have the least share of this prejudice; and when their minds can be brought to reflect upon it, I have generally observed that they soon cease to have any at all. But such a general apathy prevails and the subject is so seldom brought into view, that few are really aware how oppressively the influence of society is made to bear upon this injured class of the community. When I have related facts, that came under my own observation, I have often been listened to with surprise, which gradually increased to indignation. In order that my readers may not be ignorant of the extent of this tyrannical prejudice, I will as briefly as possible state the evidence, and leave them to judge of it, as their hearts and consciences may dictate.

In the first place, an unjust law exists in this Commonwealth, by which marriages between persons of different color is pronounced illegal. I am perfectly aware of the gross ridicule to which I may subject myself by alluding to this particular; but I have lived too long, and observed too much, to be disturbed by the world's mockery. In the first place, the government ought not to be invested with power to control the affections, any more than the consciences of citizens. A man has at least as good a right to choose his wife, as he has to choose his religion. His taste may not suit his neighbors; but so long as his deportment is correct, they have no right to interfere with his concerns. In the second place, this law is a *useless* disgrace to Massachusetts. Under existing circumstances, none but those whose condition in life is too low to be much affected by public opinion, will form such alliances; and they, when they choose to do so, *will* make such marriages, in spite of the law. I know two or three instances where women of the laboring class have been united to reputable, industrious colored men. These husbands regularly bring home their wages, and are kind to their families. If by some of the odd chances, which not unfrequently occur in the world, their wives should become heirs to any property, the children may be wronged out of it, because the law pronounces them illegitimate. And while this injustice exists with regard to *honest*, industrious individuals, who are merely guilty of differing from us in a matter of taste, neither the legislation nor customs of slaveholding States exert their influence against *immoral* connexions.

In one portion of our country this fact is shown in a very peculiar and striking manner. There is a numerous class at New Orleans, called Quateroons, or Quadroons, because their colored blood has for several successive generations been intermingled with the white. The women are much distinguished for personal beauty and gracefulness of motion; and their parents frequently send them to France for the advantages of an elegant education. White gentlemen of the first rank are desirous of being invited to their parties, and often become seriously in love with these fascinating but unfortunate beings. Prejudice forbids matrimony, but universal custom sanctions temporary connexions, to which a certain degree of respectability is allowed, on account of the peculiar situation of the parties. These attachments often continue for years—sometimes for life—and instances are not unfrequent of exemplary constancy and great propriety of deportment.

What eloquent vituperations we should pour forth, if the contending claims of nature and pride produced such a tissue of contradictions in some other country, and not in our own!

There is another Massachusetts law, which an enlightened community would not probably suffer to be carried into execution under any circumstances; but it still remains to disgrace the statutes of this Commonwealth.—It is as follows:

"No African or Negro, other than a subject of the Emperor of Morocco, or a citizen of the United States (proved so by a certificate of the Secretary of State of which he is a citizen,) shall tarry within this Commonwealth longer than two months; and on complaint a justice shall order him to depart in ten days; and if he does not then, the justice may commit such African or Negro to the House of Correction, there to be kept at hard labor; and at the next term of the Court of C. P., he shall be tried, and if convicted of remaining as aforesaid, shall be whipped not exceeding ten lashes; and if he or she shall not then depart such process shall be repeated and punishment inflicted tolies quoties" Stat. 1788, Ch. 54.

An honorable Haytian or Brazilian, who visited this country for business or information, might come under this law, unless public opinion rendered it a mere dead letter.

There is among the colored people an increasing desire for information, and a laudable ambition to be respectable in manners and appearance. Are we not foolish as well as sinful, in trying to repress a tendency so salutary to themselves, and so beneficial to the community? Several individuals of this class are very desirous to have persons of their own color qualified to teach something more than mere reading and writing. But in the public schools, colored children are subject to many discouragements and difficulties; and into the private schools they cannot gain admission. A very sensible and well-informed colored woman in a neighboring town, whose family have been brought up in a manner that excited universal remark and approbation, has been extremely desirous to obtain for her eldest daughter the advantages of a private school; but she has been resolutely repulsed, on account of her complexion. The girl is a very light mulatto, with great modesty and propriety of manners; perhaps no young person in the Commonwealth was less likely to have a bad influence on her associates. The clergyman respected the family, and he remonstrated with the instructor; but while the latter admitted the injustice of the thing, he excused himself saying such a step would occasion the loss of all his white scholars.

In a town adjoining Boston, a well-behaved colored boy was

kept out of the public school more than a year, by vote of the trustees. His mother, having some information herself, knew the importance of knowledge, and was anxious to obtain it for her family. She wrote repeatedly and urgently; and the schoolmaster himself told me that the correctness of her spelling, and the neatness of her handwriting formed a curious contrast with the notes he received from many white parents. At last, this spirited woman appeared before the committee, and reminded them that her husband, having for many years paid taxes as a citizen, had a right to the privileges of a citizen; and if her claim were refused or longer postponed, she declared her determination to seek justice from a higher source. The trustees were, of course, obliged to yield to the equality of the laws, with the best grace they could. The boy was admitted, and made good progress in his studies. Had his mother been too ignorant to know her rights, or too abject to demand them, the lad would have had a fair chance to get a living out of the State as the occupant of a workhouse, or penitentiary.

The attempt to establish a school for African girls at Canterbury, Connecticut, has made too much noise to need a detailed account in this volume. I do not know the lady who first formed the project, but I am told that she is a benevolent and religious woman. It certainly is difficult to imagine any other motives than good ones, for an undertaking so arduous and unpopular. Yet had the Pope himself attempted to establish his supremacy over that commonwealth, he could hardly have been repelled with more determined and angry resistance.—Town meetings were held, the records of which are not highly creditable to the parties concerned. Petitions were sent to the Legislature, beseeching that no African school might be allowed to admit individuals not residing in the town where said school was established; and strange to relate, this law, which makes it impossible to collect a sufficient number of pupils, was sanctioned by the State. A colored girl, who availed herself of this opportunity to gain instruction, was warned out of town and fined for not complying; and the instructress was imprisoned for persevering in her benevolent plan.

It is said, in excuse, that Canterbury will be inundated with vicious characters, who will corrupt the morals of the young men; that such a school will break down the distinctions between black and white; and that marriages between people of different colors will be the probable result. Yet they seem to assume the ground

that colored people *must* always be an inferior and degraded class—
that the prejudice against them *must* be eternal; being deeply
founded in the laws of God and nature.—Finally, they endeavored
to represent the school as one of the *incendiary* proceedings of the
Anti-Slavery Society; and they appeal to the Colonization Society,
as an aggrieved child is wont to appeal to its parent.

The objection with regard to the introduction of vicious
characters into a village, certainly has some force; but are such
persons likely to leave cities for a quiet country town, in search of
moral and intellectual improvement? Is it not obvious that the *best*
portion of the colored class are the very ones to prize such an
opportunity for instruction? Grant that a large proportion of these
unfortunate people *are* vicious—is it not our duty, and of course
our wisest policy, to try to make them otherwise? And what will so
effectually elevate their character and condition, as knowledge? I
beseech you, my countrymen, think of these things wisely, and in
season.

As for intermarriages, if there be such a repugnance between the
two races, founded in the laws of *nature*, me thinks there is a small
reason to dread their frequency.

The breaking down of distinctions in society, by means of
extended information, is an objection which appropriately belongs
to the Emperor of Austria, or the Sultan of Egypt.

I do not know how the affair of Canterbury is *generally* considered; but I have heard individuals of all parties and all opinions
speak of it—and never without merriment or indignation. Fifty
years hence, the *black* laws of Connecticut, will be a greater source
of amusement to the antiquarian, than her famous *blue* laws.

A similar, though less violent opposition arose in consequence of
the attempt to establish a college for colored people at New
Haven. A young colored man, who tried to obtain education at
the Wesleyan college in Middleton, was obliged to relinquish the
attempt on account of the persecution of his fellow students. Some
collegians from the South objected to a colored associate in their
recitations; and those from New England promptly and zealously
joined in the hue and cry. A small but firm party were in favor of
giving the colored man, a chance to pursue his studies without
insult or interruption; and I am told that this manly and
disinterested band were all Southerners. As for those individuals,

who exerted their influence to exclude an unoffending fellow-citizen from privileges which ought to be equally open to all, it is to be hoped that age will make them wiser—and that they will learn, before they die, to be ashamed of a step attended with more important results than usually belong to youthful follies.

* * *

Let us seriously consider what injury a negro college could possibly do us. It is certainly a fair presumption that the scholars would be from the better portion of the colored population; and it is an equally fair presumption that knowledge would improve their characters. There are already many hundreds of colored people in the city of Boston.—In the street they generally appear neat and respectable; and in our houses they do not "come between the wind and our nobility." Would the addition of one or two hundred more even be perceived? As for giving offence to the Southerners by allowing such establishments—they have no right to interfere with our internal concerns, any more than we have with theirs.—Why should they not give up slavery to please us, by the same rule that we must refrain from educating the negroes to please them? If they are at liberty to do wrong, we certainly ought to be at liberty to do right. They may talk and publish as much about us as they please; and we ask for no other influence over them.

* * *

A fierce excitement prevailed, not long since, because a colored man had bought a pew in one of our churches. I heard a very kind-hearted and zealous democrat declare his opinion that "the fellow ought to be turned out by constables, if he dared to occupy the pew he had purchased." Even at the communion-table, the mockery of human pride is mingled with the worship of Jehovah. Again and again have I seen a solitary negro come up to the altar, meekly and timidly, after all the white communicants had retired. One Episcopal clergyman of this city, forms an honorable exception to this remark. When there is room at the alter, Mr.   often makes a signal to the colored members of his church to kneel beside their white brethren; and once, when two white infants and one colored one were to be baptized, and the parents of the latter bashfully lingered far behind the others, he silently rebuked the

unchristian spirit of pride, by first administering the holy ord-
inance to the little dark-skinned child of God.

* * *

[After citing several instances of discrimination against Afro-
Americans on public conveyances, Mrs. Child asks,] Will any
candid person tell my why respectable colored people should not
be allowed to make use of public conveyances, open to all who are
able and willing to pay for the privilege? Those who enter a vessel,
or a stagecoach, cannot expect to select their companions. If they
can afford to take a carriage or boat for themselves, then, and only
then, they have a right to be exclusive. I was lately talking with a
young gentleman on this subject, who professed to have no
prejudice against colored people, except so far as they were
ignorant and vulgar; but still he could not tolerate the idea of
allowing them to enter stages and steam-boats. "Yet, you allow the
same privilege to vulgar and ignorant white men, without a
murmur," I replied; "Pray give a good republican reason why a
respectable colored citizen should be less favored." For want of a
better argument, he said—pardon me, fastidious reader—he implied
that the presence of colored persons was less agreeable than Otto
of Rose, or Eau de Cologne; and this distinction, he urged was
made by God himself. I answered, "Whoever takes his chance in a
public vehicle, is liable to meet with uncleanly white passengers,
whose breath may be redolent with the fumes of American cigars,
or American gin. Neither of these articles have a fragrance
peculiarly agreeable to nerves of delicate organization. Allowing
your argument double the weight it deserves, it is utter nonsense
to pretend that the inconvenience in the case I have supposed is
not infinitely greater. But what is more to the point, do you dine
in a fashionable hotel, do you sail in a fashionable steamboat, do
you sup at a fashionable house, without having negro servants
behind your chair. Would they be any more disagreeable, as
passengers seated in the corner of a stage, or a steam-boat, than as
waiters in such immediate attendance upon your person?"

Stage-drivers are very much perplexed when they attempt to
vindicate the present tyrannical customs; and they usually give up
the point, by saying they themselves have no prejudice against
colored people—they are merely afraid of the public. But stage-
drivers should remember that in a popular government, they, in

common with every other citizen, form a part and position of the
dreaded public.

The gold was never coined for which I would barter my
individual freedom of acting and thinking upon any subject, or
knowingly interfere with the rights of the meanest human being.
The only true courage is that which impels us to do right without
regard to consequences. To fear a populace is as servile as to fear
an emperor. The only salutary restraint is the fear of doing wrong.

* * *

The state of public feeling not only makes it difficult for the
Africans to obtain information, but it prevents them from making
profitable use of what knowledge they have. A colored man,
however intelligent, is not allowed to pursue any business more
lucrative than that of a barber, a shoeblack, or a waiter. These,
and all other employments, are truly respectable, whenever the
duties connected with them are faithfully performed; but it is
unjust that a man should, on account of his complexion, be
prevented from performing more elevated uses in society. Every
citizen ought to have a fair chance to try his fortune in any line of
business, which he thinks he has ability to transact. Why should
not colored men be employed in the manufactories of various
kinds? If their ignorance is an objection, let them be enlightened,
as speedily as possible. If their moral character is not sufficiently
pure, remove the pressure of public scorn, and thus supply them
with motives for being respectable. All this can be done. It merely
requires an earnest wish to overcome a prejudice, which has
"grown with our growth and strengthened with our strength," but
which is in fact opposed to the spirit of our religion and contrary
to the instinctive good feelings of our nature. When examined by
the clear light of reason, it disappears. Prejudices of all kinds have
their strongest holds in the minds of the vulgar and the ignorant.
In a community, so enlightened as our own, they must gradually
melt away under the influence of public discussion. There is no
want of kind feelings and liberal sentiment in the American
people; the simple fact is they have not *thought* upon this subject.—
An active and enterprising community are not apt to concern
themselves about laws and customs, which do not obviously
interfere with their interests or convenience; and various political
and prudential motives have combined to fetter free inquiry in
this direction. Thus we have gone on, year after year,

thoughtlessly sanctioning, by our silence and indifference, evils which our hearts and consciences are far enough from approving.

* * *

Is it asked what can be done? I answer, much, very much, can be effected, if each individual will try to serve the commendation bestowed by our Savior on the woman of old—"She hath done what she could."

The Quakers,—always remarkable for fearless obedience to the inward light of conscience,—early gave an example worthy of being followed. At their annual meeting in Pennsylvania in 1688, many individuals urged the incompatibility of slavery, and Christianity; and their zeal continued until, in 1776, all Quakers who bought or sold a slave, or refused to emancipate those they already owned, were excluded from communion with the society. Had it not been for the early exertions of these excellent people, the fair and flourishing State of Pennsylvania might now, perchance, be withering under the effects of slavery. To this day, the Society of Friends, both in England and America, omit no opportunity, public or private, of discountenancing this bad system; and the Methodists (at least in England) have earnestly labored in the same glorious cause.

The famous Anthony Benezet, a Quaker in Philadelphia, has left us a noble example of what may be done for conscience' sake. Being a teacher, he took effectual care that his scholars should have ample knowledge and christian impressions concerning the nature of slavery; he caused articles to be inserted in the almanacs likely to arrest public attention upon the subject; he talked about it, and wrote letters about it; he published and distributed tracts at his own expense; if any person was going a journey, his first thought was how he could make him instrumental in favor of his benevolent purposes; he addressed a petition to the Queen for the suppression of the slave-trade; and another to the good Countess of Huntingdon beseeching that the rice and indigo plantations belonging to the orphan-house, which she had endowed near Savannah, in Georgia, might not be cultivated by those who encouraged the slave trade; he took care to increase the comforts and elevate the character of the colored people within his influence; he zealously promoted the establishment of an African school, and devoted much of the last two years of his life to personal attendance upon his pupils. By fifty years of constant industry he had amassed a small fortune; and this was left, after the decease of his widow, to the support of the African school.

Similar exertions, though on a less extensive scale, were made by the late excellent John Kenrick, of Newton, Mass. For more than thirty years the constant object of his thoughts, and the chief purpose of his life, was the abolition of slavery. His earnest conversation aroused many other minds to think and act upon the subject. He wrote letters, inserted articles in the newspapers, gave liberal donations, and circulated pamphlets at his own expense.

Cowper contributed much to the cause when he wrote the "Negro's Complaint," and thus excited the compassion of his numerous readers. Wedgewood aided the work, when he caused cameos to be struck, representing a kneeling African in chains, and thus made even capricious fashion an avenue to the heart. Clarkson assisted by patient investigation of evidence; and Fox and Wilberforce by eloquent speeches. Mungo Park gave his powerful influence by the kind and liberal manner in which he always represented the Africans. The Duchess of Devonshire wrote verses and caused them to be set to music; and wherever these lines were sung, some hearts were touched in favor of the oppressed. This fascinating woman made even her far-famed beauty serve in the cause of benevolence. Fox was returned for Parliament through her influence, and she is said to have procured more than one vote, by allowing the yeomanry of England to kiss her beautiful cheek.

All are not able to do so much as Anthony Benezet and John Kenrick have done; but we can all do something. We can speak kindly and respectfully of colored people upon all occasions; we can repeat to our children such traits as are honorable in their character and history; we can avoid making odious caricatures of negroes; we can teach boys that it is unmanly and contemptible to insult an unfortunate class of people by the vulgar outcry of "Nigger!—Nigger!"—Even Mahmoud of Turkey rivals us in liberality—for he long ago ordered a fine to be levied upon those who called a Christian a dog; and in his dominions the *prejudice* is so great that a Christian must be a degraded being. A residence in Turkey might be profitable to those Christians who patronize the eternity of prejudice; it would afford all an opportunity of testing the goodness of the rule, by showing how it works both ways.

If we are not able to contribute to African schools, or do not choose to do so, we can at least refrain from opposing them. If it be disagreeable to allow colored people the same rights and privileges as other citizens, we can do with our prejudice, what most of us often do with better feelings—we can conceal it.

Our almanacs and newspapers can fairly show both sides of the question; and if they lean to either party, let it not be to the strongest. Our preachers can speak of slavery, as they do of other evils. Our poets can find in this subject abundant room for sentiment and pathos. Our orators (provided they do not want office) may venture an allusion to our *in*-"glorious institutions."

The union of individual influence produces a vast amount of moral force, which is not the less powerful because it is often unperceived. A mere change in the *direction* of our efforts, without any increased exertion, would in the course of a few years, produce an entire revolution of public feeling. This slow but sure way of doing good is almost the only means by which benevolence can effect its purpose.

Sixty thousand petitions have been addressed to the English parliament on the subject of slavery, and a large number of them were signed by women. The same steps here would be, with one exception, useless and injudicious; because the general government has no control over the legislatures of individual States. But the District of Columbia forms an exception to this rule.— *There* the United States have power to abolish slavery; and it is the duty of the citizens to petition year after year, until a reformation is effected. But who will present remonstrances against slavery? The Hon. John Q. Adams was intrusted with fifteen petitions for the abolition of slavery in the District of Columbia; yet, clearly as that gentleman sees and defines the pernicious effects of the system, he offered the petitions only to protest against them! Another petition to the same effect intrusted to another Massachusetts representative, was never noticed at all. "Brutus is an honorable man:—So are thay all—all honorable men." Nevertheless, there is, in this popular government, a subject on which it is *impossible* for the people to make themselves heard.

By publishing this book I have put my mite into the treasury. The expectation of displeasing all classes has not been unaccompanied with pain. But it has been strongly impressed upon my mind that it was a duty to fulfill this task; and earthly considerations should never stifle the voice of conscience.

11 FROM　　　　　　　*Wendell Phillips*
The Proclamation, How To Make It Efficient

Many such mites, as Mrs. Child called her book, were put in the antislavery treasury, and eventually they became a wealth of propaganda that informed the American people about slavery and race prejudice. This information did not mean, however, that when the Civil War finally came, the black man would automatically be freed. Abolitionists were increasingly angry with Abraham Lincoln for not making the war a crusade against slavery. As late as August 1, 1862, Wendell Phillips was excoriating the president as a "first rate second-rate man" who acted as if he were more concerned for the South's interests than for those of the black man. It was with considerable joy and some surprise, therefore, that abolitionists read Lincoln's preliminary Emancipation Proclamation on September 22, 1862. They realized the conditional nature of the document, but they were nevertheless encouraged. And when the Proclamation was finally issued on January 1, 1863, abolitionists were jubilant. Although the emancipation applied only to areas in rebellion against the United States, it was believed to be a significant change in the government's war aims and, therefore, its relationship to black people everywhere. It was with this in mind that Wendell Phillips mounted the speaker's platform at the Music Hall in Boston on Sunday, January 4, 1863, to applaud the Proclamation and to explain to his fellow abolitionists what it meant.

What can I say, friends, worthy of such an hour and such an audience! For a hundred days, your ears have listened to every word from Washington—your hearts have been full of this Proclamation. Every possible phase of thought must have been anticipated; every hope, every fear canvassed. What can mortal lips add to the anxiety or to the joy of twenty millions of people? This is the second time that I have spoken under the United States

SOURCE. Wendell Phillips, "The Proclamation, How To Make It Efficient," *The Liberator*, January 9, 1863.

banner. Nearly two years ago, for the first time in my life, I was
overshadowed by it in this hall, when the first gun—the first slave
gun—was fired at Sumter. Twenty months or more have rolled
away, and for the first time, that slave gun is answered. The
President's Proclamation is the retort of Freedom upon the first
onset of the slave system against our nationality. Fitting it is that
at last, today, we should surround ourselves again with the
emblems of the Union. During these long and weary months, the
hand of the people has groped its way—tireless, but still groping
amid the delays of law givers, the chicanery of cabinets, the
prejudices of the President until at last it grasps the hilt of the
weapon firmly, and unsheaths the glittering blade. What the result
is to be, God only knows. Our rejoicing today is that at last the
nation unsheaths its sword, and announces its determined purpose
to be a nation. The French minister said "I know you have the
power; I know as well, that you will never dare to use it." To-day
America answers to that taunt. She takes her first step in the
pathway of using the right which belongs to her.

What vast progress in these two years! What immense progress!
And all of it the PEOPLE'S progress. My hope today [is] in reading
that Proclamation because I look upon it as wrung by the
determined heart of the masses from the reluctance of [their]
leaders. I say, the people are fighting this battle; and this
Proclamation—the first step, only the first step in the direction of a
Union that every man may rightfully love and die for—this
Proclamation is the reluctant gift of the leaders to the masses. Two
years of mere claim on the part of the people has driven the
Government to this point. I believe in success, because I believe
that in another year, that some determined heart of the people will
drive the government to the very goal. Look at it! Two years ago—
hardly two years ago—the Congress of the United States almost
unanimously resolved, that this war had nothing whatsoever to do
with slavery; that the non-slaveholding States had no constitutional right to legislate upon or to interfere with slavery in the
States of this Union; that those persons in the North who did not
subscribe to this proposition were too insignificant in numbers and
influence to excite the serious attention or alarm of any portion of
the people; and that the increase of their numbers did not keep
pace with the aggregate increase of the population of the Union.
On the very day that Congress assembled in Washington, and

proclaimed to the world that there was something more sacred than Nationality, and that was Bondage—on that very day, the man whose name I have read with so much triumph at the close of this Proclamation, left his home in Springfield to take charge of the destinies of the Republic; and the first word that the expectant nation heard from his lips was at Cleveland, when he pledged himself to sustain and to execute the Fugitive Slave Law of the Republic. Disguised and hunted, he reached the capital of the Union, and the first word heard from his General, as he entered Virginia, was a pledge to put down insurrection "with an iron hand." Two years ago! Months rolled on, from his besieged outpost in Missouri, Fremont uttered the statesman-like word that was to cure the evils of the Republic, and a timid Cabinet hastened to cashier him. Time rolled on, and again and again the heart of the nation sickened over conciliation and submission. The President of the United States on the 23d of September, dared only to say to the rebel, in the voice of Congress,! "If you rebel, we confiscate; keep on in your treason, and we punish for we will take from you the slave that gives you bread." Then, turning half round, with a side glance at the anxious millions who watched his countenance, all he could say to them was—"In case you should be freed, would you promise to go instantly away?" The 23d day of September, 1862, after Bull Run and Ball's Bluff, after defeats and victories, after insults from abroad and outrages at home, the nation reached only that understanding of its position which attempted to punish treason by taking away its strength. The first day of January dawned, and the bright sun brings us a different message. Mark you! this Proclamation is not the punishment of rebels. It is no echo of the statutes of Congress, saying that if in certain localities there be a traitor, the Union will clutch from him the means of harming us. It is no sidelong appeal to a nuisance, to a burden, to an intrusive race, to take itself away from the centre of the conflict. O no; it is the act of a great nation, linking its cause to the throne of the Almighty proclaiming Liberty as an act of justice and abolishing a system found to be inconsistent with the perpetuity of the Republic. (Applause) It does not say, "The slaves of rebels are emancipated." It says, "Every slave in rebel States is a free man. We believe it to be dictated by justice, we know it to be essential to the safety of the country." "Will you go away, if I venture to free you?" said the President on the 22d of

September. "May I colonize you among the sickly deserts or the vast jungles of South America?" On the first day of January, he says to the same four million, "Let me colonize you to the forts of the Union, and put rifles in your hands! (Applause) Give us your hand to defend the perpetuity of the Union!" To that colonization, I have no criticism to suggest. (Applause)

Progress! Ordinarily, we must take some microscope to watch it. We look at the dial, and see no change in the shadow, though we know that at last twelve o'clock will come. So it is with the [human] race, unless we take in the sweep of ages. But here one must project himself afar from the present, in order to get distance sufficient to take in the magic proportions of the edifice which rises from the clouds of the battlefield (Loud Applause). The distinguishing element and great characteristic of the act of the first of January is, that it recognized for the first time in our struggle, not that the slave of a particular person may be taken from him, but that slavery as an institution, the policy of States, is inconsistent with the life of the Union, and incompatible with the success of the Government. At last, Nationality means Justice; the Union is synonomous with Liberty. The crisis of that long struggle which Mr. Lincoln proclaimed in June 1858, as then going on, and which he said could only cease in the triumph of one section or the other—a struggle between different positions of a nation half slave and half free, and which he said must become either wholly slave or wholly free—at last the crisis of that struggle is over, and the voice of the nation proclaims that hereafter it is to be wholly free! (Enthusiasm) "Hitherto hath the Lord helped us. Here we set up our Ebenezer." The long doubt whether this flag meant liberty is ended. The people never doubted it. The masses always meant it; but the Cabinet, the leaders of both parties, meant it not. I am not certain that they mean it to-day. The great effort of all our politicians, Republican and Democratic, up to this hour, has been to preserve the Union with the slightest change possible. As far as interest in the battle went, the Democrat had as keen a heart for the contest, and keener than the Republican. The new Governor of the Empire State means as loyally as ours does that this Union to the Gulf shall be preserved; but the difference between his creed and that of Massachusetts is, that he holds that the Union is to be preserved, if possible, by submission to the rebels, by conciliation, that shall bring back the Union as it was; while the Bay State scorns submission, and tramples conciliation under her feet.

Now, revolutions never go back, but they oscillate. It is by no means certain whether that Proclamation is to be law today or fifty years hence. Men make a distinction whether they wish slavery the object of this war or Union. If a man bounds his view within ten years, there is a difference; if he looks a generation ahead—fifty years—there is no difference. Slavery existing, there can be no Union; slavery abolished, there can be no disunion. (Applause) No other power can keep these States apart. Root up that system, and like kindred drops we must melt together. Battle fields like that of Manassas rankling in the heart of North, battle fields like that of Corinth writing defeat on the brow of the rebels, are both and all of them the cement of a more enduring Union. Out of this bloody contest is to come a mutual respect between the sections such as has never existed since 1776. The battles fought together against a foreign foe cemented the Union of '87; and the North and South fighting, as they think, the one for liberty and the other for bondage, are the upper and nether millstone—the mill of God, grinding slavery to atoms. The battle between such sections is but the prelude to the reconciliation which precedes an immortal marriage. The Union of the future is to be as indestructible as the granite that underlies the continent; and the cement is not to be what Webster called it, the blood of the slave; it is the blood of the brave hearts that have made Virginia more than equal to Belgium, the battle-field of a purer contest now sleeping under the glory of one sublime struggle for a Union worthy to lead the world.

I said that the significance of this hour was, that it was the people's triumph. In defiance of the Cabinet and of Major-Generals, over the head of the President, their irresistible will has carried this measure. Remember, the same means that *secured* must watch to make it efficient. Without fitting measures, this paper is worth little to our generation. I dare not yet fully believe that the *heart* either of the President or of his Cabinet is in this Proclamation. I say to the masses, Watch! Save your own child! If your vigilance, your tireless urging fail, the hour and measure are lost. Long before this, there should have been created a "Bureau of Freedmen," to guard and aid the advent of these millions into the conditions of free men. We have bureaus to guard the rights of

Indians. Here are four million about to be born into the State. How absurd this childish bo-peep game of the Executive to keep his purpose a secret—the only secret ever yet kept at Washington—when Congress ought to have spent the last thirty days in maturing the machinery which should make this change in our social and civil life easy, peaceful—like the still gliding of a noble vessel off of well-prepared stocks into her native element. Work enough then for the future. Open and secret foes watch now every misstep, to make it a short-coming of the negro, to make it a matter of accusation against this measure and discredit it in the nation's eyes; to cloud our faith and perplex our steps. The *usual aid* of Government should have been at hand to avert such perils. Watch, then your leaders with Argus eyes! Keep a hundred hands constantly stretched out to drag them onward in the right path, which so many of them hate!

Yet for all this, I am hopeful. All that blunders in the Cabinet and in the field could do to kill our cause has been done. All that treason could do in either place has been done. As Boerhaave said of the doctors, "there were some good ones, but the world's health would be better if the whole profession were abolished," so in spite of Hooker and Burnside and Hunter, if every West Pointer had betrayed us openly and at once we should have saved millions of money and thousands of lives, and months of time. Still I hope. . . . It does not seem possible this territory can have, finally, more than one government; and if so, we must be that government; for brains, justice, God, are on our side. Every natural law works for us. We have secured the laws of the universe on our side. Every broken heart prays for us. The poor and the friendless are sacred. Once their curses weighed us down. Now the blessing of him that was ready to perish is come upon us, for we break the jaw of the wicked, and pluck the spoil out of his teeth. Surely, now we shall die in our nest and multiply our days like the sand.

I have no doubt, therefore, of the absolute future, and how much it will do for us now. It is not so much a step onward as it is launching into a new channel. Let the news of it reach Europe before France and England have *decided* on intervention, and it will probably leave us our whole field, in the future untroubled by any foreign interference. What nation will earn the scorn of the world and of all time by marshalling her banners against a flag hapless of races? I am not to stop here, today, to argue the rightfulness of this Proclamation. The slave is either a man or a thing. If he is a man, the Union in its utmost peril has a right to enroll all its citizens. If he is a thing, the Union in its utmost peril has a right to every dollar within its grasp. (Applause) No matter in which light you consider him the right of the nation to his service and his right hand is perfect on either. Bear that for ever in memory! Let no chicanery of politicians make you forget the alternative. The father of the General who now looks into the eyes of Burnside, on the other bank of the Rappahannock, a bankrupt, built his house on the dividing line betwixt Maryland and Virginia in order to avoid arrest from either. Just so the statesmanship of the South and Democracy put the slave on the dividing line betwixt property and citizenship, and defy us to use him. This Proclamation avoids the question. It calls upon the slave, in the name of Justice, to fight for the nation that asks his aid. The "everlasting negro" of whom politicians begged God to deliver them! what is that? (holding up the Proclamation) The nation at his feet, after two years of defeated struggle, asking his weight in our scale to insure victory! (Applause) Nationality! It is built up of races. The despised negro for whom we hoped to open a door wide enough, amid the prejudices of contending races, to admit him, comes in with sound of trumpet and in the terror of the conflict to insure us success.

What is this Proclamation to do? I said it settles the question of the right. Let me advert to one other idea. We are either a nation, or we are not. If we are a nation—if we are really a unit—if, like England and France, we are one people, indivisible,—then—mark me! no parchment, even if it attempted the task, could bar us from the use of any power within our reach to save the nationality! Do you suppose any agreement could bar the King of England or the Emperor of France from saving his country in the hour of peril? How absurd! If the shores of England were beleaguered by the fleets of Europe, do you suppose the Settlement of 1788 would hold Palmerston or Russell from hurling unconstitutional thunderbolts that should sink Napoleon to the bottom of the channel? The nation knows no limits. *Solus populi suprema lex.* "The safety of the people is the highest law." If we have not the right—if we are not a nation—if we are merely a Confederacy, the Secession is right. Another alternative:—please bear it in your minds. If we have not the right to draft every living man, use every current dollar, in the way the nation pleases we are not a nation; and if we are not a nation then South Carolina has a right to secede, and every gun fired by the President is an unprincipled attack on the sovereignty of the States. If, therefore, any man doubts the power of the nation to issue that paper stop the war. Begin a nationality, however small. If it only includes this peninsula, begin! If it is only Plymouth Rock, begin! If it is only New England, begin! The vigor of a nationality, once begun, will cover the continent. A confederacy is a nuisance. (Applause.)

These are the corner-stones of that Proclamation. Everything that attacks it, admits the right of South Carolina. If we are a people, that is but the simplest act of our power. Well, what is it to do? Is it a "Pope's bull at the comet"? Let us see. One thing it has done—it has opened a million lips. Since the Proclamation, *Generals* talk fanaticism. at the head of armies. (Applause.) Banks has found out, at the mouth of the Mississippi, that the gun at Sumter proclaimed Emancipation. (Applause.) Between you and me, how well he has kept that secret for twenty months. (Laughter.) Let us hope he will be as successful in keeping his war plans secret in time to come. But, Generals talk abolition at the head of armies. Our voice is to be the proclamation of cannon. Battles are fought now for justice. Will the slave fall into rank? I think so. I have little regard to the extreme limits of what are called the distinctions of races. I find very narrow limits to those differences. Men say the Roman stands at the head of the catalogue, and the Indian and the Negro at the very foot. But I remember, that when Roman liberty was at its last gasp, the culminating vigor of the Roman character was in Cato at Utica, when he gathered his friends around him and said—"The Republic is over. There is nothing left for us but to die!" "The last utterance of freedom", says History. Go with me to Jamaica, two hundred years ago, when white feet pressed the soft Indian of the tropics back, back, through his woods-hunted, meted out, trodden down, starving with hunger, and finally driven to bay—and I will show you a cacique, Cato-like assembling the last twenty of his tribe around him, to say, in the words of the Romans—is over. Brothers, there is nothing left for us but to die!" And "Liberty together the twenty Catos of the tropics imitated the Roman at Utica. (Sensation.) How slight is the distinction of race! The

Roman Captain, when Nero bade him stab his own heart, turned pale, until his wife seized the dagger, and bathing it in her own blood, said "Petus! it is not so hard to die!" So too, when the French tryant ordered a negro of St. Domingo to take his own life, he faltered, and his wife seized the sword, and, inflicting a death wound, turned to her husband, saying—"Husband! life is worth nothing when liberty is gone!" (Profound sensation.) How near are the races to each other! The Indian of the tropics,—the Negro of the plantation,—the Roman of Utica,—and the Patriot of the Caesars! Yes, the negro will fight. But there is a deeper justice than that. This war is not a war of artillery. McClellan to the contrary notwithstanding. It is a war of ideas—it is a war of proclamations—infinitely more potent than cannon. What does this Proclamation mean? It means this: Mr. Lincoln excepts portions of Virginia, he excepts Tennessee, he excepts the lower counties of Louisiana. If it were possible for a little man in a great place to make a mistake, this had been a great one. But it is not possible to make a mistake. He cannot open his mouth in this hour, and not say Justice; he cannot move his hand, and not secure Victory. He must fight well, that beats the North and Justice allied together. (Enthusiasm.) What care the counties of Louisiana whether they are excepted by the Proclamation or not? With every surrounding locality free, how can they keep their slaves? At least, while the battle rages in Tennessee, it had been better to throw into our scale from one hundred to two hundred thousand slaves. And yet that is but the hesitation of a timid man. The Border States, after all, are nothing; mere bobs of the kite, North or South; mere counters, belonging to whichever party sweeps the board; mere pawns on the chess—board; nothing but the floating mud of the Mississippi, which the high tide carries North or South at its pleasure. They have not the possibility of making a nation, any more than the silk floss that floats on an electrical machine. Virginia! She belongs to us. What carried her South? Why, her manufactures. She breeds slaves, and of course adheres to the buyers. The white Virginian—what is he? A pedler of babies in the Southwest. (Applause.) Of course, when the market seceded, he went with it. (Renewed applause.) This Proclamation abolishes the market, (great enthusiasm,) and Virginia, without a Burnside, gravitates back where she belongs-to the North. In the opening of this struggle, there came up to my parlor a Florida slaveholder, to ask what we thought of this contest, and I said—"Will the Border States join you! "Join us!" The devil take them, let them go to you; they don't belong to us," was the reply. "We don't want them. We can't keep them. They belong to you. They are nothing but a weakness. The moment you take out the bottom of a bucket, the contents fall to the ground." The Gulf States are the bottom. Delaware, Maryland, Virginia, Kentucky, Tennessee, are not Slave States, properly speaking. The system is dead there, but for the stone wall South, that keeps it from dying, and being decently buried; and this Proclamation when it abolishes the market, with the question of the Border States out of the arena, is in fact,—as an act, not as a principle,—the abolition of slavery in the United States, all through.(Applause.)

I know the distinction between emancipating slaves and abolishing the system. The President conceives that he has a right to free slaves, but not to change laws; that he has a right to emancipate this generation of slaves, but not to forbid the holding of slaves in the separate States. It is doubtless a distinction; but with this English race of ours, it amounts to nothing, because we have never had a struggle, in England or here, that began at the outset with the study of a principle. They all began in a case—with an individual. We cure the evil, and then let posterity, if it finds occasion, attend to the principle. For instance; England, in her great Revolution, began with a question of ship-money—whether the Stuarts had a right, without Parliament, to make John Hampden pay twenty shillings. He said, No; the court said, Yes; and he paid it. Out of that grew the civil war. But do you suppose the civil war meant only ship-money? Do you suppose that Cromwell dashed into the field at Naseby, against the cohorts of Rupert, crying—"Pay me back that ship-money, with six per cent interest!" No, indeed. That was but the root out of which grew the power of the King to do acts without the consent of the people. When the Revolution began, it was "Ship-money"; but when it ended, it was "Democracy." (Applause.) So it is with us, We began with declaring certain slaves of rebels free; and if you had taken your cue from the actual orders at head-quarters you would have supposed that the war-cry of the nation was—"Give us back Sumter and make Anderson a healthy man again, and you may come in." But it did not mean that. It meant, Massachusetts, starting on the 19th of April, through the bloody streets of

Baltimore, to colonize the Carolinas; and she will not stop until it is done. (Applause.) No, not if she stays fifty years; no, not if the energy of the fight shall divide the Union for a generation. The Union is an indestructible fact; no battles can divide it. (Applause.)

> *Vain is the strife! when its fury is past,*
> *Our future shall move in one channel at last,*
> *As torrents that rush from the mountain of snow*
> *Roll mingled in peace through the valleys below.*
>
> *Our Union is river, lake, ocean, and sky;*
> *Man breaks not the medal, when God cuts the die;*
> *Though clouded with slaughter or cloven with steel,*
> *The blue arch will brighten, the waters will heal.*
>
> *Caroline! Caroline! thou child of the sun,*
> *There are battles with fate that can never be won;*
> *The star-flowering banner will never be furled,*
> *For its blossoms of light are the hope of the world!*
>   *(Loud Applause)*

Virginia and the Border States know well that . . . the significance of the Proclamation is, that it takes out the cement that binds them in the future of the South. The heart of the Rebellion—it is not Richmond; that is only a limb; the heart of the Rebellion is the rich soil of Alabama and Mississippi, that supplies the markets of the world, and keeps up the demand for what Carolina and Virginia manufacture—slaves; and the moment Banks and Hunter shall say to the blacks, in the language of the Proclamation, "The ranks of the army are open to you", the moment we garrison forts and arm vessels with black men—in other words, the moment we acknowledge the manhood of the negro, and pledge to him the mortal future of the Union, that moment we sever the bond that holds the Border States to their sisters of the Gulf. This Proclamation may be genuinely nothing today. I do not know that it will be vital a year hence. If Mr. Lincoln is as slow this year as he has been in the past, a Democratic Administration will follow him, and conciliate the South with a Supreme Court that will try to set it aside. All within the range of an easy possibility. I am not certain even yet, that Mr. Seward does not cling to the Union with a firmer grasp than to his own Proclamation; and I fear that the Democratic party would gladly set it aside, and make a Union as like as possible as the last. So speaks the Empire State; at least by the voice of her Capital, if not by her counties. But whether they mean it or not, it is impossible that it should ever come to pass for more than a moment because there is something, even to the Northern millions, more precious than Union, and that is—POWER. We have bound that motto (the Proclamation) on our frontlet. The basest nation that ever formed a footstool for a European despot would disdain a compromise which took back that pledge to a proscribed and hapless race. (Applause.) We may be beaten back until Burnside encamps north of Lake Ontario; but while New England rests on granite, the black race is sure of his freedom. (Enthusiasm.) I know what you can say, "Burnside attempted something and failed; McClellan tried nothing and succeeded." (Prolonged applause) Well, I had rather been Burnside's failure than McClellan's success. (Renewed applause) That Proclamation was written and signed in the blood that crimsoned the Rappahannock. That defeat guaranteed it to us forever. Yes, and looking back—though no single consideration excuses the Cabinet a moment—we can see the fountain of God. If we had met decided success within the first six months, doubtless the South would have emancipated, summoned Europe to her side, and been able to maintain her independence. If it is true that the intervening months have hardened the South by victory and defeat into a nationality, at the same time, every flap of the Northern flag has lifted a slave into manhood so that he comes to us half a soldier, even now. (Applause)

I know what men say about our President's omitting Tennessee from his list of rebel States, and sparing some certain Louisiana districts. No matter; he is only stopping on the edge of Niagara to pick up and save a few chips. He and they will go over together. I know also the threats of the Democratic party—the party of reaction. But they will not save any more chips than he. The mighty current is too strong for any reluctance of individuals or mad ambitions of desperate parties. Saints and sinners, we are all borne onward; and even if some eddy or close nook of a few years may delay our progress, the result is certain. God's hand has launched the nation into a voyage whose only poet is Liberty. Neither the reluctance of the captain, nor the mutiny of the cabin boys will matter much. And this is why I, once a Disunionist, cling to the Union. Once it had neither the right nor the wish to interfere with slavery. Then we sought to break it. That Sumter cannon gave us the right—*the right of war.* Every day since has ripened the *wish.* A blundering and corrupt Cabinet has made it at last an *inevitable necessity*—Liberty or Death. The cowardice of Webster's followers in the Cabinet has turned his empty rhetoric into solemn truth, and now honest men are not only at liberty, but bound, to live and die under this motto—"Liberty and Union, now and forever, one and inseparable."

But what is this that I am saying? Union. An idle word, whether on the lips of Lincoln or Seymour. Man does not make Unions, and it is hardly possible for man to break them. One would think by the way in which men talk, that a Union was made by parchment; as if marriage did not consist of loving hearts but of an imposing ceremony, and a certificate filed with the Town Clerk; as if a Union was made up of pieces of paper. Why does Connecticut never talk of seceding from Massachusetts? As well might one of the Siamese twins secede from the other; as well one drop of Massachusetts Bay secede from the north of Winthrop's Island, and another from the south. The moment you have made these people respect each other, the moment you have made the South recognize the fact that the North has an idea and will fight for it; that that idea includes the justice of God and the approval of man, prosperity and progress, vigor and strength; that moment Carolina will cling closer to Massachusetts than to Cuba, where she now belongs; and then without a convention as Philadelphia, with a *Courier* or a *Herald,* without Democrat or a Republican, this race—one in blood, one in history, one in interest, one in people, one in hope—will be one in Government, Indestructibly.

But, after all, what is the President's Proclamation to us? Nothing but a step in the progress of a people, rich, prosperous, independent in spite of the words. But let me open for you the huts of three millions of slaves, and what is that Proclamation then! The sunlight, scattering the despair of centuries. It is a voice like that of God, that gives the slave the right to work and to walk, the right to child and to wife. It is a word that makes the prayers of the poor and victim the corner-stones of the Republic. Other nations since Greece have built their nationality on a Thermopylae, or a great name—a victory, or a knighted family. Our cornerstone, thank God is the blessings of the poor. Our flag floats in the prayers of four million, who recognize it as the pledge of their freedom. The hut of the Carolinas! They may curse that paper in ceiled houses, but the blessings of the poor bear it up to the throne of God. Our flag floats in the thanksgiving of the slave. I know it will succeed. Such a breeze never wafted a banner in defeat. The old slave, who sought the "Kingfisher" at the Gulf of Mexico, thirty miles from the shore in a wretched skiff of boards, rudely nailed together when the commander asked him—"Why, didn't you know that a breath would have sent you to the bottom!"—said—"Lor, massa, God Almighty never brought me down here to send me to the bottom." So, God never brought the Union of 1787 to the height of the act, to sunder it in pieces! (Enthusiastic applause)

Thou, too, sail on, O Ship of State!
Sail on, O Union, strong and great!
Sail on, nor fear to breast the sea!
Our hearts, our hopes, are all with thee,
Our hearts, our hopes, our prayers, our tears,
Our faith, triumphant o'er our fears,
Are all with thee-are all with thee!

(Loud and prolonged applause)

12 FROM *Theodore Tilton*
The Negro: A Speech

The sense of triumph was never allowed to blot out the tragic knowledge of cruel and ever-present race prejudice. Abolitionists continued their fight, begun so many years before, against such sickness, but in reading their attacks one sometimes has the sense that they shared the prejudice of their fellow countrymen. In this selection there are examples of stereotypical thinking which could be considered to indicate racial bias; there are, however, even more indications of commitment to equality. One should add, complete equality, for the speaker asks his audience to understand this point clearly. "Remember," he says, "I do not ask simply that competent black men shall

SOURCE. Theodore Tilton, "The Negro: A Speech," 1863.

hold office. I ask that incompetent black men shall hold office—for only so will they be on a level with the whites." The speaker was Theodore Tilton(1835-1907) who began his public career as a crusading editor for Horace Greeley's New York Tribune while he was still a student at the College of the City of New York. After graduation from college, Tilton finally found his way into the editorship of the Independent, which eventually became one of the most influential journals of its day. Although his later career was damaged by a well-publicized scandal, Tilton was at the height of his powers and popularity when he delivered the following speech in 1863.

My Friends: I bring to you the Negro! Not the slave—not the contraband—not the freedman—but the negro! You and I will never meet slavery in the future as we have met it in the past. The times have changed. Like St. Margaret in Raphael's picture, our feet are now upon the Great Dragon, and the palmbranch of victory is in our hands. The cause which this May festival represents takes now a new phase. As *The Journal of Commerce* says, "The opposition is no longer to the Slave: it is to the Negro." That is, there is a sworn enmity to the black man whether in his chains or out—whether under the yoke or free. Men dislike the color of his skin—so they lift their hands to smite his cheek. Our plea, therefore, is no longer for the Slave. That argument has passed. It passed on the First of January. The needful plea now is for the Negro. That necessity still remains. "The poor ye have always with you!"

Who, then, is the Negro? What is his rank among mankind? Send men to search for the negro, and where will they look? Under other men's feet—for they keep him to trample on! Lift him up and ask who is he? and what is the answer? An inferior man—a sunken humanity—a half-gifted child of God. A white man, looking down upon a negro, straightens himself an inch higher into a fool's pride!

But settle as you will who are *above* the negro, I will tell you who are *below* him. The Esquimaux are below him. The Pacific Islanders are below him. The South American tribes poleward from the La Plata are below him. The ground castes of India are below him; for Bachman says that the head of the Negro measures three square inches more than the head of the Hindoo. The Natives of Van Dieman's Land are below him. Is the negro's skull thick? The Van Dieman's Lander breaks fir-wood over *his*! He could be his own schoolmaster! (Laughter) I can count you twenty races of men—and as many editors of newspapers—who rank below the negro (laughter).

Ethnologists say that the classes of mankind are five—just a handful! You may count them on your thumb and fingers—like the five points of Calvinism (laughter). Thus—Caucasian, Mongolian, Ethiopian, American Indian, Malay. Now I put a question: would you exchange the negroes of the South for four million Malays? Would you exchange them for four million Chinese? Ask San Francisco! Would you exchange them for four million Indians? Ask Minnesota, and read her answer in fire and massacre! So, out of the five classes of mankind, the negro is your second choice. You prefer him before three-fifths of all the world! You rank him second to the Caucasian. That is to say, you count him the next best man after yourself!

Of course, you would exchange the negroes for four million Caucasians. We have a Caucasian pride. But who are these typical Caucasians who have given their name to the best blood of the world? Who are these chief aristocrats of the earth? They borrow their name from Mt. Caucasus—their supposed native seat. Their women are like Venus—their men like Apollo—the finest known specimens of mankind. So the books used to say. But Mrs. Primrose has made a proverb, "Handsome is, that handsome does." Now what have these handsome Caucasians done in the world? I mean the pure, original stock by the Black Sea—untainted by baser blood. They have originated no new idea. They have left no record in history except their name. They have exerted no influence upon mankind. They rank like the Adam of the Scriptures—the original Caucasian of the garden—who probably had a fine figure and fair face, but who never said a single word, or thought a single thought, to leave behind him as a living influence upon mankind. Take the whole double tribe of original Caucasians— Georgians on one side, and Circassians on the other—and compare them, for influence in the world, with our American negroes. I maintain that the slaves of the single State of South Carolina have done more useful work—have written themselves a more lasting name—are exerting more influence upon their day

and generation—shaking States, changing governments, settling
ideas—than the whole tribe who look up to Mt. Caucasus to catch
its snows upon their foreheads, and its sun-flushes upon their
cheeks! Caucasian? Of the beautiful name nothing is now left but
the ugly-faced newspaper that has stolen it in this city! (Laughter)

Do you call the negro race inferior? No man can yet pronounce
that judgment safely. How will you compare races, to give each its
due rank? There is but one just way. You must compare them in
the fulfilments, not in their beginnings—in their flower, not in their
bud. How will you estimate the rank of the Roman people? By its
beginning? By its decline? By neither. You rank it at the height of
its civilization—when it attained to jurisprudence, to statesmanship, to eloquence, to the beautiful arts. Other wise you rank it
unjustly. The Germans, today, give philosophy to Europe—but you
can count the years backward when the Germans, now philosophers, were barbarians. Who could say, eight or nine centuries
ago, what was to be the intellectual rank of the French nation? So
no man can now predict the destiny of the negro race. That race is
yet so undeveloped—that destiny is yet so unfulfilled—that no man
can say, and no wise man pretends to say, what the negro race
shall finally become.

Inferior? What is human inferiority? Will you look at a child in
his cradle and say, that is an inferior man? No. You wait for his
growth—you will not judge him till his manhood. Will you look
upon a race yet in its ungrowth and say, that is an inferior
humanity? No. The time has not yet come to judge that infant
child; the time has not yet come to judge this infant race. As in
the nursery song, so these stormy times are yet only rocking its
cradle in the tree-tops. It may be that negroes—on their original
continent—in the long future—growing strong as other nations
grow weak—holding the soil in one hand and the sea in the other—
may yet stand the dominant, superior race of the world. I do not
say this will so be—but I say no man can prove that this will *not* so
be. You may read Prichard, and Pinkerton, and Morton, and
Pickering, and Latham, and all the rest—the whole library of
Ethnology—and in the confusion of knowledge one thing is plain—
and that is, science has not yet proved that the negro race is not to
be a high-cultured, regnant race—masters of their own continent,
and perhaps dictators to the world. Who knows but each continent may, in turn, become chief of the whole five in power and

civilization? Asia once outranked Europe, but Europe now out-ranks Asia. North America, once a wilderness, now nearly equals Europe. Who knows but Africa may yet overtop them all? For, as the least shall be greatest in the Kingdom of Heaven, it may be also that the least shall be greatest among the kingdoms of the earth. (applause)

But whatever is to be the destiny of the negro race in Africa, every man sees that the future is not to find a negro race in America—I mean a strictly negro race, of unmingled blood. We have no isolated race here, white or black, except one—the Jews. The American people are all peoples—a nation of many nations. The four quarters of the earth send us their sons and daughters. As all tongues enter into the English tongue, so all nations enter into the English-speaking race on this continent.

God, counseling with himself how to crown this people the greatest on the earth, said—"Of what fibre shall I make them?" And he poured into their veins the Saxon blood—painting their eyes with the sky, and gilding their hair with the sun. Then he mingled with it the Celtic, quickened with mercury and touched with fire. Then he poured into it the sunny wines of the South of Europe. Then, after many other gifts, he added—last but not least—a strange, mysterious current—that bleeds, when wounded, like other men's blood!—that dances in the pulse, when joy-smitten, like other men's blood!—yet that carries the blackness of darkness into men's faces in token that it should also carry the shadow of death into men's souls!

God said, "How shall I prepare a continent to be the home of such a people?" And he ribbed it through the centre with mountain-chains—that the Swiss and the Swede, coming hither, might renew their ancient fellowship with the eternal hills. He salted it on either side with two great seas—that the maritime people of Europe, coming hither, might find still fairer coasts for the ships. He laid his leveling palm upon it, that the Hollander, coming hither, might see the Zuyder Zee, touched by miracle of nature, blooming into an illimitable level of prairie-grass. Last but not least, he stretched its southern slope into the tropical heats—that the negro also, coming hither, might find a home, where he and the eagle should together look at the sun!

It is with such a people, and with such a continent under their feet, that God is working out the destiny of the New World.

Is it a wise plan? Great nations get the fibre of their strength from mixed bloods. In Europe—the most civilized of the continents—every nation stands built upon the broken fragments of former nations. God sets the centuries rolling over nationalities till in process of time all peoples lose their original identity—the nations intermingle their blood—the face of the world is changed. It is written that "God hath made of one blood all nations of men." If part of this blood becomes separated from the general current of humanity—diverted for centuries, as with the Jews, into an exclusive and narrow channel—never resupplied out of the great reservoir of the race—history shows that it loses some element of richness, of vitality, of capacity for national greatness. What have the Jews gained by being miserly of their blood? Since Solomon, they have so treasured their nationality that none has run to waste. But have they, in consequence, transmitted the wisdom of Solomon? When the Jews die, will wisdom die with them? Solomon says that wisdom is gold. If the Jews were to drop off, I think gold would go down (laughter). But I cast no shadow upon the Jews— wanderers in the earth having no rest for the soles of their feet. There is a christian doctrine that you and I must practice, "Honor *all* men." Races belong to each other. No race was meant only for itself. Shut up to clannishness, a tribe becomes defrauded of its just growth. Stocks that perpetually exclude themselves from all others remain unchanged from generation to generation—or fade out of the earth. The veins of nations must constantly borrow fresh blood—else the current stagnates. A nation cannot live always upon itself except in poverty of soul. As a single family, marrying within itself, violates the equities of nature, so a nation which keeps itself forever as an exclusive family among nations holds back its own progress, and prevents its greatness. The history of the world's civilization is written in one word— which many are afraid to speak—which many more are afraid to hear—and that is, Amalgamation. Barred out from the rest of mankind, the Chinese are no fuller grown to day than of old when they sat like children at the feet of Confucius. If an Arab of Abraham's time were to rise from the dead, no traveler could tell him from the Arab of last summer's tour. The Africans at the sources of the Nile are unchanged in character and habits from the morning of history. Only those nations have made progress that have joined their blood with others. This is God's beautiful provision against human selfishness—ordaining that one nation shall not rise without lifting others with it. And whichsoever will not raise another, shall fall itself. Will the Jews have no dealings with the Samaritans! The Jews themselves become losers. But following the true law, great nations grow from small beginnings. The British are a great people—in spite of their own modesty in never mentioning it! But when a philosopher argued before the British Association of Science that negroes are fit only to be slaves, a negro who was present, having escaped from his chains in the South, quoted Julius Caesar, who said he found the British too stupid even to be fit for slaves! So it is idle to fix the rank of races—for behold! time will change all your measurings. Looked at through centuries, the question of races sinks into insignificance. The only generalization that will stand is not that there are five races of men, or seven, or twelve, but only one—the universal human race in which all men are brothers, and God is father over all!

Meanwhile, what is the spectacle of races in this country? Was there ever such a motley multitude as compose this nation! Were there ever such intergraftings of many stocks? Saxon blood is split into Anglo Saxon veins. Celtic blood hides in many a man's heart who has never dreamed himself an Irishman—and never will till we have war with England (laughter). Feel the pulse of our American nationality—open the channel of its veins—question the blood concerning its pedigree-nay, look only at men's features as you meet them day by day—here a trace of German descent, there an unmistakable Scotch feature, there a borrowing from the Spanish, there a token of Huguenot ancestry—why the map of the whole world is written upon the faces of the men who daily walk the streets of New York!

Three stupendous processes of intermingling are going forward in this country. First, we are absorbing the Irish race. Second, we are absorbing the German race. Third, are we absorbing the Negro race? No, just the opposite. Look at the facts. It is not black blood that pours itself into white veins. It is white blood that pours itself into black veins. It is not, therefore, a philosophical statement to say, as Pres. Sturtevant says, that the negro race is being absorbed by the white. On the contrary, the negro race is receiving and absorbing part of the white. A large fraction of the white race of the South is melting away into the black. I am not stating any theory on the subject—I am stating only the fact. And this is the plain fact, which no man can gainsay.

Our fathers, in writing the Constitution, said in the preamble that it was to secure the blessings of liberty "for ourselves and our posterity." Southern interpreters claim that these blessings are only for white men, not for black. But who are the posterity of Southern white men? They are Southern half-black men (laughter). If God were now to step visibly into the land, holding that preamble in His hand, calling out, "As many as are here named, let them come forth." how many would answer? A hand-writing in milk, held to the fire will grow plain. So the record of white blood written in the black race of this country, if suddenly summoned to play tell-tale with its secret, would give answer in the faces of three-quarters of the four million slaves! I say three-quarters! These figures are not a guess. They are a careful estimate—based upon good authority—upon many inquiries—and believed to understate rather than to overstate the truth.

Have you not seen with your own eyes—no man can have escaped it—that the black race in this country is losing its typical blackness? Go into any social company of colored people. I was lately among them at a wedding—for, they, too, marry, and are given in marriage. Not one in twenty of the colored persons present had either the pure African hue or feature. What does this argue? That the negro race is passing away, like the Indian? No! the Indian is dying out—the Negro is only changing color! Men who by and by shall ask for the Indians, will be pointed to their graves—"There lie their ashes." Men who by and by shall ask for the negroes, will be told, "There they go, clad in white men's skins!" The negro dying out? Vain thought! The race has not only its own blood to keep it alive, but is taking to itself the blood of the aristocracy of the South. The negro is filling his veins from two fountains of life! A hundred years ago a mulatto was a curiosity—now the mulattoes are half a million. You can yourself predict the future! Mr. Phillips last evening held in his hand, on this platform, an early white May blossom of the coming harvest! [Referring to the little white slavegirl whom Mr. Beecher had baptized the Sunday before.]

I am not advocating the union of whites and blacks. This is taking place without advocacy. It neither waits for the permission of an argument in favor of it, nor stays at the barrier of an argument against it. I am often asked, "Would you marry a black woman?" I reply, "I have a wife already, and therefore will not." I am asked, "Do you think that a white man ought ever marry a black woman?" I reply, "When a man and a woman want to be married, it is *their* business, not mine, nor anybody's else." Is not that plain sense? But to read what some newspapers say of the "monstrous doctrine of amalgamation," one would think it consisted in stationing a provost marshal at street-corners, to seize first a white man and then a black woman, and to marry them on the spot against their will, for a testimony to human equality. But I will venture to advance the opinion as holding good in morals, that a slave-woman's master who makes himself father of her children is in honor bound to make himself her husband. So far from denouncing the marriage of blacks and whites, I would be glad if the banns of a hundred thousand such marriages could be published next Sunday, that in many a slave's cabin or master's mansion the unrepaired wrong might be righted and the fallen honor raised. But whether in marriage or in shame, the fact grows broader every day that the whites and blacks of this country are coloring; or to use the more horrible word, amalgamating. In Slavery, this amalgamation proceeds rapidly; in Freedom, slowly; but it proceeds, nor will it stop. And in the far future, the negro will wash his face into paleness with the blood of white men's veins.

Meanwhile, before the American negro becomes a white man, he ought to remain a negro as long as he can. I will tell you why. Although, after a lapse of time, all nationalities lose their identity and merge in each other, they meanwhile have an important object in preserving and intensifying this individuality. The farmer, though he means to cut down his corn-stalk next Fall, nevertheless stimulates it to its best growth during the long Summer, God means that a nation, though it shall not retain its identity forever, yet shall develop its individual peculiarity of growth to the fullest bloom and fruit. The earth is covered with many distinct nationalities. What comes of this variety? It broadens and diversifies human character. The thoughts of the Infinite Mind are so great that it takes many symbols to express the divine meaning. What is God's idea of a flower? Is it a daisy? Is it a lily? Is it a rose? It is none of these by itself. It takes the whole garden of the earth—every flower that grows, every blossom that bursts in

May—all these, gathered out of every clime, the world around—to illustrate the breath of God's conception when he made the flowers of the field. Now, man—who is *he*? Is he a Frenchman? A Spaniard? An Asiatic? A Sea-islander? An Indian? A Negro? None of these by himself. It takes all men to make Man! It takes all tongues and tribes and races to mass up God's grand idea of humanity!

Look at Europe! What a diversity of races—yet every race different from every other—and each, in some peculiar characteristic, superior to every other. Now strike out the German mind from the world—strike out the French mind—strike out the Scotch mind—strike out the English mind—and you impoverish the world by just so much as you destroy any of its varying types of mankind. Now I maintain that, as you cannot afford to strike out any of these, so you cannot afford to strike out the Negro (applause).

In the first place, the negro is the most religious man among men. Is not the religious nature the highest part of human nature? Destroy the negro then, and you destroy the highest development of the highest part of human nature. If the Christian system were to perish out of wise men's knowledge it could be reconstructed by plantation slaves. In Solomon's Song, the Bride is made to say, " "I am black, for the sun hath looked at me." Do you take the Bride to mean the Church—as Commentators say—and Christ the Head? Then is there not here a suggestion that the Church of Christ is preeminently the black race—the religious race of the world?

It is a mistake to rank men only according to superiority of intellectual faculties. God has given to man a higher dignity than the reason. It is the moral nature. Compare the moral nature of the negro race with that of other men. Baron Larry says that the most perfect human skull is the Arab's. What is the Arab's religious nature? In the Academy of Design on Broadway is a picture of an Arab kneeling in the sand before the Sphinx, his ear at its lips, waiting in superstitious awe for the whispering of the secret which the dumb image will never divulge. But the negro of the plantation-whom men call the meanest of the human race- knows better than the perfect-brained Arab, because, bowing down before no stone image, he lifts his face up to the Living God, saying in the fervor of his devotion, "The entrance of Thy Word giveth light: it giveth understanding to the simple" (applause).

In all those intellectual activities which take a strange quickening from the moral faculties—processes which we call instincts, or intuitions—the negro is superior to the white man—equal to the white woman. The negro race is the feminine race of the world. Africa is the woman among the nations. This is not only because of the negro's social and affectional nature but because he possesses that strange moral, instinctive insight that belongs more to women than to men. I suppose the brain of Daniel Webster weighed five pounds. Daniel Webster said, "It is useless to reenact the laws of God." Frederick Douglass replied, "It is worse than useless to reenact any other." I think the black man's remark morally more profound than the white's.

We have need of the negro for his Mirth—because he carries about in his bosom a "cheerful heart that doeth good like a medicine." A negro's laugh has a summer day's sunshine in it (laughter).

We have need of the negro for his Imitative Faculty—which, not working toward constructiveness—not making him a mechanic or inventor (I mean as a class), works toward the aesthetic faculties and makes him a true dramatic actor, though banished from the stage. Shakespeare drew Othello with an art so true to nature that the play will never be perfectly represented until you permit the negro to come upon the boards to represent it.

We have need of the negro for his music—unto whom, in his bondage, as unto Paul and Silas in their prison-house, God has mercifully given songs in the night!

But let us stop questioning whether the negro is a man. In many respects, he is a superior man. In a few respects, he is the greatest of men. I think he is certainly greater than those men who clamor against giving him a chance in the world, as if they feared something from the competition (laughter).

Now what is it that I ask for the negro? I ask nothing more than for myself—nothing less. First of all, I ask that he shall not be held as a slave. Break the yokes; burst the chains; open the prison-doors; let the oppressed go free! (Applause.) I ask, then, that after he is free, he shall not be oppressed by those cruel laws which degrade him to a secondary slavery in the free States. I ask that in the State of New York he shall go to the ballot-box, subject to the same restrictions as white men, and subject to no other (applause). On the day when the people of this State gave, with their right

hand, 100,000 majority for Abraham Lincoln, they gave, with
their left, 100,000 majority against negro suffrage. Now we must
help the negro up from under the weight of that injustice
(applause). I ask, also, that he shall take his seat in the jury-box, to
perform a part in those honorable services from which no white
man escapes. Do you say that he is too humble? Well, I have
known a million dollars—the interests of a great corporation—to
hang for decision in a jury-room upon the assenting voice of a
twelfth juror, and he a poor humble mechanic earning a dollar a
day. It was a sublime spectacle! I ask, also, that the negro shall be
eligible to every political office to which white men are eligible. I
do not say that he shall *hold* office, only that he shall be *eligible.*
Then, after nomination, if you don't like him, vote-him down—as
you vote down other decent men (laughter). Are negroes capable
of holding office? Capable of governing States? Well, for instance,
for the next Presidency, as between Gen. McClellan and Frederick
Douglass—who is your choice? (Applause.) In the British Island of
Jamaica the ablest man in the government is Sir Edward Jordon—
and he is a negro. I hope to see the day when South Carolina shall
be governed by some educated negro, lifted to that high position
by the generous majority of a free people (applause). But, remember, I do not ask simply that *competent* black men shall hold office. I
ask that *incompetent* black men shall hold office—for only so will
they be on a level with the whites (laughter).

I ask that the negro shall receive the respect of the best society.
He always does—for that only is the best society that honors the
poor! (Applause.) Ask him into your pew at church. Let him ride
at your side in the cars. Give him the right hand of fellowship—as,
indeed God ordained, for He made the inside of the negro's hand
white, for clasping a white man's (laughter). The finest sight I ever
saw in Central Park was an old wagon drawn by an old horse,
with an Irishman and a Negro sitting side by side on one seat,
taking a fashionable drive (laughter). That team and its teamsters,
I thought, drove farther toward the millennium than all the
guilded cavalcade that whirled by! (Laughter and applause.)

Now, after these views of the character of the negro, and of his
rights, what are the signs of the times? What are the hopes that
this character will be acknowledged, and these rights maintained?
A new era came in with Sumter. That fortress of Charleston
harbor was built upon a foundation of New England granite; that

State of South Carolina shall be rebuilt upon a foundation of New
England ideas. How the war has changed character in two years!
The Revolution of our fathers began with no idea of the independence of the colonies, but only a redress of grievances. The war now
in that land began with no idea of the emancipation of slaves, but
only the retaking of forts. Yet how grandly has that providence—
that rules the whirlwind and directs the storm—evolved out of a
struggle to maintain the public property a grander struggle to
maintain the dignity of man! We witness the spectacle to a great
nation, staking all that it holds dear upon an issue which, stripped
of all the disguises that conceal the real meaning of the war, means
simply this—that we will no longer join hands in building up a
despotism whose corner-stone is laid upon the body of the slave!
Every flag that we send Southward is a token to the world that we
mean no longer to suffer the despoiling of the poor.

This is something new in the world's history. A nation
struggling for self-existence—that is nothing new! A nation
struggling for self-aggrandizement—that is nothing new! A nation
struggling against a rebellion—that is nothing new! But there is a
nation struggling for the rights of the meanest beggars that walk
naked and hungry up and down its desolate plantations! This is
something new. No other record equals this, in human annals.
There have been many struggles for freedom before. The world
holds sacred their memory. But what has been their aim? They
have been the contests of the common people against princes and
kings, against priests and popes. The people heard a king say, "I
am the state," and they smote the lie dead upon his lips, and ever
since have said, "We are the state." The people saw an ecclesiastical hierarchy treading upon liberty of conscience, and they
asserted the right of private judgment, and ever since have said,
"To our own Master we stand or fall!" The people, looking up,
saw kings above them, and drew them down; saw a privileged
class above them, and cast it down; saw the various aristocracies
of birth and wealth above them, and smote them all down.

The struggle for liberty in the past has found the common
people lifting up their hands above their heads to pull down to
their own level the high, the noble, the proud. The struggle for
liberty now finds the common people reaching down their hands
under their feet to lift up to their own level the low, the poor, the
enslaved! (Applause.) This it is that constitutes the Christian

marvel of these times. This it is that distinguishes this war from every other war ever waged. Four million slaves are under our feet; they are to stand at our side!—each a child of God!—each having a birthright here, and an inheritance there!—each crowned with the strange, immortal dignity that falls like a coronet out of the heavens upon whomsoever God loves! (Applause.)

We speak of social equality and inequality—of high and low—of rich and poor—of white and black. If you had walked down Broadway at six o'clock this evening—stemming that stream of humanity that pours hitherward after the mill-wheels of the day's work are stopped—you would have seen the merchant, the scholar, the lawyer,—you would have seen the mechanic, the beggar, the outcast—all grades of men. You would have reordered them varying respect according to their varying grade. But how soon shall all these distinctions fade away, and all men stand equal before the bar of Him who is no respecter of persons? If, then, these distinctions avail so little there, why should they avail so much here? My thought wanders out to that great multitude of God's lowly children who are soon to be lifted to a higher estate on earth—that great race who, for 240 years, have been slaves on the same soil where we are free—whose bondage is thrice older than the Republic—whose fathers, for eight generations, have worn the chain, and borne the burden, and gone down with sorrow into merciful graves! What a record will be revealed against this guilty nation in that day when the books shall be opened, and the graves shall burst, and God shall avenge his own elect! I dare not think of it! Veil the picture! It is too awful for human sight!" Look, rather, toward the far South, to the living children of these eight generations of the dead—children more blessed than their fathers, having now a hope in this world! Behold them emerging out of the valley of the shadow of death into the light and liberty of the sons of God! My countrymen, give them a greeting of good cheer! Throw words of Christian welcome like roses under their feet, to make fragrant the pathway of their coming! For they come guided of Him whose reward is with Him—who has said, "Inasmuch as ye do it unto the least of these, my little ones, ye do it unto me"(applause).

13 FROM *Frederick Douglass*
What the Black Man Wants

The most eloquent spokesman for the black man, however, was not the white abolitionist but the black. And the most eloquent black abolitionist was Frederick Douglass (1817-1895). A former slave, an impressive orator, a persistent critic, Douglass worked for black solidarity and racial equality in ways not always approved by white abolitionists—they feared he might split the movement. They probably smarted also under Douglass' accusations that too often white reformers forgot that race prejudice just as much as slavery was the enemy. Equality was the goal of the black man, he said, and he would fight for it.

Mr. President—I came here, as I come always to the meetings in New England, as a listener, and not as a speaker; and one of the reasons why I have not been more frequently to the meetings of this society [The Massachusetts Anti-Slavery Society], has been because of the disposition on the part of some of my friends to call me out upon the platform, even when they knew that there was some difference of opinion and of feeling between those who rightfully belong to this platform and myself; and for fear of being misconstrued, as desiring to interrupt or disturb the proceedings of these meetings, I have usually kept away, and have thus been deprived of that educating influence, which I am always free to confess is of the highest order, descending from this platform. I have felt, since I have lived out West, that in going there I parted from a great deal that was valuable; and I feel, every time I come to these meetings, that I have lost a great deal by making my home west of Boston, west of Massachusetts; for, if anywhere in the country there is to be found the highest sense of justice, or the truest demands for my race, I look for it in the East, I look for it here. The ablest discussions of the whole question of our rights occur here, and to be deprived of the privilege of listening to those discussions is a great deprivation.

SOURCE. Frederick Douglass, "What the Black Man Wants," 1865.

I do not know, from what has been said, that there is any
difference of opinion as to the duty of abolitionists, at the present
moment. How can we get up any difference at this point, or at any
point, where we are so united, so agreed? I went especially,
however, with that word of Mr. Phillips, which is the criticism of
Gen. Banks and Gen. Bank's policy. I hold that that policy is our
chief danger at the present moment; that it practically enslaves
the negro, and makes the Proclamation of 1863 a mockery and
delusion. What is freedom! It is the *right to choose one's own
employment.* Certainly it means that, if it means anything; and when
any individual or combination of individuals, undertakes to decide
for any man when he shall work, where he shall work, at what he
shall work, and for what he shall work, he or they practically
reduce him to slavery.(Applause.) He is a slave. That I understand
Gen. Banks to do—to determine for the so-called freedman, when,
and where, and at what, and for how much he shall work, when he
shall be punished, and by whom punished. It is absolute slavery. It
defeats the beneficent intentions of the Government, if it has
beneficent intentions, in regard to the freedom of our people.

I have had but one idea for the last three years, to present to the
American people, and the phraseology in which I clothe it is the
old abolition phraseology. *I am for the "immediate, unconditional, and
universal" enfranchisement of the black man, in every State in the Union.*
(Loud applause.) Without this, his liberty is a mockery; without
this, you might as well almost retain the old name of slavery for
his condition; for, in fact, if he is not the slave of the individual
master he is the slave of society, and holds his liberty as a
privilege, not as a right. He is at the mercy of the mob, and has no
means of protecting himself.

It may be objected, however, that this pressing of the negro's
right to suffrage is premature. Let us have slavery abolished, it
may be said, let us have labor organized, and then, in the natural
course of events, the right of suffrage will be extended to the negro.
I do not agree with this. The constitution of the human mind is
such, that if it once disregards the conviction forced upon it by a
revelation of truth, it requires the exercise of a higher power to
produce the same conviction afterwards. The American people are
now in tears. The Shenandoah has run blood—the best blood of
the North. All around Richmond, the blood of New England and

of the North has been shed—of your sons, your brothers and your fathers. We all feel, in the existence of this Rebellion, that judgments terrible, wide-spread, far-reaching, overwhelming, are abroad in the land; and we feel, in view of these judgments, just now, a disposition to learn righteousness. This is the hour. Our streets are in mourning, tears are falling at every fireside, and under the chastisement of this Rebellion we have almost come up to the point of conceding this great, this all-important right of suffrage. I fear that if we fail to do it now, if abolitionists fail to press it now, we may not see, for centuries to come, the same disposition that exists at this moment.(Applause.) Hence, I say, *now is the time to press this right.*

It may be asked, "Why do you want it? Some men have got along very well without it. Women have not this right." Shall we justify one wrong by another? That is a sufficient answer. Shall we at this moment justify the deprivation of the negro of the right to vote, because some one else is deprived of that privilege? I hold that women, as well as men, have the right to vote (applause) and my heart and my voice go with the movement to extend suffrage to woman; but that question rests upon another basis than that on which our right rests. We may be asked, I say, why we want it. I will tell you why we want it. We want it because it is our *right*, first of all. (Applause.) No class of men can, without insulting their own nature, be content with any deprivation of their rights. We want it, again, *as a means for educating our race.* Men are so constituted that they derive their conviction of their own possibilities largely from the estimate formed of them by others. If nothing is expected of a people, that people will find it difficult to contradict that expectation. *By depriving us of suffrage, you affirm our incapacity to form an intelligent judgment respecting public men and public measures;* you declare before the world that we are unfit to exercise the elective franchise, and by this means lead us to undervalue ourselves, to put a low estimate upon ourselves, and to feel that we have no possibilities like other men. Again, I want the elective franchise, for one, as a colored man, *because ours is a peculiar government, based upon a peculiar idea, and that idea is universal suffrage.* If I were in a monarchical government, or an autocratic or aristocratic government, where the few bore rule and the many were subject, there would be no special stigma resting upon me, because

I did not exercise the elective franchise. It would do me no great
violence. Mingling with the mass, I should partake of the strength
of the mass; I should be supported by the mass, and I should have
the same incentives to endeavor with the mass of my fellow-men; it
would be no particular burden, no particular deprivation; but
here, where universal suffrage is the rule, where that is the
fundamental idea of the Government, to rule us out is to make us
an exception, to brand us with the stigma of inferiority, and to
invite to our heads the missiles of those about us; therefore, I want
the franchise for the black man.

There are, however, other reasons, not derived from any consideration merely of our rights, but arising out of the condition of the
South, and of the country—considerations which have already
been referred to by Mr. Phillips—considerations which must arrest
the attention of statesmen. I believe that when the tall heads of
this Rebellion shall have been swept down, as they will be swept
down, when the Davises and Toombses and Stephenses, and others
who are leading in this Rebellion shall have been blotted out,
there will be this rank undergrowth of treason, to which reference
has been made, growing up there, and interfering with, and
thwarting the quiet operation of the Federal Government in those
States. You will see those traitors handing down, from sire to son,
the same malignant spirit which they have manifested, and which
they are now exhibiting, with malicious hearts, broad blades, and
bloody hands in the field, against our sons and brothers. That
spirit will still remain; and whoever sees the Federal Government
extended over those Southern States will see that Government in a
strange land, and not only in a strange land, but in an enemy's
land. A post-master of the United States in the South will find
himself surrounded by a hostile spirit; a collector in a Southern
port will find himself surrounded by a hostile spirit; a United
States marshal or United States judge will be surrounded there by
a hostile element. *That enmity will not die out in a year, will not die out
in an age.* The Federal Government will be looked upon in those
States precisely as the Governments of Austria and France are
looked upon in Italy at the present moment. They will endeavor to
circumvent, they will endeavor to destroy, the peaceful operation
of this Government. *Now, where will you find the strength to counterbal-
ance this spirit, if you do not find it in the negroes of the South?* They are

your friends, and have always been your friends. They were your
friends even when the Government did not regard them as such.
They comprehended the genius of this war before you did. It is a
significant fact, it is a marvelous fact, it seems almost to imply a
direct interposition of Providence, that this war, which began in
the interest of slavery on both sides, bids fair to end in the interest
of liberty on both sides. (Applause.) It was begun, I say, in the
interest of slavery on both sides. The South was fighting to take
slavery out of the Union, and the North fighting to keep it in the
Union; the South fighting to get it beyond the limits of the United
States Constitution, and the North fighting to retain it within
those limits; the South fighting for new guarantees, and the North
fighting for the old guarantees;—both despising the negro, both
insulting the negro. Yet, the negro, apparently endowed with
wisdom from on high, saw more clearly the end from the beginning
than we did. When Seward said the status of no man in the
country would be changed by the war, the negro did not believe
him. (Applause.) When our generals sent their underlings in
shoulder-straps to hunt the flying negro back from our lines into
the jaws of slavery, from which he had escaped, the negroes
thought that a mistake had been made, and that the intentions of
the Government had not been rightly understood by our officers in
shoulder-straps, and they continued to come into our lines,
threading their way through bogs and fens, over briefs and thorns,
fording streams, swimming rivers, bringing us tidings as to the safe
path to march, and pointing out the dangers that threatened us.
*They are our only friends in the South, and we should be true to them in this
their trial hour, and see to it that they have the elective franchise.*

I know that we are inferior to you in some things—virtually
inferior. We walk about among you like dwarfs among giants. Our
heads are scarcely seen above the great sea of humanity. The
Germans are superior to us; the Irish are superior to us; the
Yankees are superior to us (laughter); they can do what we
cannot, that is, what we have not hitherto been allowed to do. But
while I make this admission, *I utterly deny that we are originally, or
naturally, or practically, or in any way, or in any important sense, inferior to
anybody on this globe.* (Loud applause.) *This charge of inferiority is an
old dodge.* It has been made available for oppression on many
occasions. It is only about six centuries since the blue-eyed and
fair-haired Anglo-Saxons were considered inferior by the haughty

Normans, who once trampled upon them. If you read the history
of the Norman Conquest, you will find that this proud Anglo-
Saxon was once looked upon as of coarser clay than his Norman
master, and might be found in the highways and byways of old
England laboring with a brass collar on his neck, and the name of
his master marked upon it. *You* were down then! (Laughter and
applause.) You are up now. I am glad you are up, and I want you
to be glad to help us up also. (Applause.)

The story *of our inferiority* is an old dodge, as I have said; for
wherever men oppress their fellows, wherever they enslave them,
they will endeavor to find the needed apology for such enslavement and oppression in the character of the people oppressed
and enslaved. When we wanted, a few years ago, a slice of Mexico,
it was hinted that the Mexicans were an inferior race, that the old
Castilian blood had become so weak that it would scarcely run
down hill, and that Mexico needed the long, strong and beneficent
arm of the Anglo-Saxon care extended over it. We said that it was
necessary to its salvation, and a part of the "manifest destiny" of
this Republic, to extend our arm over that dilapidated government. So, too, when Russia wanted to take possession of a part of
the Ottoman Empire, the Turks were "an inferior race." So, too,
when England wants to set the heel of her power more firmly in
the quivering heart of old Ireland, the Celts are an "inferior race."
*So, too, the negro, when he is to be robbed of any right which is justly his, is
an "inferior man."* It is said that we are ignorant; I admit it. But if
we know enough to be hung, we know enough to vote. If the negro
knows enough to pay taxes to support the government, he knows
enough to vote; taxation and representation should go together. If
he knows enough to shoulder a musket and fight for the flag, fight
for the government, he knows enough to vote. If he knows as much
when he is sober as an Irishman knows when drunk, he knows
enough to vote, on good American principles.(Laughter and
applause.)

But I was saying that you needed a counterpoise in the persons
of the slaves to the enmity that would exist at the South after the
Rebellion is put down. *I hold that the American people are bound, not
only in self-defense, to extend this right to the freedom of the South, but they
are bound by their love of country, and by all their regard for the future safety
of those Southern States, to do this—to do it as a measure essential to the
preservation of peace there.* But I will not dwell upon this. I put it to

the American sense of honor. The honor of a nation is an important thing. It is said in the Scriptures, "What doth it profit a man if he gain the whole world, and lose his own soul?" It may be said, also, What doth it profit a nation if it gain the whole world, but lose its honor? I hold that the American government has taken upon itself a solemn obligation of honor, to see that this war—let it be long or let it be short, let it cost much or let it cost little—that this war shall not cease until every freedman at the South has the right to vote. (Applause.) It has bound itself to it. What have you asked the black men of the South, the black men of the whole country, to do? Why, you have asked them to incur the deadly enmity of their masters, in order to befriend you and to befriend this Government. You have asked us to call down, not only upon ourselves, but upon our children's children, the deadly hate of the entire Southern people. You have called upon us to turn our backs upon our masters, to abandon their cause and espouse yours; to turn against the South and in favor of the North; to shoot down the Confederacy and uphold the flag—the American flag. You have called upon us to expose ourselves to all the subtle machinations of their malignity for all time. And now, what do you propose to do when you come to make peace? To reward your enemies, and trample in the dust your friends? Do you intend to sacrifice the very men who have come to the rescue of your banner in the South, and incurred the lasting displeasure of their masters thereby? Do you intend to sacrifice them and reward your enemies? Do you mean to give your enemies the right to vote, and take it away from your friends. Is that wise policy? Is that honorable? Could American honor withstand such a blow? I do not believe you will do it. I think you will see to it that we have the right to vote. There is something too mean in looking upon the negro, when you are in trouble, as a citizen, and when you are free from trouble, as an alien. When this nation was in trouble, in its early struggles, it looked upon the negro as a citizen. In 1776 he was a citizen. At the time of the formation of the Constitution the negro had the right to vote in eleven States out of the old thirteen. In your trouble you have made us citizens. In 1812 Gen. Jackson addressed us as citizens—"fellow-citizens." He wanted us to fight. We were citizens then! And now when you come to frame a conscription bill, the negro is a citizen again. He has been a citizen just three times in the history of this government, and it has always been in time of trouble. *In time of trouble we are citizens. Shall we be citizens in war, and aliens in peace? Would that be just?*

I ask my friends who are apologizing for not insisting upon this right, where can the black man look, in this country, for the assertion of this right, if he may not look to the Massachusetts Anti-Slavery Society? Where under the whole heavens can he look for sympathy, in asserting this right, if he may not look to the Massachusetts Anti-Slavery Society? Where under the whole heavens can he look for sympathy, in asserting this right, if he may not look to this platform? Have you lifted us up to a certain height to see that we are men, and then are any disposed to leave us there, without seeing that we are put in possession of all our rights? We look naturally to this platform for the assertion of all our rights, and for this one especially. I understand the anti-slavery societies of this country to be based on two principles,— first, the freedom of the blacks of this country; and, second, the elevation of them. Let me not be misunderstood here. I am not asking for sympathy at the hands of abolitionists, sympathy at the hands of any. I think the American people are disposed often to be generous rather than just. I look over this country at the present time, and I see Educational Societies, Sanitary Commissions, Freedmen's Associations, and the like,—all very good: but in regard to the colored people there is always more that is benevolent, I perceive, than just, manifested towards us. What I ask for the negro is not benevolence, not pity, not sympathy, but simply *justice.* (Applause.) The American people have always been anxious to know what they shall do with us. Gen. Banks was distressed with solicitude as to what he should do with the negro. Everybody has asked the question, and they learned to ask it early of the abolitionists, "What shall we do with the negro?" I have had but one answer from the beginning. Do nothing with us! Your doing with us has already played the mischief with us. Do nothing with us! If the apples will not remain on the tree of their own strength, if they are worm-eaten at the core, if they are early ripe and disposed to fall, let them fall! I am not for tying or fastening them on the tree in any way, except by nature's plan, and if they will not stay there, let them fall. And if the negro cannot stand on his own legs, let him fall also. All I ask is, give him a chance to stand on his own legs! Let him alone! If you see him on his way to school, let him alone,—don't disturb him! If you see him going to the dinner-table at a hotel, let him go! If you see him going to the ballot-box, let him alone,—don't disturb him! (Applause.) If you see him going into a work-shop, just let him alone,—your interfer-ence is doing him a positive injury. Gen. Bank's "preparation" is of a piece with this attempt to prop up the negro. Let him fall if he cannot stand alone! If the negro cannot live by the line of eternal justice, so beautifully pictured to you in the illustration used by Mr. Phillips, the fault will not be yours, it will be his who made the negro, and established that line for his government. (Applause.) Let him live or die by that. If you will only untie his hands, and give him a chance, I think he will live. He will work as readily for himself as the white man. A great many delusions have been swept away by this war. One was, that the negro would not work; he has proved his ability to work. Another was, that the negro would not fight; that he possessed only the most sheepish attributes of humanity; was a perfect lamb, or an "Uncle Tom;" disposed to take off his coat whenever required, fold his hands, and be whipped by anybody who wanted to whip him. But the war has proved that there is a great deal of human nature in the negro, and that "he will fight," as Mr. Quincy, our President, said, in earlier days than these, "when there is a reasonable probability of his whipping anybody." (Laughter and applause.)

14 FROM *Wendell Phillips*
The Fulfillment of Our Pledge

In April 1870 the abolitionists met in New York to disband the American Anti-Slavery Society. The Fifteenth Amendment giving black men the right to vote had just become part of the Constitution; the Thirteenth Amendment and the Fourteenth Amendment had long since been made a part of the supreme law. To be sure, discrimination and prejudice still existed, but there was considerable hope among abolitionists that the governmental machinery provided by statutory and constitutional law would gradually destroy the remnants of slavery. Such hope was guarded by the abolitionists' knowledge of the difficulties ahead—although it might be argued that their knowledge was not, perhaps, could not be, very profound on this point. Wendell Phillips warned his fellow reformers that even with the dissolution of their society, "the Negro will need the special sympathy of his friends." The end of the American Anti-Slavery Society was simply the beginning of the struggle for equality. Nevertheless, argued Phillips, the abolitionists had fulfilled their pledge.

The purpose and pledge of the Anti-Slavery movement was to secure for the black race equality before the law with other races,—to strike the word "white" from our Laws and Constitutions,—to put the Negro in possession of the same civil and political rights as are enjoyed by other citizens.

The New England Anti-Slavery Society—the parent of all the rest—formed in 1832—stated its object to be, "to effect the Abolition of Slavery in the United States, to improve the character and condition of the free people of color, to inform and correct public opinion in relation to their situation and rights and OBTAIN FOR THEM EQUAL CIVIL AND POLITICAL RIGHTS AND PRIVILEGES WITH THE WHITES."

The American Anti-Slavery Society, formed in 1833, aimed to secure the Black an "equality with the whites of civil and religious privileges." Its Declaration of Sentiments pledged it "to Secure to the Colored Population of the United States all the rights and privileges which belong to them as Men and as Americans."

The ratification of the Fifteenth Amendment accomplishes this purpose and fulfils this pledge. In consequence of social prejudice and of other obstacles the exercise of these rights may be, for a longer or shorter time, neither easy nor wholly safe. But the law recognizes them, and the whole power of the Nation is pledged to the Negro's protection in the exercise of them. He holds at last his sufficient shield in his own hands, that which has always sufficed, in the long run, for the protection of an oppressed class. Thwarted at one moment, bullied or starved at another, the voter, if true to himself, always conquers and dictates his own fate and position in the end. Though this Constitutional Amendment does not cover all it ought, in present circumstances,—still it contains within itself the cure for its own defects. A man with the ballot in his hand is the master of the situation. He defines all his other rights. What is not already given him, he takes. As soon as the negro holds the ballot at the South, whatever he suffers will be largely now, and in [the] future wholly, his own fault. At present, the anarchy in those States, the rule of assassins, social prejudice, his own poverty,

SOURCE. Wendell Phillips, "The Fulfillment of Our Pledge," *National Anti-Slavery Standard,* April 16, 1870.

ignorance and lack of combination will postpone the full use of his power; but, in the end, the ballot makes every class sovereign over its own fate. Corruption may steal from a man his independence. Capital may starve and intrigue fetter him at times. But against all these his vote, intelligently and honestly cast, is, in the long run, his full protection. If in the struggle his fort surrenders, it is only because it is betrayed from within. No power ever permanently wronged a voting class without its own consent.

Today, therefore, the Anti-Slavery movement may fairly leave its client to the broad influences of civilization and society. The AMERICAN ANTI-SLAVERY SOCIETY may dissolve, or adjourn indefinitely, only to be called together in case of some unexpected emergency.

No description can do justice to the wonderful influence—the far-reaching results of the Anti-Slavery movement, here and in Europe, since CLARKSON started it. Hardly anything in history surpasses it. We are not yet distant enough to measure the majestic sweep of this marvellous power. Its influence on Biblical criticism,—on the study of races,—on questions of Constitutional and International Law,—in promoting a deeper study of History, of the duties of a citizen and his relation to Government and Law,—in rousing the Church from its long sleep and broadening its idea of its own function,—on the study of Ethics,—in the development of Democratic Institutions, and recognizing the rights of the masses,— in drawing attention to the rights of Woman and hastening their recognition—its influence in all these channels only future History can fitly measure.

The results of the movement in this country have been as great as anywhere else. But though thoughtful men did not doubt the effect, there was, before 1861, no trustworthy test of its full measure. We had seen the movement break great parties to pieces, tear asunder powerful sects, destroy colossal reputations, abasing the proud and lifting up the humble and making the whole land heave with angry convulsion. Still beyond a leavening of public sentiment, a few changes in State Law, and one or two triumphs in party politics more than balanced, apparently, by gain on the opposite side, we had no palpable results, no milestones to mark its progress. Indeed sometimes it seemed as if the Slave Power grew faster than its opponent. In 1861 the most sanguine were surprised at the loyal readiness of the masses.

So good a judge as Mr. Lincoln did not dare to rest any measure on the strength of an Anti-Slavery purpose in the people.

At first he hardly dared to risk Emancipation, even as a war measure. Until 1863 he thought it necessary, in view of popular prejudice, to offer to accept the Union with slavery or without, as the rebels preferred. Events have showed that he miscalculated; that he might have relied more on the Anti-Slavery conscience of the people. But the mistake of a judge, so fairminded as he, is very suggestive as showing how unable we were then to estimate the effects of Anti-Slavery labor. The ploughshare of that reform had been much more deep, wide and thorough than we dared to hope. It had not reeducated the people but it had fully prepared them for the stern lessons of the war and made them apt learners. That teaching has set the seal to the effort and swept from American Law the odious distinction of race. In the catalogue of great popular movements among men of Saxon blood, no one, except the Protestant Reformation, can claim to stand by the side of this when measured by beneficial and permanent results. Its triumph marks a sublime epoch in our history.

The occasion naturally brings to mind the difference of opinion in our ranks in May 1865; when some thought that the state of public affairs would justify a dissolution of the Society. A glance at the course of events since that date will show, we think, how wise was the resolution of the Society to continue its organized work.

No one among us doubted the right of the Negro to suffrage. No one denied its grave importance to him. To have left him without its protection in a land where every other man votes, would have been most perilous. We all agreed that his freedom in such circumstances would have been almost a mockery. The only difference of opinion was whether it was necessary to insist on the recognition of his right to suffrage before any rebel State was admitted to the Union, or whether the rebels themselves, readmitted to the Union, could safely be left to decide if the negro should vote or not in their States. And again, whether if the first alternative was to be insisted on, our remaining together would contribute toward securing that result.

Probably no American, at this hour, looking back on the last five years, would deny that to have left rebels to settle the question of a negro's voting, would have been madness, and a total surrender of that race into the hands of its enraged masters.

Yet in 1865 and 1866 that was the avowed policy even of the Republican leaders at the North. Just before his death, in April,

1865, Mr. Lincoln urged the admission of Louisiana on this plan—leaving the Negro's civil and political rights to be settled by his late master. Most earnestly did Mr. Lincoln press this policy upon Congress. At the same time, *The Liberator*, the leader of the Abolitionists, advocated such an admission of Louisiana, and would hardly allow any criticism of Gen. Banks' system of negro-serfdom and apprenticeship there. Of course a large and influential portion of the Republican press supported the plan. Meanwhile the majority of the Senate seemed to favor it. Mr. Sumner prevented the admission of that State by talking against time and using, then only in his life, all the obstructive machinery of parliamentary law. No scene in American Parliamentary history so closely resembles the younger PITT struggling, almost sin-glehanded, during those grand seventy days, against Fox and the Coalition, as SUMNER and his half-score of comrades in our Senate Chamber checkmating President and Senate, and saving the Loyal cause. Such a scene was proof enough of the critical and confused state of public opinion, rendering it indispensable to press into service and save all means fitted to hold the Nation back from such a fatal and irretraceable step.

Then to show still further the indecisive and halting state of public purpose on such a vital point, the people of Connecticut in October, 1865, while choosing a Republican Governor, voted down a proposition to give the Negro a vote. Wisconsin and Minnesota followed her example the next month.

Repeatedly as the subject was brought to their attention in 1864, 1865, and 1866, still down to December, 1866, both Houses of Congress steadily refused to grant suffrage to the Negro, even where they exercise exclusive legislation; as in the District of Columbia and the Territories, as Idaho, for instance. Roused by Johnson's treason, Congress granted suffrage to the Negro in the District of Columbia, in January, 1867, and secured it to him in the new State of Nebraska about the same time. Still, Ohio, a Republican State, in October, 1867, voted down an Amendment to her Constitution giving the blacks suffrage, and in November, the States of Kansas and Minnesota, both Republican States, followed the example of Ohio.

Above all, in that year 1865, began the weary night of Johnson's treason. For a time the result hung doubtful. His attempt to readmit the Rebel States without waiting for a Constitutional recognition of even the citizenship of the Negro, seemed at one time likely to succeed.

The last half of 1865 and the first of 1866, may justly be termed the darkest hours of the Rebellion. The hot enthusiasm of battle was over. Men's minds were weary and confused. Old prejudices began to revive. There was no doubt that the loyal North disavowed Johnson. But it was for some time [a] matter of grave doubt whether it could be rallied unanimously and promptly enough to prevent fatal steps, which once taken could never be retraced. The immediate and overwhelming influence of the Executive was brought to bear with success in many quarters. Beside this, the surrender of forfeited estates to their former and rebel owners—the wholesale pardon of rebels, and other similar acts were productive of most disastrous consequences, and once done no power could recall them. Slowly, with hesitation and much conflict of opinion, the North roused itself for this second battle. The Rebel Convention of August, 1866, in Philadelphia, will be remembered, which drew into its ranks even the Chairman of the National Republican Committee, Mr. Raymond, with other prominent members of the party. It is almost too kind a construction to say of the conduct of such a Republican leader as Senator Fessenden of Maine, that he *hesitated* between loyalty and Johnson.

Even when, in that same summer of 1866, the loyal Convention assembled in Philadelphia, the leading men from the North went there not bold nor decided enough to pledge the party to Negro Suffrage; indeed some State delegations had about resolved beforehand to oppose it. The almost tearful demand of the Southern members alone roused their Northern friends to that level.

When the Fourteenth Amendment,—proposed in June, 1866, ratified in July, 1868, securing only civil rights to the Negro,—was under discussion, the Debate showed that it was impossible to lift the Republican party or Congress to the point of suffrage. Civil rights were all they were ready to guarantee. Even that half-way Amendment was with some difficulty secured.

The late debate, between Senators Sumner and Trumbull, has revealed the fact that, as late as the Reconstruction Act of March, 1867, the committee of Republican Senators voted down a provision to give the negro suffrage; that a few radicals in that body were obliged to fight for it against some of the strongest men in the party, and that it passed only by two votes in the caucus.

Meanwhile as events rolled on, Texas was a field of blood—Tennessee was anarchy, Kentucky in civil war. Those were the dark days when the Secretary of War dared not leave his office

day or night, fortified there against a traitor in the White House—
those were the days when Congress feared to adjourn. Day by day
it shrank from admitting States into the Union which showed that
the rebellion within their borders was still unsubdued. Even when
half admitted, Georgia flung defiance at the Nation and broke all
her pledges by expelling every negro from her Legislature, and
thus compelled Congress to remand her into military rule.

To-day, Tennessee Senators and her Republican leaders urge
that the State be remanded to military rule,—while Congress
hesitates as to the policy which the condition of Georgia demands,
and in Louisiana, Texas, and North Carolina and Georgia the
presence of United States troops is necessary to protect the lives of
loyal men and keep the peace.

When in May, 1868, the platform of the Republican party
approved of suffrage for the negro in the rebel States; leaving the
North to give it or not as she chose, Grant's majority, in the fall of
that year, was only three hundred thousand in a total vote of five
and a half millions; and such is our electing plan that the change
of thirty thousand votes would have put the rebel candidate,
Seymour, into the White House. Indeed very few men will doubt
that if Mr. Chase had been nominated on a platform which
stopped at the Fourteenth Amendment—giving the negroes civil
rights without suffrage—he would have been triumphantly elected
over Gen. Grant.

Is this the picture of a South fit to be trusted to decide whether
the Negro shall vote? Is this the picture of a North so clear in its
views, so decided in its purpose to protect the black race with the
ballot, that Abolitionists needed not further concern themselves by
any *organised* effort to help that race to its rights? Is this a North
from which it would have been safe to withdraw any influence,
however slight, to lead it to a right decision?

Only after repeated attempts to avoid this great duty has the
Nation been willing to bow to the plain necessity of its situation.
Only after every other plan had failed and difficulties thickened
round us, have we been willing to accept this basis of impartial
liberty. Five years have elapsed since Lincoln's death. It has taken
this long time and much bitter experience to show us the folly of
the half-way reconstruction which his undue tenderness for and
confidence in the South led him to favor.

No one then will deny that the condition of the black race was
perilous and uncertain in 1865; that much needed to be done and
has since been done with terrible loss and great labor. Have we,

has our organization, contributed anything to this great change? The best of the Republican leaders have again and again testified to the value and the need of such an organization as ours; confessed that its existence and labors strengthened them inside their party—and that the radical element there owed much of its success to the pressure brought to bear on its ranks by our testimony. Never, for thirty years, has THE ANTI-SLAVERY STANDARD been more closely watched or more widely copied. In the columns of the New York journals and of a hundred others, its protests have reached often a million of readers. Almost every week, during the last four years, the leading journals, all over the Nation, have quoted its opinions. It is safe to say that its influence has been three-fold what it ever was before, owing wholly to the fact that events gave terrible significance to our warnings. Whenever the Congressional history of the Fifteenth Amendment is fully written, it will be seen that The Standard's influence in removing some of the obstacles to its prompt adoption was very marked.

It is manifest from the glance we have made at the condition of affairs in 1865 and 1866, that the journals and leaders of the Republican party were no more ready at that time to claim suffrage for the Negro than their fathers were to claim his liberty in 1845. If an Anti-Slavery Society was needed in 1845 to rouse and educate the people, to watch and urge forward their leaders toward emancipation, such an organization was just as much needed in 1865, to argue the claim for suffrage and to make the Nation willing to do its study on this point.

Any suggestions, any line of argument which would excuse Abolitionists from organized effort in these last years, will prove that their holding themselves together, twenty-five years ago, was unnecessary and superfluous effort; an interference with the ordinary educators and leaders of the people which there was no emergency to justify.

Had the whole body of Abolitionists remained together, their influence in hastening and perfecting reconstruction, saving the Negro from suffering and the country from bloodshed and loss, would have outrun the most sanguine imagination. To have disbanded in 1865, events have shown us, would have been most disastrous.

Belittle the influence of the Anti-Slavery Society as much as you will, still in that dark night of 1865 and 1866 and 1867 the issues were too grave, the odds too unequal, the hour too perilous to allow us to withdraw any weight, however slight, which could help hold the country back from fatal mistakes. Not unexpectedly to be sure, but still only after most devoted, persistent and united effort, at great cost, and with excessive toil through such scenes as the assassination of Lincoln, the savage and brutal riots of New Orleans, the murders of Tennessee and Texas, the infamy of the President's journey to Chicago, the impudence and undying hate of the rebels of Georgia—has the Nation at last reached this goal. What the result might have been had the elements of the problem been changed, of course, no man can say. In any event, in any circumstances, the Nation might have triumphed. But we have the satisfaction of knowing that toward a result which has cost great sacrifices, been often in doubt, and sometimes so much in peril that even sanguine men doubted whether it would not be postponed for a generation,—toward such a result we have done our utmost personally and by *union*; by every new device and by keeping at our mast-head the old flag, constantly to warn our opponents that eyes whose watch had done so much to lift the Republican party to its best level, were still wide open, and to remind our friends also that the old "cause" needed and expected "every man to do his duty."

We have a right then, as a Society, to rejoice in the present condition of the Negro's cause. We have seen one rebel State after another half reconstructed, and then dashed to pieces by the indignation of the North. By dint of keeping the question open,—a result to which our unintermitted demand of suffrage largely contributed,—we have seen the misconduct of the South educate and rouse the North to its duty and the necessity of the hour; fortunately before it was too late to retrace heedless steps. We have the satisfaction of having held up—a hundredfold more than we could have done individually—the hands of the dozen men, in the Senate and House, whose unflinching purpose and vigilant watch have saved the Negro in spite of the weariness, the petty jealousies, the narrow technicalities, the ignorance, the prejudice, and the treason of their party fellows. We have seen the Dred Scott decision set aside and the Negro's citizenship incorporated into the Constitution. We have seen his right to State office vindicated at the point of the bayonet. We have seen him preside over State Senates and take his place on the Supreme Bench of one of the original thirteen states. We have seen a Negro fill the Senatorial chair at Washington left vacant by the chief of the Rebel Confederacy. The hitherto partial law has resumed its sacred fillet and blindfold can no longer distinguish black from white.

At length, panoplied in all the rights of citizenship, the Negro stands under a Constitution which knows nothing of race, and for the first time in our history we can read without a blush our fathers' sublime declaration, that all men are created equal. As we look back to the perils through which the path has led up to this august goal, we can have the satisfaction of knowing that no hesitation or mistake of ours increased those dangers or prolonged them one single instant. But that, on the contrary, straining every nerve, pressing into service every instrumentality, saving every tool that had in any hour availed our clients we have contributed our utmost toward making the Nation adopt the pledge of the American Anti-Slavery Society and bind itself to protect our client in "ALL THE RIGHTS AND PRIVILEGES WHICH BELONG TO THEM AS MEN AND AS AMERICANS."

Of course, in spite of this pledge, the negro, like every race just struggling into complete recognition, still needs the special sympathy and help of his friends. To be sure the great elements of political security and of industrial protection are on his side. Already the Southerners tremble when they see any thing tempt *labor* away from them. They see that a population tests the value of land and the possibility of growth. The Ocean States are even now alarmed by the increasing emigration of black labor toward the valley of the Mississippi. On this alarm rests the Negro's safety. States begin to compete with each other in tempting him by good treatment to remain within their limits.

Then the vote is a mighty bulwark. The Irish race among us still occupies, mostly, a humble place; is rarely defended by the possession of large wealth or by social position. But where does a politician dare to soil his lips with that name of contempt which used to be flung at the Irish? No, the class, a large one, has a vote; and ambitious men hunt up or invent any link which connects them with Erin. The day is close at hand, when Americans will shrink just as carefully from spelling negro with two g's. How much was made out of Gen. Jackson's Irish descent? We may yet live to see the day when a Presidential Candidate will boast his share of negro blood.

These two are chief among the strong forces which will cover the Black with an ample shield and secure him the fairest opportunity. Ploughing its laborious, but no longer doubtful, course through heavy seas, the bark of that race nears a safe harbor.

Meanwhile, in his transition, he needs counsel, aid, education, land. Our long crusade for him is not therefore really and fully ended. We may break up our ranks, but we may not yet dismiss our care nor lessen our interest.

While this generation lasts it is probable the negro will need the special sympathy of his friends. The victim of cruel prejudice, of long disfranchisement, of accumulated wrongs, debarred for centuries, not only from book education but from that better education of business and social life, he must long struggle under heavy disadvantages. Hitherto he has more than redeemed all we pledged him for; has far outrun the most sanguine hopes of us all. God has made him the cornerstone on which alone the Nation's safety could rest. With fearful exactness this stone which the builders rejected became the head of the corner. Stripped and plundered, God put it into his power to pay us back, by the very intellectual light and moral strength which the movement in his behalf gave to us, far more than we ever sacrificed for him. And now, under that same Providence, we owe him victory. The heavy debt of centuries is doubled. Bankrupt debtors we grant him nothing:—we admit him to nothing. Penitent for a guilty past, grateful for a triumphant and undeserved present, we welcome a wronged equal to the full enjoyment of a Nationality and a civilization which, under God, mysteriously, he has done more to save and perfect than we have. Far deeper than our fathers thought was the sublime truth, to which they rendered only lip service, that ALL MEN ARE CREATED EQUAL.